LIFE IN THE FAST LANE

THE EAGLES' RECKLESS RIDE
DOWN THE ROCK & ROLL HIGHWAY

LIFE IN THE FAST LANE

MICK WALL

DIVERSION
BOOKS

First published in Great Britain as *Eagles: Dark Desert Highway*
in 2023 by Trapeze, an imprint of The Orion Publishing Group Ltd.

For more information,
email info@diversionbooks.com

Diversion Books
A division of Diversion Publishing Corp.
www.diversionbooks.com

First Diversion Books Edition: July 2023
Paperback ISBN: 9781635768909
eBook ISBN: 9781635769555

Printed in the United States of America

15 16 17 18 19 6 5 4 3 2 1

CONTENTS

SIDE ONE
All the Right People

SIDE TWO

Heavenly Bills

Though thou exalt thyself as the eagle, and though thou set thy nest among the stars, thence I will bring thee down, saith the Lord.

—*Obadiah 1:4*

FAST FORWARD

Don Henley Does Not Like Books about the Eagles

He really doesn't.

From *To the Limit: The Untold Story of the Eagles* by Marc Eliot:

> Early on, I sent letters to Don Henley and [Eagles manager] Irving Azoff informing them that I was working on the book and asking for their cooperation in the form of a series of interviews. I emphasized that this was not a "tell all" and that I believed my previous work spoke for itself, and that I was giving them the opportunity to challenge or dispute any material I might uncover in my research and provide properly documented corrective material . . .
>
> Their response was to tell me to go fuck myself.

The above is part of a long afterword by the acclaimed *New York Times* writer detailing how Don Henley "turned into a modern-day Captain Ahab, so obsessed with my whale of a book that he lost all sense of reason and fairness."

In Eliot's account, Henley embarks on a long and attritional campaign to scupper the book after both he and former Eagles record label chief David Geffen manage to acquire copies of the manuscript before it is published. When Eliot asks Geffen how he got a copy, Geffen laughs and tells him, "That's how life in the real-world operates." Don Henley and Irving Azoff then prevaricate for months over giving interviews to the author in return for the chance to go through the manuscript line by line and offer corrections to any passages that they don't like.

Eventually, Henley agrees to meet Marc Eliot in return for Eliot agreeing to remove from the book a mention of the time in 1979 that Henley was arrested for contributing to the delinquency of a minor after a party at his house where a sixteen-year-old girl overdosed on cocaine and Quaaludes, because, Don says, he does not want to upset his mother. He speaks on the record about anything else Eliot wants to discuss, and afterward sometimes goes to bars with him. At one point they spend an afternoon arguing over whether Eliot can say that Henley once "had a perm."

When *To the Limit* finally comes out, in 1998, Don Henley drives around bookshops in LA that are planning to have author event signings asking them not to and, in one case, offers to have an in-person event for his next solo CD if they agree to cancel Marc Eliot's appearance. In an interview given in 2002 to the *Toronto Sun*, Henley says, "Marc Eliot is not only a bad writer but an evil person. He was a sick person who had some kind of axe to grind."

So let's get something straight right here before we get started. Don Henley probably never had a perm. Maybe Marc was thinking of Lindsey Buckingham.

Don Henley hates all Eagles books. But he especially hates the one by his former guitarist, Don Felder—the Eagle who actually came up with the musical idea for "Hotel California": *Heaven and Hell: My Life in the Eagles, 1974–2001.*

Much of Felder's history with Henley and Frey is fraught, to say the least. During the final show of Felder's first stint in the Eagles, back in 1980, Frey turns to him onstage and hisses, "When this is over, I'm gonna kill you. I can't wait."

Nonetheless Don Felder rejoins for the Hell Freezes Over tour in 1994 but is sacked again in 2001. He sues Frey and Henley for wrongful termination. Don and Glenn countersue him, and the case is settled out of court. Then Don publishes his book.

Eight years later, talking to the *Guardian* newspaper, Don Henley says: "A lot of people on the outside believe a lot of the bullshit in Don Felder's book and believe Glenn Frey and I are some kind of tyrants. The fact is, we are largely responsible both for the longevity and the success of this band. Because we did it our way, and a lot of people didn't like that. Felder's just bitter because he got kicked out of the group, so he decided to write a nasty little tell-all, which I think is a really low, cheap shot. I mean, I could write some stuff about him that would make your mustache curl."

He adds: "I believe some things should go to our graves. And some things are nobody's fuckin' business . . ."

So yeah, Don Henley does not like books about the Eagles.

SIDE ONE
All the Right People

1.

Nobody's Favorite Band

Ask anyone in America where the craziest people live, and they'll tell you California. Ask anyone in California where the craziest people live, and they'll say Los Angeles. Ask anyone in Los Angeles where the craziest people live, and they'll tell you Hollywood. Ask anyone in Hollywood where the craziest people live, and they'll say Laurel Canyon. And ask anyone in Laurel Canyon where the craziest people live, and they'll say Lookout Mountain. So I bought a house on Lookout Mountain.

—Joni Mitchell, *Vanity Fair*, 2015

The Eagles have never been anybody's favorite band. Oh sure, they may have written and recorded lots of people's favorite *song*. There are plenty of those to choose from: "Hotel California," "Lyin' Eyes," "One of These Nights," "Take It to the Limit," "New Kid in Town" . . . enough to fill the biggest-selling greatest hits album of all time. Back in the seventies, whenever one of their dirty-dozen million-sellers hit the radio, they compelled you to listen. But it was always the song that detained you, never the singer. Indeed, nobody knew what "the singer" looked like in the Eagles in their heyday. Few do even now. Wait, the beardy, grouchy-looking dude at the back on the drums? Or the truck-stop jock with the droopy stash out front? Or maybe the smug-faced older-sister's-boyfriend type next to him?

Even when crazy-ass, bad-to-the-bone Joe Walsh joined it was hard to get a mental fix on who or what the Eagles actually were. As for Bernie Leadon and Don Felder, you've gotta be kidding, right? Most people didn't even know they were in the band. Most still don't.

The really serious, big-time, seventies music journalists—and there was no bigger or more serious time to be a music journalist than the seventies—*hated* the Eagles, almost on a point of principle. The same high-priest sages whose minds had been blown by the previously thought impossible, Frankenstein-like conjoining of post-psychedelic rock and good-ole-boy American country. For these self-regarding gatekeepers, *Sweetheart of the Rodeo* by the Gram Parsons–reborn Byrds was when the Big Bang occurred. The Eagles were just a dime-store knockoff of the real deal.

Unlike the later fresh-breeze glow of early Eagles hits like "Take It Easy" and "Peaceful Easy Feeling," there was a knowing, road-weary drug-consciousness to *Sweetheart of the Rodeo*—an illicit confection of ripe Nashville cheese, soul-blood ballads, and some of the Byrds' own slo-mo, old-before-their-time originals, for when you're wasted and coming down.

Released in August 1968, a few weeks after Bob Dylan's formidable former backing group the Band released their self-consciously rootsy debut, *Music from Big Pink*, and in the same year that Dylan's bare-bones *John Wesley Harding* had signaled an unexpected departure from eye-in-the-sky, acid-rock apocalypse and a move toward a more considered, consciously "authentic" approach, *Sweetheart of the Rodeo* was not so much back to the garden as cut the shit, man, let's get high. And even though it didn't sell squat it was deemed the hippest trip you could take on your turntable, and has remained so, historically, throughout rock time. One of those historic records that everyone who knows their shit claims to have always loved but almost no one has ever really listened to.

When word spread that Gram Parsons had already left the Byrds before *Sweetheart* had even come out, it damaged sales but only added to the depth of their cool. Gram had been fired, it was whispered, for refusing to go on tour, preferring to hang out at Muscle Shoals studio with Keith Richards and Mick Jagger.

It was super cool while it lasted, the three of them lounging around stoned as they pieced together the ultimate after-dark love song, "Wild Horses." Not that Gram would get any credit for it when it came out on the Stones' *Sticky Fingers* album a year later.

"I remember we sat around originally doing this with Gram Parsons," Jagger grudgingly admitted years later. "But I was definitely very inside this piece emotionally."

Which is interesting, especially when you consider Gram would record the song first, on *Burrito Deluxe*, the second album from his new outfit, the Flying Burrito Brothers, released the year before *Sticky Fingers,* which contained the Stones' version. Jagger and Richards famously never credited anybody, not even when maybe they should. Gram didn't know that yet back then though. Instead he followed them to London.

Mick had already moved on, taking "Wild Horses" with him. That just left Keith with Gram, shacked up together at Keef's Chelsea abode, as the smack and the Jack and the hee-haw tales of rose-pink Cadillacs, blackened spoons, and cocaine cowgirls took over. In the end, it took Richards's own dark avenging angel, the witchy Anita Pallenberg, to physically throw Gram out. Imagine that: being so fucked up that Keith Richards, permanently fucked up since 1965, gets his crazy, even more fucked-up chick to throw you out the door and don't come back no time soon.

Gram didn't care. Gram barely even noticed. He just jetted back to LA, where Chris Hillman, left to burn in the now failing Byrds, jumped at the chance to hook up again with his good ole junky partner in a new, low-slung outfit Gram smirkingly named the Flying Burrito Brothers.

This was now psychedelic country rock deluxe with extra fillings of soul, gospel, and heroin. The band's debut album, *The*

Gilded Palace of Sin, released in 1969, carried on directly from where *Sweetheart of the Rodeo* left off, right down to the critical religious ecstasy—*Rolling Stone* called it "one of the best records of the year" and it was only February; Dylan, unprompted, announced it to be his favorite country rock album: "Boy, I love them," he was reported to have said, in one of the most un-Dylan-like quotes ever.

But *Palace* didn't even match the puny sales of its predecessor, selling half what *Sweetheart* did, scraping into the *Billboard* Top 200 for a week or two, then vamoosing again. Gone but never to be forgotten by the same inky tub-thumpers that would soon take pleasure in dismissing the Eagles as upstart wannabes at best, insultingly bad fakes at worst—the Monkees of country rock, only much less charming and far more anonymous.

Unlike Crosby, Stills & Nash, the first legit American supergroup. All of whom were already stars. Such stars they went out of their way *not* to be. David Van Cortlandt Crosby—Croz—was one of the original, everyone-remembers Byrds, blowing up on TV doing "Mr. Tambourine Man," "Turn, Turn, Turn," "Eight Miles High" . . . the actual templates for folk rock, country rock, psychedelic pop, meaningful jingle-jangle. Americana thirty years early.

Promoted as the American Beatles, the Byrds inspired Dylan to lose his rock 'n' roll virginity and "go electric," the Beach Boys to get off the beach and allow mild and crazy Brian Wilson to invent pop opera, and every kid under twenty-one to sell their souls for a pair of those rimless blue rectangular sunglasses that Roger McGuinn looked so heavenly cooool in on *The Ed Sullivan Show*.

Dig it. The Byrds were the now sound of tomorrow today. Something the Eagles would never be.

But then tall, twenty-year-old going-on-forty singer and resident tortured genius, Gene Clark, split the scene and the suits got involved trying to keep the cash machine whirring and suddenly they were releasing candy-ass covers of ready-made hits like the Goffin and King, Tin Pan Alley chestnut, "Goin' Back." A major moment for a dozen artists over a half-century period. But not for the Byrds.

That's when Croz bailed too. By then he'd been everywhere, man, knew everyone worth knowing, okay? Making an unannounced appearance onstage at Monterey Pop, ranting about who really shot JFK, filling in for the absent Neil Young with Buffalo Springfield the following night—at the request of the equally "spontaneous" Stephen Stills.

It was Croz who gave a home to Joni Mitchell in Laurel Canyon before anyone else had heard of her. It was Croz who held open house at his humble hippy homestead on Lookout Mountain for any passing musician or musician's best friend or good-buddy drug dealer who beat the trail from freak-show Sunset Boulevard up to this new world paradise of eucalyptus trees, single-track lanes, and quaint, crumbling shacks. Joni, Neil Young, Jim Morrison, Micky Dolenz, Cass Elliot, Peter Fonda, Arthur Lee . . . come on in, the spiked water's fine.

Crazy motherfucker Croz really wasn't in it for the money. That made him dangerous. Sang like an angel and could write a devilishly catchy tune. Walked around with a small woodsman's knife dangling from his belt. Could talk fuck-you and metaphysics in the same interpolated sentence. Deal with it.

Stephen Stills was a tough son-of-a-bitch army brat from Dallas who absolutely positively knew he was a star long before anyone else did, more fool them. Even when Neil Young was at the mic in Buffalo Springfield blasting out "Mr. Soul," Stephen would mug for the camera in the background, wearing a cowboy hat and doing little "that-boy-is-crazy" dance steps.

Stephen had auditioned for the part Peter Tork eventually got in the Monkees: the amiable blond dork with the lopsided grin.

Stephen's chipped front tooth was the only reason he didn't get the gig. Realizing he couldn't rely on his looks, Stephen instead became a master guitarist, hipster singer-songwriter, sorcerer producer, and . . . just do it the way I goddamned showed you, okay?

Okay, Stephen.

His best scene-steal came with the Buffalo Springfield's only big chart hit, "For What It's Worth," which Stephen wrote and sang. But not even that prevented the world from seeing Neil as the true star of that band.

The runt of the litter was Graham Nash. He'd had giant hit singles up the wazoo with British beat group the Hollies, including four top 10 hits in America, three of which he'd co-written and sung. Pretty enough to be a pop star, his soul born with a star embossed upon it, the only thing he lacked was credibility.

Graham thought the Hollies could have been the Beatles. But whenever he talked like that the others just looked at him. When he tried to indoctrinate them into the efficacious delights of LSD and marijuana, they picked up their pints of bitter and moved to another table. After the band then rejected "some interesting songs" that he'd written, including "Marrakesh Express" and "Lady of the Island," both later to adorn the first CS&N album, he decided he "couldn't handle it" anymore and split.

That's when Graham found California—or when California found him, as he might say. Introduced to Croz by Mama Cass, falling instantly in love with Joni, with whom he set up his own Laurel Canyon hang. Best of all for Graham, CS&N were credibility magnified, instant maxed-out cachet. Debuted at Woodstock. First album a stone-cold, five-million-selling classic. CS&N played acoustic-electric . . . folk? Country? Not really. What, then? Something new and earthy and bewitching.

Then Neil Young joined, and they became even bigger and yet more fashionable. Crosby, Stills, Nash *and* Young. One album,

Déjà Vu, which sold twice what the *Crosby, Stills & Nash* album had. One hit single, another Hollies reject written and sung by Nash called "Teach Your Children" and one hit single written and sung by Young in direct response to the Kent State shootings of May 4, 1970, "Ohio."

With Dylan in cloistered retreat from the business of writing momentous music and the breakup of the Beatles now official, CSN&Y were now regarded as the only massively popular group left with a bleeding-edge conscience.

Then came cocaine.

Here the Eagles did bear comparison. Big time. But that was only looking back later, too gacked out of their minds to give a shit anymore anyway.

2.

Scenes from the Troubadour,
Late 1970

The Troubadour, sited at 9081 Santa Monica Boulevard since 1961, has missed out on the slow death of the freaks-and-geeks Sunset Strip music scene. The hippies and heads melt away around the same time Charlie Manson is holed up at Spahn Ranch thinking about offing Terry Melcher because that capitalist pig fucker won't make him the star that he was surely destined to be, and the bands that brought the neon nights alive in the sixties have either gotten too big and too famous to cram themselves back into the Whisky a Go Go, or they're dead or long since split.

As Michelle Phillips, cool-blonde, California-dreaming LA-lady of the Mamas & the Papas, later put it: "Before 1969, my memories were nothing but fun and excitement and shooting to the top of the charts and loving every minute of it. The Manson murders ruined the LA music scene. That was the nail in the coffin of the freewheeling, 'Let's get high, everybody's welcome, come on in, sit right down.' Everyone was terrified. I carried a gun in my purse. And I never invited anybody over to my house again."

But down on Santa Monica, the Troubadour is like a magnet for the new post-hippy, double-denimed singer-songwriter crowd that scatter back up into the canyons when the dawn breaks. Doe-eyed girls in floaty gingham dresses, soulful country rock cowboys in bell bottoms and shades; heavy drinkers, dope thinkers, and flat-out stinkers hang tough at the Troubadour. You go there to write songs, get spotted, get signed. You go there to get drunk, get loaded, and get laid. You go for the hang. Linda Ronstadt—cute cut-off denim shorts and sweet brown doll's eyes, the Troubadour girl with the sunny small-town smile and the voice of a cactus mountain goddess, the super-groovy chick that all the would-be groovy guys want the most—says there are two sets of Troubadour regulars, "the musician pool and the sex pool."

Linda's cool new friend, Eve Babitz, gorgeous, glorious, Hollywood demi-monde artist and writer, who was famously photographed playing chess naked with Marcel Duchamp—her, not him, obviously—is another familiar pretty face at the bar of the Troub.

Eve Babitz, who Jim Morrison wanted to teach him about classical music and who taught him instead not to always want to fuck your mother. Eve, who occasionally designs album covers for Linda and also Buffalo Springfield, is another tough, smart queen of the hive who knows exactly why hot boys and girls go to the Troubadour.

"You can smell the semen out on the street," she shrugs. Or as one of the waitresses, Susan Smith, put it: "You had to wear a diaphragm just to walk through—it was enough to get you pregnant just standing there."

Eve has another special friend in new dick on the block Glenn Frey. "It seemed like Glenn and I had been hanging out drinking tequila in the corner of the bar forever, and that we never went home."

Who else is here at the ash-end of 1970? Well, who isn't? Fat Jim Morrison of the Doors likes to drink whiskey in its dark corners—until he splits for Paris and an ingloriously graffitied early grave in Père Lachaise. Jackson Browne, with his puppy-dog eyes and his cheekbones from heaven, hangs loose by the bar. He's twenty-two but looks fifteen. Everyone says Jackson is a great young songwriter but no label in town wants to sign him. The folk rock boom is over, pretty boy.

Lost former Byrds genius Gene Clark stares soulfully into the distance and wonders where the good times have gone. Born-to-be-background-artists Bernie Leadon and Randy Meisner bullshit and haggle over who has the best-paying side hustle. Bernie is twenty-three and plays guitar, banjo, anything with strings. He keeps coming close but no cigar, first with the doomed Clark, in Dillard & Clark, who everyone loved but nobody bought, now the Flying Burrito Brothers, who nobody likes anymore since they nixed Gram Parsons, and nobody bought anyway.

Randy is twenty-four, a bass player who sings—unusual for that scene—and a co-founding member of Poco, yet another Buffalo Springfield off-cut, country rock lite, who everyone kinda digs and no one actually buys—come on, man. Randy is not-so-secretly glad. He'd walked out before their first album was released, pissed off at being excluded from the final mix sessions. Lately he's been a member of Ricky Nelson's Stone Canyon Band, whose live album, *In Concert at the Troubadour, 1969*, is another way-cool release the general public has largely overlooked.

There's Arlo Guthrie, twenty-three-year-old son of Woody, still trying to parlay his 1967 counterculture anthem, "Alice's Restaurant," into a solid recording career. His latest album, *Washington County*, stalls just outside the top 30 but offers temporary shelter to Ry Cooder, Doug Dillard, and various members, past and future, of the Byrds, the Burritos, and Little Feat. Arlo is just a little too New York for this crowd, but everyone feels they owe fealty to his dead dad Woody, so his son gets a free pass into LA hipsterdom.

There's Steve Martin, comedian-cum-banjo-player, nursing a solitary white wine alone at the bar, looking for a break. He was making beaucoup bucks writing hip-to-be-square sketches for the

Smothers Brothers Comedy Hour—until CBS canceled the show for being just a little *too* hip for all the squares upstairs in the boardroom. Steve now opens for rock groups, doing loopy magic tricks and pretending to mess up on the banjo. You don't have to be stoned to find Steve funny, but if you are he's fucking hysterical.

There are the waitresses, Big Tit Sue, Bigger Tit Sue, and Black Sylvia. (What it says on the label.) Towering above it all, sometimes naked on the stage, forty-three-year-old Doug Weston, owner, standing six foot six inches (the "tallest queer I ever knew," according to Ted Markland, who played Reno in NBC's hit TV western, *The High Chaparral*).

The Troubadour is where Harry Dean Stanton would hang out. Where rising stars like Kris Kristofferson would hang with Hollywood hipster Jack Nicholson. Where Janis Joplin showed up just a few days before she died, sitting at a table looking gone already.

If you've ever played a show for Doug, then he'll have your nuts in a vice. Stars come back to play the Troubadour because Doug pays a thousand bucks a gig (worth around $7,500 in 2023) but signs them to a five-year contract. Even Don McLean, happy just to be there in 1970 but about to become a megastar a year later, selling out arenas, can't do a damn thing about it. Welcome back, Don.

There are other regulars, singers and songwriters not destined for stardom but nevertheless possessed of enough talent to parlay them into steady if unremarkable recording careers. Cats like Ned Doheny and David Blue, David Ackles and Jack Wilce. Not all of them came from LA, but they all somehow now belonged there.

When the Troub first opened in 1957 as a coffeehouse on La Cienega, it was about the Beats. Cool jazz, French cigarettes, beat poetry—being hip to the trip, daddio. By the time it relocated a few miles up the boulevard to Santa Monica, the Troub was about folk singers with earnest faces, then singer-songwriters with long hair.

It's a young nonconformist scene. Grass is in, baby. Lenny Bruce was arrested there in 1962 for obscenity, after using the word "schmuck" onstage—Yiddish slang for "penis," as in stoopid prick. But then Lenny with his golden arm full of narcotics and his head full of "dirty talk" was always in trouble for something.

Now in the early seventies it's a whole new cast of young music rebels showing up looking for meaningful kicks. Longhaired, dope-smoking, Sons of the Second World War, children of the rock revolution, born in the backs of taxis wearing shades, the Troubadour becomes the place to hang again whether you are another unsigned Laurel Canyon hippy laureate or someone who already has a name but just really digs the hang, man. The Troub's bar was the place where the regulars plunged into "over-boogie," as they called it.

Unlike his bedeviled predecessor, when Richard Pryor—no less an addict and even more outspoken than the now deceased, gone too soon Bruce—releases his debut album, *Richard Pryor*, a recording of his Troubadour appearance in September 1968, he feels free to express himself honestly and explicitly, in the process not only breaking taboos but making the material even funnier. Because the audience has changed, this new post-love, post-Beatles, post-Manson, post-pill, post-dope, post-man-on-the-moon society has now given them permission.

Monday night is Hoot Night, just a dollar to get in, and the joint has always been packed for that. A showcase for anyone brave enough to get high on that low stage. If you get to sing three numbers you're winning. For locals and out-of-towners. Low-powered blonde chicks with tans and Marlboros and the clearest skin anyone has ever seen, eyes shining bluer than the Pacific. Young guys already stoned from smoking weed out back, laughing cos everything's funny when you're nineteen and from the LA burbs. Young buck musos from places with gen-u-wine cowboy cred like Lubbock and El Paso also mill around the bar, enjoying rubbing shoulders with the West LA cats that matter.

Glenn Frey and his good buddies J. D. Souther and Jackson Browne would be hanging around somewhere in the middle. Glenn with his vicious tongue, giving it to the straights, Jackson with his sweet, everyone-loves-Jackson eyelashes and cheekbones, and J.D. with his quick-draw, hanging-judge's eye.

The Troubadour becomes the center for this new-style, electrified blend of country and rock with its added layer of pop harmonies and jagged-edge guitars. It's bitter, brilliant lyrics about the shitty guys in other bands and the chicks who don't know their names yet. The world that will one day bow down before them. It's the journey from cheap moonshine whiskey and bad-woman blues to the bong-sucking, acid-gobbling, coke-snortin' scene that everyone at the club under twenty-five is now into.

It's rock but with a more "authentic" country aspect, ya dig? It's country but with its outlaw guns strapped on again. Sunny on the outside, pitch black on the inside. Just the thing for the new decade that is emerging from the clouds of love-love-love into a more uncertain, conflicted age—Tricky Dicky Nixon sending nukes fizzing into Russian airspace, Elvis heading reluctantly to Vegas to kick-start his fat jumpsuit years, the Beatles suddenly bailing out without warning, segued into Joni Mitchell releasing *Ladies of the Canyon*, Jagger and Richards hooking up with Gram Parsons to write "Wild Horses," even Led Zeppelin now doing cool country-folk-roots licks when they're not, as singer Robert Plant describes it, "eating women and spitting the bones out the window."

But while the vibes are always up, they are also darker, hiding in plain sight right at the heart of the feel-good factor, everything heading west, blown by the stink of prevailing cross-cultural winds, everyone and their monkey packing up, moving out—going to

California, baby. In their cars. In their minds. Thumbs ahoy. So long, priestly Ginsberg; hello, evil twin Bukowski.

The cool daddy of the scene is supposed to be David Crosby. David is twenty-nine—old in pop-dog years—but he's been a star since he was twenty-four and in the Byrds. Now he's an even bigger star in Crosby, Stills, Nash & Young. David's done the do. Sold the T-shirt. But it was Gene Clark, dubbed the "hillbilly Shakespeare" by his one-time bassist John York, who got all the credit for the Byrds, and David is determined to finally make his mark. Except he knows everything better than anybody else, whoever the hell they think they are. He'll take your Linda Ronstadt and raise you a Joni Mitchell. Hater of pretention, epitomized for Croz by the Doors, who he will tell you "basically sucked." That Jim Morrison was "no fucking good as a singer or poet." As for the Eagles, they simply "were and are a commercial band." The ultimate Croz put-down. Not only that, "but they are really, really good at it." Wow.

What Croz doesn't understand is that this new generation of SoCal hippy singer-songwriters do not see themselves as musical pioneers, as he and his original Laurel Canyon cohorts did, these new kids in town are *settlers*. They aren't reaching for the unknown. They know exactly where they want their music to take them. That's why they're here now and nowhere else.

John David "J.D." Souther is one such longhaired, guitar-strumming Troub dude lurking on the fringes in 1970. Born on the edge in Detroit, same as his future best bud Glenn Frey, J.D. had blown in from Amarillo, Texas, where he'd been raised, in 1968. He'd played guitar, led a band, scored a deal, released two flop-peroo singles, then tried his luck in New York. When that didn't pan out either, he came back to LA and was "doing some house painting . . . and general carpentry" between nights hanging out at the Troubadour looking for an in.

J.D. was twenty-five, tall and lean, and ready to roll the dice. It felt like now or never for him. His luck changed when he met a beautiful blonde singer, also from Detroit, named Alexandra Sliwin. She was in a vocal group with her sister Joanie called Honey Ltd. They would release seven honey-sweet singles between 1967 and 1970, none of which were hits. But Honey Ltd. were cute and sexy and very "with it," and they made several appearances on TV, bopping sweet for the moms and dads on *The Ed Sullivan Show*, *The Joey Bishop Show*, *The Jerry Lewis Show*, and *The Andy Williams Show*.

Then Joanie shows up one day, followed by her lovestruck new boyfriend, twenty-two-year-old Glenn Frey. J.D., with his Texas hold 'em reserve, sees that Glenn thinks he's James Dean, rolling his cigarette pack into the sleeve of his T-shirt, flipping one into his mouth when he wants a smoke, something he's obviously spent quality time practicing. He also seems to know every song out of Motown by ear—unusual for that white-bread musical milieu. Is he putting it on? No, the boy just loves his Detroit soul. Glenn is funny as all hell. Doesn't really fit in at all. J.D. digs that about him.

Alex and Joanie get a place together. Honey Ltd. are doing well. J.D. and Glenn are now inseparable, the faded double denim and long, freshly shampooed hair interchangeable, the two guitar-cradling bromancers permanently residing at the Troubadour along with their third wheel, Jackson Browne, the boys guzzling bottles of sticky brown Dos Equis with chunks of lime jammed down their necks.

Soon the three amigos have a cool-dude pad together. Not above the Strip like Linda, now perched in an apartment upstairs from Doug Dillard on the sunny side of the street, nor high up on Lookout Mountain with the space-captain cowboys and their fully loaded old ladies. But way down the wrong end of Sunset, amigo, in scuzzville, Echo Park, a known LA gang hotspot, bordered by

Chinatown to the east, sandwiched between Filipino Town and Angelino Heights.

The guys rent a pale, two-story box at 1020 Laguna Avenue, where Jackson takes the ground floor converted garage with no windows and J.D. and Glenn the small apartment above with the double locks on the door, all for $60 a month. Okay, you're living it up in Crazy Town, especially after dark when even the LAPD and their night-sight choppers keep outta the way, but at that price it's a steal, right?

Glenn toughs it out. He's seen worse, he shrugs. But Glenn is not really from Detroit; he was born there but raised in nearby Royal Oak. There were no mean streets in Royal Oak. Indeed, there was precious little Detroit steel on show anywhere growing up. Glenn studied piano from the age of five, then got on to the guitar. Had a high school band he called the Subterraneans, after Kerouac's daring, harum-scarum head-rush follow-up to *On the Road*. Glenn reads books, plays music, *knows* stuff.

But he likes to play the Detroit tough guy card whenever it suits him. "I grew up running in Detroit," Frey remembered in one interview after he became a star. "I went to school with the sons and daughters of automobile factory workers—fathers who beat their wives and beat their kids. The kids would then go to school and beat on me. My father was a machinist in a shop that built the machines that built car parts."

Other than that, he had to admit, "I had a pretty normal childhood. My parents weren't drinkers. I always had clothes. I always went to camp for a week in the summer. My parents didn't have enough money to buy me a car when I turned sixteen, but I had a great childhood."

Enrolled at Oakland Community College in Michigan, he band-hops, learns to sing harmonies in the Four of Us, learns to kick ass in the Mushrooms, and makes a little headway as a hotshot local guitarist, getting looks from the girls and pissing off the boys. With his long, center-parted hair and angular hooked nose, he actually *looked* like a goddamned American eagle, swooping down to hook its prey.

When he later gets to LA, he will discover he is just an average guitar player, but here in Detroit in the prehistoric sixties, Glenn is seen as a crazy-skilled kid on the scene. He is introduced as such to Bob Seger, who is already on his way to becoming a real name in the Motor City. Bob is three and a half years older and assumes a father-figure role, letting Glenn sit in with him sometimes, which is a gas for the kid, and kool kudos for Bob.

Pretty soon though, Glenn feels the same magnetic pull that Bob and everyone else who wants this seriously does—the "California consciousness," as he later calls it—and when Joanie and her sister drop out of Wayne State University and head boldly for Los Angeles, Glenn does likewise. You betcha bottom dollar.

"We all watched the sun set in the west every night of adolescence and thought someday about coming out here," Frey would one day rhapsodize in the *LA Times*. "It all seemed so romantic . . . The *Life* magazine articles about Golden Gate Park and the Sunset Strip . . . And the music: the Beach Boys, the Byrds, Buffalo Springfield. It was definitely the archetype of the most beautiful place in the world."

J.D. quickly hips Glenn to country music, the cool new stuff, shows him how it's done, how it works when you let it, and Glenn gets it. Really *gets* it, man. "I'd just quit my band and he'd just quit his band," recalled J.D. "And we wanted to write songs, so we started writing songs together."

Not just any songs. Taking their cue from the prevailing lone-gunman-with-geetar vibe of the Troub, they mix gentle-touch folk with loud-twang country and come up with frolicking early Frey fare like "Run, Boy, Run" and soulful J.D. smoothies like "Rebecca."

Soon they have a band—well, not exactly a band, just the two of them—that J.D. suggests calling Longbranch and Glenn suggests calling Pennywhistle. They settle on Longbranch Pennywhistle and wangle an indie deal with Amos Records, where they become label mates with wild-eyed rock 'n' roll anti-hero Bing Crosby who they hope they never have to meet. Amos had been started the year before by former rockabilly singer Jimmy Bowen (one hit in 1957: "I'm Stickin' With You," which Bowen co-wrote), latterly turned producer for Frank Sinatra at Ol' Blue Eyes's Warner-backed Reprise label.

Charged with bringing Sinatra and his pals—Dean Martin and Sammy Davis Jr.—back from the bow-tie doldrums of the late fifties into the post-Beatles, everything-in-color sixties, it was Bowen in his role as go-getter young producer who brought Sinatra "Strangers in the Night," which went to Number 1 in the US and UK in 1966 and won three Grammy Awards, including Record of the Year for Bowen. He started Amos off the back of such success.

But while Bowen clearly saw the writing on the wall, in terms of the direction pop music was heading in the late sixties, when the self-titled Longbranch Pennywhistle album was released sometime in 1969, it instantly disappeared without a trace. Here today, gone later today, as Croz liked to say.

Not knowing what to do, J.D. and Glenn sat around in Echo Park waiting for something else to happen, while downstairs Jackson was showing them how it's done, working endlessly on his songs, his hardworking old piano drifting up through the courtyard day and night.

Jackson is the same age as Glenn and three years younger than J.D., but he is California-raised and has been singing his own songs at the Troubadour since he was an old-before-his-time teenager at school. He can't get a deal. Instead his songs become hits for others. He was sixteen when he wrote "These Days," an achingly beautiful song about deep loss and lifelong regret. A song so gothically self-absorbed the ghostly Nico was drawn to cover it for *Chelsea Girl*, her first solo album after being chased out of the Velvet Underground by an insanely jealous Lou Reed.

Thirty-eight-year-old Nico was the most beautiful blonde in Cologne, where she was born Christa Päffgen, the daughter of a *Wehrmacht* conscript, before becoming Nico, the most beautiful blonde in Rome, when she appeared as her new self in Federico Fellini's 1960 satirical comedy-drama, *La Dolce Vita*, then the most beautiful blonde in New York when Andy Warhol put her first in the Velvet Underground then *Chelsea Girls*, the latest of his experimental, art-trash-underground-trip-out sex movies, but the first to become a major commercial hit. Nico was the most beautiful blonde you had ever seen wherever she went, before the drugs got to her and finished all that off quick.

The ice queen had "dated" eighteen-year-old Jackson in New York in 1967, where he'd backed her on guitar at coffeehouse gigs. He would play on five of *Chelsea Girl*'s ten tracks and co-write the sweetly sour album opener "The Fairest of the Seasons." Then she dumped him. Since then Jackson had been with Joni. Been with a lot of different girls. Tom Rush did a version of "These Days" that did okay, paid a little rent. The doozy though was the soul-superior Gregg Allman version on his 1973 album, *Laid Back*. Jackson said he didn't know how the song should really sound, really be sung, until he heard badass Gregg laying it down so rich and true.

Here in 1970, though, Jackson has already been around long enough to know that the Troubadour vibe will eventually drag them all down if they let it. There's something about the place, something that seems to still time and fog creativity. It lets you think you're doing something great, getting somewhere real, but it's all after-dark delusion, all dust and dreams. Years later, Browne will claim, "The Troubadour was a big thing then, but I don't think there was ever a *scene* . . ."

The key, as Jackson saw it, was less about the Troubadour, and all about Laurel Canyon. "Places become a focal point for breaking out of convention," he said. "What was happening in Laurel Canyon was the universe cracking open and revealing its secrets. It was just about a time, a creative awakening [and] with the Byrds and the Burritos came a whole resurgence of interest in country music that led eventually to the Eagles."

An impossibly old head on ridiculously young shoulders, by the time Jackson finally gets a record deal in 1971, he has already met his future wife, actress-model Phyllis Major, who he will have a son with, Ethan. Jackson doesn't pretend to have a foolproof plan; he just knows you have to keep moving forward.

Glenn takes heed and starts to see into the dark of the Troubadour's corners. Starts to take in all the has-beens and never-wills bar-flying around the place, talking themselves up, coke-jivin', pot-blowin', singing the same old song to themselves, hoping someone else will sing along too. Feels the fear of getting sucked into the Troubadour quicksand, where everyone is just about to do this . . . see a guy about that . . . "Hey man, maybe we should get together and write some songs . . ."

Glenn knows deep down in the coldest part of his hard, fake city heart that it ain't going to work.

But what is? What works now it's 1970 and it's all been done already? And where do you go to get it? How much does it cost? Glenn intends to find out. Or die trying like the brown-dirt cowboy he actually believes he is.

3.

Asylum and the Lunatics That Run It

D avid Geffen is twenty-six years old, just a couple of years older than J.D. Souther, but he doesn't live in a cruddy shared shack out in Echo Park. He is already a millionaire twice over. Favors faded blue jeans and Western-cut shirts with floral patterns. Drives a Rolls-Royce Corniche. Already knows he is gay but also knows that being gay is the one personal freedom the freedom-flag-waving hippies will not tolerate. Knows, too, that that will change over time. Except David Geffen is not a "sit around waiting" type of guy. He's not a "hang at the Troubadour talking shit" type of guy (although he does quietly lurk at the Troubadour, in his freshly laundered and pressed chinos, looking like some camp, preppie dork who has just seen the Monkees on TV and decided this pop group stuff looks neat).

No, David Geffen is a "leave New York and get a job in Hollywood in the William Morris showbiz talent agency mailroom by faking your qualifications" kind of guy. He's a "get in at 6:30 a.m. and read everyone else's memos so you know every deal that is going down at the company" kind of guy. David's the kind of guy who sees the world as something to be claimed and believes California is ripe for its next gold rush, a place filled with barely hidden treasure as long as you're prepared to get down on your knees and dig it out with your bare, bloody hands.

In Hollywood, David quickly realizes, everyone has a shot at the big time. But, he notes, few take it. Geffen sees himself, rightly, as one of the self-chosen few.

In the William Morris mailroom he meets Elliot Roberts, another *geshikt* young Jewish guy from NYC but with a marginally better-concealed ambition. Elliot is funny and clever, more of stoner than David; hipper, at least on the surface. Elliot gets a gig as a junior agent at another firm, Chartoff-Winkler, where one of his clients is Buffy Sainte-Marie. Buffy came out of the same claustrophobic Toronto folk scene that Leonard Cohen and Neil Young later emerged from; now she's news in New York. But not *chart* news, so newbie Elliot gets given the job of taking care of her.

Buffy bosses Elliot into listening to a tape of this singer-songwriter she knows from Toronto, who happens to be in town doing a show in Greenwich Village that night. Elliot can't refuse, obviously; he wouldn't know how to say no to an artist yet, though he will quickly have to learn. So along he goes—and has his mind totally blown by one Roberta Joan Mitchell, Joni to her friends.

Elliot quits his job at Chartoff-Winkler the very next day in order to manage the twenty-four-year-old mystery blonde, books her a tour and then, on the word-to-the-wise advice of David Crosby, brings her to LA rather than New York, after Croz convinces him that LA is where it's all going to be happening now the sixties are dead and no one knows anything anymore.

Croz takes Joni in at his supershack in Laurel Canyon and starts showing her off like an exotic bird of paradise. They fall in and out of love. Elliot gets Joni a record deal with Warner Brothers' Reprise label and has Crosby produce her album.

"I didn't so much produce it as make sure nobody tried to fuck with it," he explained. "I just let her play and recorded it." A loose setup that captured too much ambient noise, resulting in excessive tape hiss. The only way to fix it was in post-production, at the cost of the high end of the audio range, resulting in the finished album sounding, as one critic put it, "as flat as a witch's tit."

Meanwhile, back on Lookout Mountain, where when the weather's good, you can see right into the future, David and Joni introduce Elliot to her old Toronto friend Neil Young, who wants out of Buffalo Springfield but doesn't know how to do it.

Elliot says he knows and takes Neil on as a client. Then he signs Croz too. Suddenly he's all in. Takes a Laurel Canyon house actually called the Lookout and bases his operation there. Drop by any time of the day or night and you'll run into Dennis Hopper, Mama Cass, Jack Nicholson, Michelle Phillips, Arthur Lee, Harry Dean Stanton, Micky Dolenz, Bonnie Raitt, Peter Fonda, Harry Nilsson, Joni, and Croz . . . Coke and grass, acid and acoustic guitars, sex and symbolism . . . Croz calls it "a model environment," which is one way of looking out from the Lookout.

David Geffen sees what Elliot is doing and quickly realizes he has to make a move too and finds a female singer-songwriter of his own, twenty-one-year-old Laura Nyro. He begins managing her shortly after she gives a career-shattering performance at the Monterey Pop Festival, where she is booed off. But Laura is gothically beautiful, writes songs of purest gold, and has a three-octave mezzo-soprano vocal range. When Laura sings, bluebirds flutter all around. The moon appears in daylight and the sun hides in shame.

David gets Laura a proper record deal with Clive Davis, president of Columbia Records. Then Geffen sets up a publishing company, Tuna Fish, in which he and Nyro have equal shares. Although Laura is too individual and careless of commerciality for the big time, her next two albums contain original songs that become huge American hits for more chart-friendly acts like Three Dog Night;

Blood, Sweat and Tears; and the 5th Dimension. That's when David pulls his biggest stroke yet and sells Tuna Fish to Clive Davis for $4.5 million (over $35 million in 2022) and both he and Laura become millionaires overnight.

While this is happening, Elliot books Joni into a four-night residency at the Troubadour and the shows become the launch pad for her second album, *Clouds*, which sneaks into the US top 30 in the summer of '69, nudged by the Judy Collins hit version of "Both Sides Now" from the year before, and the superior production courtesy of Doors recording guru and big pal of Crosby's, Paul A. Rothchild.

Joni's been singing at hootenannies and round campfires since she was a teenager in Saskatoon, Canada. Had a baby at twenty-one, gave it up for adoption, and fled to the folk clubs of Ontario and Toronto before fleeing again in 1965 for the real America, starting in New York and landing in Los Angeles. She has never been further from home nor felt closer to her past.

The same month *Clouds* is released, Geffen helps Elliot really hit the jackpot with the *Crosby, Stills & Nash* album. Crosby had been talking about forming some kind of folk-rock, country-blues, big-stuff "supergroup" with Stephen Stills, who was looking for something real to get his teeth into after Buffalo Springfield turned into a one-hit wonder, and Graham Nash, who has just fled England and the Hollies.

Together the three harmonize like fallen angels, an almost occult synthesis of musical minds, instantly appealing to anyone who hears them. It's certainly instantly clear to them. They know this is something. But they all have different record deals and publishing contracts that are getting in the way, they all have bullshit obligations bringing them down, man, a legal Gordian knot.

Elliot realizes he can't untangle them all by himself, and so he thinks again of David Geffen, who is probably the only person

Elliot knows in LA who could talk his way through that amount of bullshit and come out with a rose between his teeth.

Geffen can't wait to get started. Goes first to Clive Davis, who went to Monterey Pop as Barbra Streisand's go-to label guy and came back with Santana and Janis Joplin, the first of a new rock empire Davis would preside over on Columbia's behalf. Clive already has Croz signed to one of Columbia's subsidiaries and immediately grasps the concept of Crosby, Stills & Nash. So then Geffen hustles over to Atlantic to negotiate the release of Stephen Stills. Atlantic supremo-producer, legend-and-don't-you-forget-it Jerry Wexler throws him out. Jerry is all about Aretha Franklin and Dusty Springfield, not this white, druggy, hippy horseshit.

But Jerry's only living god, Ahmet Ertegun, who has just sold a million records with the debut album from his other white, druggy, hippy-horseshit signing, Led Zeppelin, and already has pre-orders of five million for their next album, listens carefully to what Geffen has to say. Geffen goes into full swing. CS&N might be selling music for the mind, he tells Ahmet, but those minds will pay top dollar.

Ahmet, who first got his beak wet with loud white rock groups when he signed Cream to the label in 1966, has just green-lit Atlantic to pay $7 million for the rights to distribute Rolling Stones Records—the band's newly formed boutique vanity label— throughout North America and Canada. The debut release under the new deal is *Sticky Fingers*, the first of eight consecutive Stones albums to go to No.1 in America.

Ahmet knows the good shit when he hears it, regardless of genre or ethnicity, and decides that, actually, fuck Jerry, he *would* like Crosby, Stills & Nash on Atlantic Records. He smiles that seductive, reptilian smile of his and lets bushy-tailed David know this could be the start of a beautiful friendship. So then Geffen runs panting back to Clive Davis, in a hurry to get a bidding war started. But Clive blindsides him by admitting he's had a downer on Croz since—the way Clive sees it—he plotted to get himself thrown out of the Byrds, leaving them to rot. Clive tells David he is actually quite happy to be rid of the bastard.

This is when David Geffen finally seizes his moment, telling Elliot that he's had enough of being an agent, that if Elliot partners up with him in a management company, he'll make him twice the money he can make on his own. The same night, they shake hands on the Geffen-Roberts Company.

Well, that first Crosby, Stills & Nash album *sold*—two million copies, baby, one of the biggest records of the year. Becoming the soundtrack to the summer of 1969 for a new generation of wiser-time heads. Their first big show was at the Woodstock festival, after which they sold a million more albums. By the time the Woodstock movie came out in 1970 they had sold another million. The same month their second album, *Déjà Vu*, went straight to Number 1 and sold another three, four, five million. Then three times that in the coming years.

But nothing stays the same forever, and by the end of 1970 David Geffen has discovered that management is fundamentally unsuited to a big-picture personality like his. He's too smart, too restless, too ruthless, too intolerant of fools and their fucking girlfriends and boyfriends and other no-gooders, especially those mishearing hope for dope, and when Crosby, Stills & Nash bolt on Neil Young to boost their sound and become a real, genuine, live, living nightmare of a band, he begins to wonder why he is the schmuck out there dealing with all their other shit day after day, night in, night out. The nights in particular. Being used that time as an unwitting drug mule by fucking Crosby—carrying weed cross-country—has him thinking that, you know what, maybe Clive Davis was the smart one.

The other three are no picnic either. Stephen Stills is a control freak who thinks Neil Young is taking the group away from him. Neil Young is a control freak who is trying to take the group away from Stephen Stills. Croz can't keep his sarcastic, know-all mouth shut. Stephen and Graham are both still suffering in the aftermath of "complicated" relationships, Stephen with Judy Collins, whose rejection results in two of Stills's most moving songs, "Suite: Judy Blue Eyes" and "Hopelessly Hoping," heartbreak highlights of the first CS&N album.

"It was fireworks," Collins recalled of their relationship. "[Stephen] hated New York and he hated therapy. And I was in both." When Stills played her "Suite: Judy Blue Eyes," they both listened and cried. Then Collins told him: "Oh, Stephen, it's such a beautiful song. But it's not winning me back."

Graham Nash had first met Joni Mitchell long before either of them got to Lookout Mountain—at a Hollies show in Ottawa in 1967. He recalled: "She picked up a guitar and played me fifteen of the best songs I'd ever heard, and then we spent the night together. It was magical on so many different levels."

When they met again a year later, this time at Crosby's place in Laurel Canyon, where the inevitable all-night-every-night party was going on, Joni grabbed Graham's arm and whispered: "Come to my house and I'll take care of you." He moved in with her that same night.

As with Stills, some great songs emerged from the Nash–Mitchell romance, including "Our House," which Graham wrote on Joni's piano after another blissed-out day together at home in the Canyon. They spoke occasionally of marriage. But things had soured by the time the first CS&N album caught fire. After yet another row, she poured a bowl of cornflakes and milk over his head. He put her over his knee and spanked her. "With all due respect," he later recalled, "she took it very well." By the time recording began on *Déjà Vu* the romance was over.

Then real tragedy struck when Crosby's twenty-one-year-old girlfriend, Christine Hinton, was killed in a car crash. Croz and

Chris had been together going back to the Byrds. She was a hippy chick, liked to go naked on the beach, roll a tight doobie, and make love all night. But then Croz fell for Joni because everyone fell for Joni, and they broke up. After Nash moved in, Croz and Chris got back together. In September 1969, she borrowed David's VW van to take her two cats to the vet. When one of them jumped into her lap while she was driving, she lost control and collided with an oncoming school bus, killing her.

Friends say that was the day the best part of David Crosby died too. The day when cocaine and, soon after, heroin became more important to Croz. Much more important. "David went to identify the body and he's never been the same since," Nash told the group's photographer, Dave Zimmer.

To try to deal with it, he and Nash took a long trip on Crosby's boat, *The Mayan*, sailing 3,000 miles from Fort Lauderdale, Florida, to San Francisco. Croz wanted to scatter Christine's ashes in the ocean. They spent seven weeks at sea with what Nash described as a "bottomless supply of weed and coke." It didn't help.

Nash was back home in LA, lying on the kitchen floor, when he got a telegram from Joni: "If you hold sand too tightly in your hand, it will run through your fingers. Love, Joan."

How is Geffen supposed to deal with this kind of next-level horror show? Geffen's real environment is the office, the quick-draw telephone, one in each hand, two more ringing hot on the desk, where he can let loose: be a monster, a shark, a cold-blooded killer. Be himself.

He and Elliot have their technique all down. They create an intoxicating bubble of stardom around their clients by keeping reality at bay. Then Geffen, always thinking, begins to resent all the money their acts are making for the record companies. He begins to wonder out loud why *they* couldn't be the record label, too?

David tells Elliot they should sweep away the old guys in their ivory towers and build some of their own to sit in. But bigger, and with more ivory. Geffen now works even harder than before. He lives at his Sunset Boulevard office. On the phones, in the car, breaking down doors. His week beats your year.

One day a letter-size package arrives in the mail. Inside it is a black-and-white headshot and a demo cassette tape. The letter is very long and blah-blah-blah, so David who's heard it all before throws it in the garbage. But the picture catches the eye of his secretary Dodie Smith, who thinks the guy looks cute, and so she takes the letter back out again and reads it.

It is sweet, sincere. So she pulls the tape out and plays it. It is a young Cadillac-clown named Jackson Browne who'd been singing and writing LA-verité since he was sixteen. The track is called "Song for Adam." Just voice and acoustic guitar. And the ghost of tortured memory, of Adam.

Dodie, David, and Elliot are utterly floored. They play the tape back and are astonished all over again. David now makes it his job to find this kid Jackson and nurture him. The first place he goes to look is the Troubadour and . . . bingo!

Jackson is down to his last borrowed dollar and it's an easy win. David introduces Jackson to Laura Nyro and they begin an intensely sexual affair. Everything seems to be going their way, stars crashing in the sky. But when David urges Ahmet Ertegun to sign Jackson, Ahmet, to David's disbelief, says no.

"But Ahmet," David pleads, aghast, "you'll make a lot of money . . ."

"David," Ahmet says, adjusting his tinted glasses, "I *have* a lot of money. Why don't you start a label, then you'll have a lot of money, too?"

David gets it. David *always* gets it. They strike a deal. David will start a new record label, in cahoots with Elliot. They call it

Asylum—they like the double meaning. Ahmet pays start-up costs and Atlantic handles distribution in return for 50 percent of the profits.

The only downer: Laura Nyro, who Geffen still manages and has helped make a millionaire. Laura was going to be Asylum's marquee signing, David promising her the world. But Laura reneged on the deal and, without telling Geffen, signed a new deal directly with Clive Davis at Columbia. David would later describe it as the biggest betrayal of his life up to that point and that he "cried for days" afterward.

Then David goes to work. Within weeks Asylum have signed Linda Ronstadt, J.D. Souther, Joni Mitchell, native Los Angelino singer-songwriter Judee Sill, a Greenwich Village folk-scene outcast with slow-burning talent named David Blue—and another outside-chancer named Glenn Frey.

Geffen doesn't see Glenn as a star, he tells him straight: he will need a band. Then signs him after Glenn comes back a few weeks later with his buddies Don Henley, Bernie Leadon, and Randy Meisner and says, how about this for a band?

In a revealing interview with Cameron Crowe for *Rolling Stone* in 1975, Frey explained that David Geffen had told him point blank that, "I shouldn't make a record by myself and that maybe I should join a band." Before he could fully absorb this bombshell, he landed a gig in Linda Ronstadt's touring band. When they hadn't found a drummer with just two days left before the band was to begin rehearsing, Frey suggested his new pal, Don Henley. Running into Don at the Troub, Frey "struck up a conversation with him. I told him my whole trip was just stalled. I had all these songs and couldn't make a record and I wanted to put together a band, but I was going on the road with Linda. Henley said that he was fucked up, too." The guitarist in the band he was then in, Shiloh, had just left to join the Burritos, Don told Glenn. "So he joined Linda's group, too," Frey told Crowe. "The first night of our tour, we decided to start a band."

"Glenn asked if I'd like to go on the road with Linda Ronstadt's band, and I said: 'You bet I do,'" Henley recalled of their first, fateful connection. "I was broke, and here was a chance for two hundred dollars a week. We went out for a month or two, and Glenn and I struck up this great friendship. That's when we started plotting to put a band together."

Back in LA at the end of the Ronstadt tour, after just their third rehearsal with their new band, Frey turned to Henley and said conspiratorially: "We're going to have to run things . . ."

4.

Everyone Dies Famous in a Small Town

The first time Don Henley's baby-blues lit on the thirteen-story Capitol "Stack of Records" Tower—the one that looks like it's come out of a kids' sci-fi cartoon, *The Jetsons* or some shit, beamed down onto the ninety-eight-degree streets of Hollywood and Vine—he actually gets *shivers*, man. It is June 1970. Donald Hugh Henley, from Texas, is a month short of his twenty-third birthday and feels like he has finally arrived in the Promised Land. The tra-la-land of the Byrds and the Beach Boys, a go-go get-to only glimpsed on TV shows and in magazines . . . until now.

Here he is, Don Henley, lantern-jawed young Texan, a look on his face like he's counting gift-horse teeth, a belligerent blend of Irish, Scots, and English blood, but still wet behind the ears, about to begin his very own American Gothic fable. He'd dreamed of being a football player—until his high school coach broke the news: he was too short. So he wandered over to the music class where there were a lot of chicks. Somethin' ta do. Realized he was good at it. Started thinking. Dreaming.

Now here he was in the place where dreams are bought and sold every day. LA, I tell you what. It's all out there, if you know where to look in this haunted city, with its scorched mountains and killer canyons, its sheltered valley secrets and its blond and busty beaches, stretched out so far that the only way to get anywhere is to drive it, cruising on the wide boulevards and endless freeways ... it's already there, if you rip back the silver screen, there in the shooting of RFK at the Ambassador Hotel ... in the murders on Cielo Drive ... in the cipher codes of the Zodiac Killer being printed in the newspapers, this creeping undercurrent of paranoia and fear that finds its full expression here in the armed private security patrols that move through the weird, hushed calm of Beverley Hills, in the LA cops running undercover stake-outs in borrowed Rolls-Royces, the movie stars and studio execs reinforcing their tall gates and upgrading their spy cameras, trying to ride out the new unease and panic that is sweeping away one culture and bringing in another. The sixties are over, baby. The seventies are here to stay. Blow me.

If you're an artist, you feel it even if you're not trying to, even if you don't want to, sometimes especially when you don't want to— feel this new darkness that occupies all the spaces around you. Stanley Kubrick feels it as he calls action on *A Clockwork Orange*— then later withdraws the film from circulation after several copycat attacks occur in Britain. So do Don Siegel and Clint Eastwood as they film *Dirty Harry* (Eastwood's rock 'n' roll detective Harry Callaghan hunts a killer called Scorpio, a nod to the Zodiac, who is still out there killing). Billy Friedkin feels the same and makes *The French Connection* and then *The Exorcist*. Sixties dream turned seventies nightmare. And Robert Altman, who makes *McCabe & Mrs. Miller*. The Wild West, not as movie mythos but sordid cowboy-vivant.

Suddenly what happened last night feels like a long time ago, and Don Henley chooses this precise moment to push open the saloon doors and swing into town, spurs jangling.

From Linden, via North Texas State University in Denton, his life like a coming-of-age movie directed by Mike Nichols. Fifties

Linden, population a thousand or so—that's a lot of *cousins*—was archetypal Republican, small-town rural America. Don's parents C.J. and Hughlene were both Texas natives. After the Second World War, C.J. opened an auto parts store. Hughlene was a schoolteacher until only child Don came along.

Don's parents are good people. Don is a good and dutiful son. In high school he joins the Future Farmers of America and tends an acre of cucumbers. He plays football until the coach inadvertently does him a solid. Music, Don recognizes, is something he had grown up around, his mom and dad have all the big band records—Glenn Miller, the daddy; Benny Goodman, king of swing; Harry James, who gave the scrawny young Sinatra his big break.

C.J. loves country music, too, has always got KWKH blaring in the car, his favorite show: *Louisiana Hayride*. Hank Williams and Elvis *in excelsis*. Then there is church music and all the spirituals, flood tides of music, and then comes a record player of his own, an RCA connector, and the 45s Hughlene picks up for him: Ricky Nelson, the Everly Brothers, Jerry Lee Lewis, Bobby Freeman, and then the Beatles . . . Oh God, the Beatles. Don *loved* them!

So young Don tries out the trombone, but I mean, c'mon . . . he soon switches, this time to percussion, a drum. He's not a big hitter but Don has a certain feeling for time, and the kid is good right away in the way that the naturally talented are, and soon he has his first full kit and begins to play every chance he gets.

Every chance he gets, that is, when he's not out eyeing up cars. Big-finned Caddies and long-nosed Chevy 'vettes. Anything with four wheels and a bad attitude. Don starts off with a go-kart that he builds from a kit, then he inherits C.J.'s '48 Dodge ("Slept in it, threw up in it, hunted in it," he'll happily tell you), which he actually wins a drag-racing trophy in that he will keep forever.

Don's a car stud all right all right all right. See him come fiending round those tight bends. Hear his tires scream.

Young Don is an only child and kind of a loner. He has that special only-child power to absorb himself for long hours in solitary pursuits. In his case, music or cars, same difference—cucumbers if he has to, even *reading*—and in redneck Texas circa nineteen sixty-nowhere, that didn't hold much water.

Young Don wants to prove his manliness, but he can't do it through his physicality, and the right cars cost too much money, so he gets deeper into the music. His closest friend is Richard Bowden, a big, outgoing, friendly fella with a huge Texas-shaped heart, who plays guitar a little bit.

"Mrs. Henley was a real fine lady, but she never had any control over Don," Bowden told *Rolling Stone* magazine when they profiled the band in 1976. "Not that he didn't respect her, he just always did what he wanted. And his father would have to come down on him. They couldn't get along for years. Don always felt he had to prove something to him."

Don's father was a worrier, too, a hardworking man who saved twenty-five cents a week for Henley's college fund. A serious guy with his own points to prove, Don would inherit his father's mistrust for the opinions of others. Years later, a so-called friend will recollect, "[Don] just had to constantly prove he could do whatever he wanted. He had to prove he wasn't still that dorky kid."

In that amorphous, casual way of the early sixties, Don joins a band run by Richard's father, Elmer, a Dixieland-type deal. Not exactly Don's scene, but, hey, it's an actual band playing actual shows in front of actual people. When Pappy leaves, Don, Richard, and another school pal, Jerry Surratt, become the foundation of a party-cum-covers act that play frat houses, bars, high school proms, anything that pays a few bucks, in and around Austin and Dallas.

Like small-ad hookers, they keep changing their name to make it seem like they're a new act, settling longest on the Four Speeds.

It's while they are playing four-hour sets to party-hearty kids that it happens, this magic thing, the discovery that will define Don Henley's career and thus the rest of his life; that will light the way at last toward that dark desert highway, and will show him the first steps he has to take on that fabulous and fucked-up Yellow Brick Road that only the very few, the Chosen, get to tread.

Don Henley opens his mouth and starts to sing—and everybody stops what they're doing and listens. First of all at the frat parties where the jocks 'n' frocks demand the hot R & B hits of the day, the stuff you can dance to, that brings the girls out onto the floor, the Wilson Pickett and James Brown stuff, Otis Redding and Bobby Bland, Marvin Gaye and Smoky Robinson, the stuff that a skinny white boy in an old plaid shirt and dusty cowboy boots shouldn't be able to sing but somehow *can*.

It's a goddamned miracle, I tell you what, right there on Main Street.

This becomes Don Henley's training ground, a boot camp for what will become one of the greatest and most distinguishable voices in music, and it starts here in the Lone Star bars and after-hours shindigs of the Texas Triangle. After a while, it's so obvious, this thing that Don has, that the rest of the band, now laboring under the unenviable name of the Felicity, vote him in as their full-time singer.

They know what everyone knows, even in these early, raw days of the music business: you can learn to play drums. But you can't learn to sing the way Don Henley can, a pure low tenor voice with a high G falsetto, just the right amount of grit in the oyster to make the pearl, a voice that only comes along a few times in each generation.

Don begins writing his own songs with the band, even though the get-down party crowds do not want to hear them. One of their early efforts, credited on the label to Richard but which Don should have had at least a co-credit for, "Hurtin'," kicks off their recording career when one of the local producers-cum-label owners looking for a cheap fix, puts it out, and it goes absolutely nowhere but at least it's there, at least it exists. Something Don can hold in his hands and show people. Show his parents. Show himself.

The Felicity became Shiloh, a name that at least hints at the direction of travel, and then everyone hits eighteen and Don enrolls in college because C.J. has set aside that precious twenty-five cents a week since his son was born to make sure that he can. "He had to quit school in the eighth grade," Don recalled of his father, "and he wanted me to have a better life than he had."

Don moves to Stephen F. Austin State University, in the small East Texas city of Nacogdoches, along with his high school sweetheart, Jana, who is the first of the great many very beautiful girls who will share Don's life and the first who ruffles the feathers of the other, cooler guys who wonder what in hell a red-hot chick like Jana is doing with a badly dressed no-shot loser like Don. "Guys would ask her out all the time," he recalled ruefully. "It's one of the reasons I transferred to another school . . ."

At Don's insistence he and Jana head for North Texas State. By now, Don is almost twenty and he has seen and heard the Byrds, bought *Sgt. Pepper*, dropped acid, smoked the good shit, encountered and grasped the significance of the work two of his literary heroes, Thomas Hardy—who wrote poems as effortlessly as he wrote lyrics, ballads, novels, satire—and Ralph Waldo Emerson, another essayist and poet who championed individuality and personal freedom over everything, seeing God not in the heavens above but deep in a man's soul.

Don studies for three semesters at North Texas before Hughlene sends word that C.J.'s health is deteriorating fast due to a serious heart condition. The car parts business is sold and Don returns to Linden to spend as much time with C.J. and Hughlene as he can while his father is still here with them on earth.

There aren't many upsides to times like that, but one is that Don can play a little more often again with Shiloh, who are still gigging. One night at the Studio Club in Dallas, in walks a bona fide Texas music star looking for the next big thing. Kenny Rogers, late of the First Edition, is now a budding producer scouting for his friend and First Edition producer Jimmy Bowen, who has a deal with Frank Sinatra's Reprise label out in LA. Kenny hears Shiloh and thinks just maybe they could be the band he's looking for.

They strike up a kind of friendship, and they cut a song for Kenny called "Jennifer." The signs are all good. Then Jerry Surratt comes out of the rehearsal room in Linden one day, gets on his dirt bike, and is killed instantly as he is crossing the highway, struck by an oncoming car. His mom, his sister, and his bandmates all see it happen. The car is driven by a kid they all know, who was distracted for a brief moment by seeing his friends standing by the side of Kenny Rogers's tour bus.

It's a small-town death, a small-town tragedy, and everyone in that small town takes it very, very hard.

After a lot of ass scratching, they decide to carry on with the band. It's what Jerry would have wanted, they tell themselves.

Don finds Jim Ed Norman, who plays keyboards and also went to North Texas State, and Al Perkins, who plays pedal steel and is a friend of Kenny Rogers, and Shiloh clamber up onto their feet. As Don says, "It took two talented guys to replace Jerry." Meanwhile, after some hard thinking, Don breaks it off with Jana, because she wants to get married and settle down and he is not ready yet to commit his life to just one girl in just one place.

In the summer of 1970, the call comes from Kenny Rogers, letting Shiloh know it's time to pack their bags and say their so-longs, time to come out to LA, boys, where you are going to make a record.

His life already scarred by an early death, and knowing C.J. is becoming sicker by the day, Don agonizes about leaving Hughlene to deal with all this shit on her own.

In the end though, Don knows what he has to do, which direction life is pulling him in, and he departs the world of, as he puts it, "the Baptists and the Methodists and the Southern purgatory they laid on me."

No muss, no fuss. Just packs up his 1967 Chevelle, gathers the guys and steps on it, leading Richard's Buick, Jim Ed's Ford van, and a rented U-Haul carrying their few possessions.

Heading west, going to California, any troublesome objects in the rearview mirror rapidly fading behind them.

They sure hope so anyway.

5.

The Overwhelming Odds against Anyone Ever Becoming the Eagles

So from the point of view of all previous highly regarded rock orthodoxies penned by well-meaning but hopelessly academic *music* journalists—the kind the Eagles held a blood-hatred for—this is where our fledgling outlaws, Glenn Frey and Don Henley, unveil their cunning plan. First we take the Troubadour, then we take the world. But it wasn't the music that molded them into the yin-yang of the Eagles. It was the sheer bloody-minded determination to make this thing they were building work.

Dark side. Light side. Sun and moon. Fire and water. Not so much good cop bad cop, though, as enjoying taking turns. Ganging up together. It is established early on that Frey and Henley, Glenn and Don, are the A-Team, the golden geese, the gruesome two-some, the alpha-and-omega, fuck-you-very-much.

Frey, the instinctive, hedonistic, hard-driving Motor City greaser whose copper-bottomed philosophy he summed up in that one line he wrote and sang in the first ever Eagles million-seller, "Take It Easy": "Lighten up while you still can," he breezes. "Don't even try to understand . . ."

Henley the cerebral, hard-driving country boy, radically different from Glenn but completely the same, both of them full of their own top-shelf brands of angels and demons, both in Los Angeles selling their wares, both heading in a similar direction, come hell or high water, soon to meet at the place where everyone meets—the devil's crossroads that they call the Troubadour.

What a cosmic fucking fluke it is, what an infinitesimally small chance that these two drifters should come together at this particular time in this specific place, on this mad planet three stoned steps from the sun. Imagine all of the small coincidences, big decisions, and random life events that have to coalesce for them to even *meet*, let alone entwine their fates together.

Imagine the further elements that brought David Geffen and Elliot Roberts to this point in their lives, to this moment, where they are out looking for exactly what Glenn and Don will become. It's enough to make you believe in karma, or kismet, or destiny, or Disney, or whatever you want to call it, especially when you think about all of the people who do not meet, who never come together in a sudden flash combination that proves irresistible to the world, all of the bands and songs and gigs and records that never happen, that are not even conceived, because lives did not collide in exactly the right way, or time or headspace, in exactly the way they are about to for Glenn Frey and Don Henley.

Don and Shiloh drive into Los Angeles in June 1970 and head straight for Kenny Rogers's place in Encino. It's a sweet crib, gotta swimming pool and everything, but after a few weeks of crashing on the floor, they're in hotels and motels, playing shows here and there—the Valley, the beaches, any bar that'll have them—while Kenny finds them a label for the album he wants to record.

Coincidentally, the label Kenny is doing such a fine job for, Amos Records, was also the home until recently to Longbranch Pennywhistle. Don and Shiloh head to Larrabee Sound in Manhattan Beach to make a record, but after a couple of singles Amos Records folds and Shiloh are left hanging. Kenny is sorry fellas but, hey, what can you do? That's showbiz, I tell you what.

Shiloh turn up for the Hoot Night they've been told about at
the Troubadour, get to play a couple of songs, go down not bad,
nobody dies, then split to the bar. That's when the collisions
really start, stars crashing into one another, burning fuses, bringing it all together to create this tiny new universe that will keep
expanding rapidly until it becomes its own impossible-to-measure
black hole.

In the audience this night are Glenn Frey and Jackson Browne,
Linda Ronstadt, and J.D. Souther, and although Shiloh go down
well, it is not quite well enough for Don, who is the first of the band
to conclude that they may have been good enough to escape from
Texas, but they are not quite good enough to make it here in the
city of the hot bright lights, facing off against the future where it
really counts.

Also feeling the slow disheartening grind of things never quite
working out, the weight of failure dragging at her heels, is Linda
Ronstadt, who everyone can hear plain as day is one of the greatest
singers on the scene, but who can't seem to shake off the labels they
want to put on her. Her folk-pop trio, the Stone Poneys, released
three albums on Capitol between 1967 and '68 and none of them
caught fire.

There was a top 20 one-hit wonder in their manicured version of
Mike Nesmith's delightfully defiant "Different Drum," Linda's
mountain-dew voice with a harpsichord solo draped over it like an
old-lady shawl. A kind of Judith Durham trip for the groovy kids.
Only it's not the groovy kids who buy the record, it's their moms
and pops.

Capitol has a rethink. Offers Linda, still only twenty-two, a solo
contract. She can still have the other two boys from the Poneys on
the record, but this is now Linda's story, and against advice she
decides she's now on a country rock trip. She never liked the old
Nashville wigs-and-cleavage deal, never considered country music

at all, in fact. But she digs what's going on at the Troubadour. Thinks maybe there's a seat at the table for her too.

There's an album, *Hand Sown . . . Home Grown*, a mix of contemporary Dylan and Randy Newman covers and old-school Nashville selections from the likes of Jack Rhodes and Wayne Raney, plus an original from the Poneys' multi-instrumentalist Kenny Edwards. It's a *nice* record. It disappears without a trace.

A year later there's a second album, *Silk Purse*, this time recorded in Nashville, for extra authenticity—the only album Linda will ever make there. Produced by Elliot F. Mazer, off the back of working with other folk-area, rock-curious artists like Gordon Lightfoot, Jake Holmes, and Richie Havens. He's also nabbed a credit on *Cheap Thrills*, the last Big Brother and the Holding Company album to feature Janis Joplin, which spent eight weeks at Number 1 in the US charts in 1968. This surely is the guy who will know what to do for Linda Ronstadt. On the basis of a personal recommendation from Janis, Linda gets Capitol to hire him.

Sure enough, it's more obviously "country" than her first album, with the safety net of a cover of Carole King's sure-fire-hit "Will You Still Love Me Tomorrow"—which pointedly isn't a hit when it's released as the first single. Instead, that honor goes to a song Ronstadt had to fight Capitol tooth and nail to allow her to record, "Long, Long Time," a ballad-with-strings by Texan Gary White, which climbs to Number 21 when it's released as the album's second single in the summer of 1970.

Capitol chiefs tried everything to dissuade Linda from including it on the album. It was either too country or not country enough. It was certainly more easy listening than country rock. But the label hated it and actively forbade her to seek out any other material of a similar ilk. If Capitol had a plan, it was difficult to discern. Even the cover shot of *Silk Purse* was decidedly off—a non-ironic shot of lovely Linda sitting in a pigsty. Silk purse—pigsty, geddit?

Christ. It shows a base-level lack of understanding of who Linda is, as an artist and as a woman. She does not fit into any of the pre-marked boxes that in 1970, year of *The Female Eunuch*, are about to be challenged and dismantled. She is an artist, who, like other true artists, defines her own limits. She has played with the Doors and Neil Young. She can and will sing anything from hard rock to light opera. She tells everyone who will listen that *her* music is not country music, not folk and not rock, but "California music." As Linda's producer-cum-manager-cum-boyfriend John Boylan puts it, "A lot of people in LA were trying to figure out the perfect country rock sound. And we knew that if we could get the songs right and the combination right, we could have something big." All of these small, bright stars in their own constellations, slowly drawing into one another's orbits.

Boylan was another paid-up member of the Troubadour brotherhood, but at twenty-nine older than most. A musician, composer, producer, he was the permanently hot-running New Yorker let loose among the LA lotus-eaters. He'd come through Tin Pan Alley, where one of his songs, "Suzanne on a Sunday Morning" became a modest hit for fifties teenage heartthrob Rick Nelson. He wafted down to California, found himself in LA scoring the soundtrack to Ali MacGraw's movie hit *Goodbye, Columbus*, and becoming a full-time record producer. When one night early on he found the Troubadour—and had lived there ever since.

Word soon got around. Boylan was not like the others. He was a musical maverick who, unlike most self-avowed musical mavericks, also understood how the business worked. In 1969, he produced the fifth album, self-titled, by the Association, the "California sunshine" collective that had performed on the *Goodbye, Columbus* soundtrack. The Association had already had two Number 1 singles and were the opening act at Monterey Pop. Their music comprised dippy-sappy, feel-good pop confections that appealed to young hippies who didn't inhale yet. Same crowd as Monkees fans, Archies, clean-cut and very, very catchy.

But as the sixties sullied, so did their career.

The big idea was that John Boylan, this full-on New York production stud would facilitate that kind of decidedly more right-on album needed to bring the Association up to date. In 1969, that meant the Band, *All Things Have Passed*, CS&N, the first full flowering of the Laurel Canyon songwriters' love-in.

You'd have to say he succeeded too. Gone was the wispy whimsy and aimless, forced smiles. In came musical grit and lyrical authenticity. In came genuine charm. The album tiptoed elegantly to Number 32 and subsequently vanished. But John Boylan's rep now preceded him.

His passion shone through. He would tell the younger bucks at the Troub bar, how the best damn group he'd ever worked with were the Dillards, and they'd assume he was joking and laugh along. Boylan meant every word. The Dillards were a true-life American bluegrass band from Salem, Missouri. In their only promotional picture at the time, one of them looked cross-eyed and one of them—the bald one—smoked a pipe. Two of them looked like goofy guys just darned pleased to meetcha. Only one of them, a big cuddly bear with a big hairy bear chest, lush lampshade head-hair, and thick Axminster wraparound rug-beard with added hair, had any charisma.

But it was one of the goofy guys who would stand out: thirty-three-year-old banjo player Doug Dillard. By the time Boylan saw him again he was co-fronting Dillard & Clark with beautiful but bewildered former Byrd Gene Clark, and everyone thought they were the Second Coming. Or maybe the third or fourth. But definitely right up there this week.

For Boylan it was the Dillards that were truly something else. "They had great bluegrass harmonies and were a tremendous influence on everyone around here and never get proper credit. Crosby, Stills & Nash, Poco, and the Eagles all stole their harmonies from Dillards. They used to play the Troubadour."

For John Boylan, when the Dillards invited him to produce their 1970 album, *Copperfields*, "that gave me credibility."

Boylan seems to know something, and Linda listens to him. John tells Linda what she needs is her own band. She and John are now living together in John's own Laurel Canyon hang, falling for one another, then falling out with one another romantically but striking up a powerful musical relationship that will survive the scene.

Linda and John go looking for "good players" to join her band, starting of course at the Troubadour. It's there one night in 1970 that Linda hears Shiloh perform "Silver Threads and Golden Needles" from her *Hand Sown . . . Home Grown* record, and though she's unsure if it's her version or someone else's—there have been a lot, including one, coincidentally, or cosmically, if you don't believe in coincidence, which no one in Laurel Canyon does, by a girl group called Honey Ltd.—it sounds *right*, like Linda always heard it in her head.

At the same time, Boylan immediately identifies Glenn Frey of Longbranch Pennywhistle as another potential recruit. Boylan notes approvingly that Glenn plays guitar "the right way" and can sing harmony as well as lead. One evening he and Linda are having dinner with Glenn and J.D. Souther at Nucleus Nuance, the clubby new jazz eatery on Melrose where Howard Hughes likes to go undercover to nibble on their specialty, "Ra, The Untouchable" (a steak), when J.D. suggests out of the blue that Glenn hook up with Linda. There's not much happening with Longbranch Pennywhistle now that Amos is about to fold. Boylan offers Glenn $200 a week to join Linda's new touring band, "and I jumped at it," Glenn recalled, "it was more than I'd seen in about three years in California. I got so excited because I'd never been on the road before . . ."

They all remember it differently now, of course, but either Glenn suggests Don should join up too, or John suggests it, or maybe it was Linda, it doesn't really matter—these nascent stars were now coming together, colliding into stars, drawn by the mysterious universe they inhabit.

Boylan went to check out Shiloh play at Hollywood's Aquarius. Impressed, he went back after the show and made Don a straight offer of $200 a week to join Linda's band. Don recalled it a little differently, when speaking with Marc Eliot years later. He said it was Glenn who introduced him. An audition was arranged at her small wooden shack in Laurel Canyon. "I went up there and ran through several numbers with Glenn, Linda, John Boylan and the others," remembered Don. "I was hired on the spot."

"Glenn was our suggestion," Linda later clarified, "but he was the one who discovered Henley could sing. He called Don his secret weapon."

There are two significant others orbiting in this new band of Linda's. Bernie Leadon is from Minnesota, wears a great frizz of hair and a Zapata mustache that makes him look like an albino bandito. Bernie can play anything with strings—guitar, banjo, mandolin, pedal steel, dobro—and he can sing and write, and more than that, he has a nose for the great ones. He knows how to make them better, how to reflect the rays of their glory.

Bernie just glows badass. You don't wanna tangle. He has been in Dillard & Clark with Gene Clark, working on the seminal country rock release *The Fantastic Expedition of Dillard & Clark*; most people have never heard of it, but then he goes to the Flying Burrito Brothers and works with the fragile, self-destructive genius that is Gram Parsons, where he watches as Gram burns through his trust fund while he parties with the Stones.

Bernie plays at Altamont with the Burritos, feels like the scoutmaster to a bunch of scared kids, realizes that if he's going to get anywhere, he needs to ditch the fragile genius guys and find some other kind of geniuses, the kick-ass, fuck you, we want all the money, fame, and women you can get us kind—the Mick and Keef kind, rather than the Gene and Gram kind. He doesn't know if that's exactly who Linda Ronstadt is, but he sees she is not possessed by demons or shooting up smack, and that's a big improvement. That and a guaranteed weekly paycheck from the tour means big gangly Bernie's in—no further questions, your honor.

Then there's Randall Herman Meisner. Randy has grown up on a farm in Nebraska, the second child and only boy of hardworking German Russian immigrants, Herman and Emilie, which is about as far removed as you can get from the life he is about to start living in LA.

He has long, straight hair and a folksy, hippy disposition, and he plays bass just fine and can sing pretty great, actually. He looks and is and sees himself as a good guy. From honest Volga German bones.

His folks produce corn, alfalfa, sweet beets, beans, all that good shit. Mom sings around the house all day and grandfather might play the violin. But music is an indulgence for when the day's work is done. Then, when he is ten years old, Randy sees Elvis Presley blowing the shit out of "Hound Dog" on *The Ed Sullivan Show* and his tiny farm-boy mind is blown.

Randy persuades his folks to stump up for an acoustic guitar, which he practices on and poses with in his bedroom, playing along to "Don't Be Cruel" and "All Shook Up." He tries on the Elvis voice for size uh-huh-uh-huh but can't quite make it. Instead he discovers he can produce sweet harmonies, really hitting those high notes. Starts getting into R & B, race records, and playing in high school outfits geared to the hits of the day, same as all the others. Randy doesn't locate his own special superpower until his music teacher at Scottsbluff High School suggests he might like to try his hand at bass.

Unlike guitar, which, because he couldn't read music, he would use to pick apart and learn songs by ear, "my bass playing came real naturally." Inspired by the standout playing of Motown's boss-bass, badass James Jamerson, his style developed quickly. He was fifteen when he joined his first semipro outfit, the Dynamics (later the Driving Dynamics). In 1965 they pressed up 500 copies of a four-track EP, on which Randy sang Sam Cooke's "You Send Me"—and didn't fuck it up! Randy could *sing*, man. He just didn't crow about it.

After the usual early days dicking around with local heroes, he made it out to LA with a band called the Soul Survivors, soon to be renamed the Poor—and never was a band more aptly named. Randy has to walk everywhere and live on five bucks a day at the Tropicana, this divey place just outside of West Hollywood, and gets by dealing a little grass. But at least the Poor share management with Buffalo Springfield and Sonny and Cher, and one time they even get a gig supporting Jimi Hendrix in New York. That doesn't go too well, and the Poor have to threaten all sorts of violent shit to the club owner just to get their plane tickets home.

Randy makes a little extra money handing out copies of the *Los Angeles Free Press* on Sunset, but the only way he can get any decent food is to find the Diggers, a right-on charitable group that rescues out-of-date supermarket stock from the trash in dumpsters at the back of stores and distributes it to whoever needs it. At least the weather's good.

Randy finally gets a break when he auditions for Poco, which features a couple of ex–Buffalo Springfield cats, Jim Messina and Richie Furay. They make a pretty good first record called *Pickin' Up the Pieces*, almost as good as *Sweetheart of the Rodeo*, some misty-eyed critics boldly claim, but then it all turns to shit for Randy. He is super pissed off when Richie and Jim cut him out of the final mixing sessions. He lets his feelings be known and quits.

To spite him, Richie and Jim remove Randy's lead vocals from the record and replace his picture on the sleeve with a painting of a dog.

A fucking dog.

Randy keeps going, holding down the beat, singing with a mile-high smile. He immediately gets a gig in Ricky Nelson's Stone Canyon Band and goes on tour, appears on a couple of records, even has a song of his own on one of them, and gets some session work, appearing on dreamy James Taylor's *Sweet Baby James* and Waylon Jennings's *Singer of Sad Songs*.

Now after a shitty tour of Europe with Stone Canyon, Randy has had enough and goes home to Nebraska to sell John Deere tractors and try to save his marriage to his high school sweetheart, Jennifer, who will soon have twins to join their older son, Dana. It's only when Randy Meisner returns to LA to give it one last shot that he finally gets some of that good God's good luck he's been hearing about all his life but never yet seen.

So that's Randy and that's Bernie. They collide, too, collide with Don and Glenn and with Linda and John, when, after a first round of touring, Linda's other backing musos, Kenny Bloom and Casey Van Beek, split because John can't afford to pay them during any down time.

Meanwhile, back on the farm, where no one was looking, or not very hard, Linda has a new boyfriend she's openly calling the love of her life—it's Mr. John David Souther. And all his friends.

While Linda and J.D. hang with Don and Glenn, John Boylan, who is not blowing the scene just over a chick, thinks instead of easy-going Randy Meisner and calls inviting him to come hang out, plug in his bass. Glenn is very impressed. He remembers watching from the foot of the stage when Randy was in Poco, and to him Randy is a rock star, not a wannabe or a pretender, definitely a step up for the Linda Ronstadt band.

It is July 12, 1971, and the stars have rear-ended. As if sending an augury from the heavens, Glenn Frey, Don Henley, Randy Meisner, and Bernie Leadon quietly step onto a stage together for the first time . . . at Disneyland. It's a one-off show before Linda hits the road again, and the only part of the run that features all four of those musicians in combination. As Boylan recalled, "various combinations played behind Linda. But those four, what I consider the dream configuration for the tour, only played one gig."

As with all the great bands, together this fabulous new four are able to summon whatever near-mystical spell it is that transforms civilians into shooting stars. As singers and musicians they are all tip-top in their own right, but together they are something else. That's the hallmark of quality, of dealing with the real deal. The thing that money can't buy, the stuff you can strive a lifetime to achieve and not even catch sight of all the while you're striving. The kind of flash-fire alchemy that only happens in a particular combination—they all feel it, the glow, and are taken aback by it.

J.D. Souther gets it immediately. Sees the sea of possibilities.

He saw Frey was "a great natural country singer," while Don "could sing anything he wrapped his voice around." He dubbed him the Secret Weapon "because he sat back there behind all those drums [and] that insanely beautiful voice . . . was incredible to hear, even if you didn't know where it was coming from." He rated Randy and Bernie highly, too, grasped immediately what they would bring to the band. Randy's "singing on the high end" was immaculate. Bernie was "one of the best and most overlooked guitar players around. When you heard them, you knew."

Everybody knew.

b.

The Right Advice

It was beautiful right from the start, but being beautiful wasn't going to pay the rent. Right from the start, Glenn Frey was a believer in the music business's defining principle, its cardinal virtue and guiding credo:

ART FOR ART'S SAKE

HIT SINGLES FOR FUCK'S SAKE

Take that and spray-paint it on your wall, because it's what is going to separate the Eagles from the Pocos of this world, from the Buffalo Springfields and the Flying Burrito Brothers and all the rest of the nearly men and also-rans, the fragile and delicate geniuses who could never quite keep their shit together long enough to do anything other than please a few critics and scenesters.

As Glenn confessed to Cameron Crowe: "We wanted it all. Peer respect. AM and FM success. Number 1 singles and albums, great music, and a lot of money." Frey had been dreaming big since he was little. Don wouldn't have said so out loud, but he felt exactly the same way.

First, Glenn and the boys undertake the delicate task of telling Linda they are going to leave and form a band of their own. They play with her for six months, all the while talking to one another about the band that they will form without her. They tell J.D. first. J.D. says, "Great idea." He sees the look in Glenn's eye and knows that whatever he says won't make a blind bit of difference to that boy anyway, but he *does* think it's a great idea. They tell John and Linda, who give their blessing too. "I really respect Linda Ronstadt," Don will say later. "She's got a good heart. She's never been selfish enough to hold anybody back."

But first the band that will become the Eagles make their recording debut together on various parts of her third solo record, *Linda Ronstadt*, which will come out in January 1972 and flop spectacularly, causing her and John to flee Capitol Records once their contract has run itself down.

It doesn't flop because of the music, however. Glenn and Don are across six tracks; J.D., Randy, and Bernie a few more. There are three songs recorded live at the Troubadour, including a cover of Jackson's "Rock Me on the Water." It's another pioneering record for Linda's "California music"—a gen-u-wine country rock forerunner—and it doesn't have a picture of her squatting in a pig pen and pretending to like it on the cover. But the world is not quite ready for this, not just . . . yet.

Jackson has already signed to Geffen and Roberts's new Asylum label, and J.D. Souther is about to join him. Linda will follow soon, although she will have to fulfill her contract with Capitol first, and the record that she fulfills it with, *Heart Like a Wheel*, oh sweet irony, will become her breakthrough release. Her *big* breakthrough release—Number 1 on the US mainstream album chart, Number 1 on the US country chart, with a big fuck-off Number 1 hit single to go with it: her richly varnished soft rock version of the Clint Ballard Jr. cool-groove classic, "You're No Good."

Once again, the Eagles hovered over the project. Don and Glenn both cameo on James Taylor's "You Can Close Your Eyes," which Linda closes the album with. (Trivia freaks note: Future Eagle Timothy B. Schmit also appeared on the track.) Eve Babitz handled photography. The standout was Linda's river-deep version of "Faithless Love," one of the most affecting ballads J.D. ever wrote, sitting alone at night in the dark, listening to his hero Tim Hardin's *Bird on a Wire*.

There is one more obvious collision that does not happen, however, one connection that goes unmade. As Don, Glenn, Randy, and Bernie rehearse together they consider adding J.D. to the band. There's not one good reason why they shouldn't—after all, J.D. more than fits Glenn's "look good, play good, sing good, and write good" criteria. It's lot of little things. J.D. has a solo deal for one thing, and he is just a natural loner. He and Glenn have a connection that precedes Glenn's connection with the other three band members, so if he joined the band where would that leave Don, exactly? Plus, musically, J.D. doesn't do anything the guys in the band don't do already—except take orders. It's all of those little things that keep J.D. out, although his destiny will remain very much entwined with theirs.

"Glenn wanted [Longbranch Pennywhistle] to be bigger," J.D. recalled twenty-five years later. "He wanted to make a band out of it instead of just a duo. And I just sort of wanted to stay home and write songs, I felt like I was just starting to get a handle on how to do that."

Unlike Glenn, J.D. "didn't think much in terms of career." Speaking in 1997 to writer Debbie Kruger, he elaborated: "I had just as much respect for Harold Arlen and Jimmy Van Heusen and the Gershwins and Cole Porter and Matt Dennis and all those guys, as I did for Hank Williams and Tim Hardin and Graham [Nash] and Chris [Hillman] and the guys that we already sounded more like. The musical themes of those songs [are] timeless. And I think I always wanted to do that; I wanted to write songs that would outlive me."

He didn't join the gang—deliberately didn't become an Eagle—but "that was the genesis of their band, and, in a way, it was a big stepping stone for me as a writer, because then I really was alone—home trying to figure out how to do this by myself. I'd already met Jackson and I saw that there was something about this one-man kind of introspective songwriting that appealed to me, that was already in my nature, it would just improve my whole world if I tried to write songs that way instead of aiming them at necessarily getting them recorded or performing them or something." It was the most honest and insightful account of his early career that J.D. had ever given.

So it is that the four as yet unnamed Eagles headed for 9130 Sunset Boulevard, home of Asylum Records, to see David Geffen and Elliot Roberts. "We marched into David's office," recalled Bernie Leadon, "and we said, 'Do you want us or not?' He came down to a rehearsal and said yes, he did . . ."

Geffen, Roberts, and their assistant manager John Hartmann catch a rehearsal out in the San Fernando Valley that has their combined antennae twitching, and Geffen goes straight to work. He goes to Amos Records and buys out the Longbranch Pennywhistle contract for $15,000 and Shiloh's for $12,500. David knows what he wants and knows how to get it. Glenn and Don are mighty impressed.

One afternoon in August 1971, he has Don and Glenn over to his place on Alto Cedro Drive. Beverly Hills, baby. They sit in David's sauna, sweating their asses off, and David tells them that Asylum's policy—*his* policy—is never to have more acts than he can fit into this sauna. That way, those that he does have will always get his full attention.

Don and Glenn say they like the sound of that. But what about walking-around money? It's agreed the band will each get $200 a week from a fund of $125,000 set up to cover costs while they rehearse and record an album. The money is to cover everything: buying a van, employing a road crew, even getting their teeth fixed, which they do. Fully recoupable, natch.

7.

Eagles, No Definite Article

They hear about Gram Parsons and his crew heading out to Joshua Tree, taking peyote, and staring at the great rock formations and the twisted trees, while above them, in the endless desert skies, strange things are happening.

"We should fuckin' do that, man . . ." mumbles someone.

"Desert trip . . ." mumbles someone else.

"Death trip . . ." mumbles someone else.

Smirking, they load up and take off. Maybe some booze and maybe some grass. Maybe some acid, maybe nothing at all. Off they go, four young guys now somehow pulling together in this thing. Pooling resources.

The size and the silence are what hit them most about Joshua Tree. A place that can rightly be described as awesome, vast, and flat and dry, the horizon sketched by the jagged mountains. They are truly alone. Together truly alone.

Maybe they get loaded. Maybe they get high. Maybe they drink peyote tea and slug tequila. Maybe it's just the fucking eternal mystery of the place and they really don't need any of that earthly shit to dig it. Who knows? In the years that follow, they will all have their own wildly differing stories to tell.

One thing they agree on at the time. They are lost and now found. They are a little closer to the seeds of creation. They feel the *breeze, allow the sun to bake their skin, raise their eyes to the heavens, a burning imprint on their retinas against the arc of the heavens above them. It is blue and it is white. It is yellow and it is brown. They are small. They are nothing. About to be reborn as something. This place could eat you, take you over, kill you. This place could make you. This place could fill you. Wow.*

The desert gives them something. A message. A gift. An augury. Glenn Frey, from Detroit, lies on his back in the California desert and looks up into the scorched heavens. In the sky he watches a giant bird of prey ride the dizzy thermals that exist in the lower air. "Eagles . . ." he says. "EAGLES . . ."

Eagles are not a common sight out here in the desert, but it is not wholly unknown. That's how Glenn remembers it anyhow.

Or maybe it's Bernie, who says something about Carlos Castaneda and separate realities, and about the eagle being above all others because it flies closest to the sun. Or maybe it's Don or even Randy rambling away as they lie around soaking up the uniquely lysergic vibes of the Joshua Tree house party. It's definitely one of them who hears Glenn saying the word "Eagles" out loud, and they all take their cue from it. Suddenly it's obvious. What they should call the band.

Eagles. Like the great bird of prey that presides over the earth's celestial boundaries like a king, looking down on us from a realm we can only imagine.

Eagles. No definite article. Glenn is very clear about that, right from the start. They are not "The Eagles." They are "Eagles."

They return from the desert new men. They return from the desert as a band of brothers. Flying in formation.

They can't wait to tell David Geffen all about it. David decides he likes the name "Eagles." David decides he digs their desert visions. David points out that most American banknotes have an eagle on them too. Another good omen. Right on.

Their first real rehearsal is a crash landing when it dawns on them that they have no songs. "We were mostly jamming on things like Chuck Berry songs," Bernie remembered. "Then at the end, Glenn sat down with his guitar and sang a song he'd just written called 'Most of Us Are Sad.' On the album, Randy ended up singing it. I thought, 'Well, that's a really interesting song.' It really does express something truthful—that a lot of people probably are sad but don't express it."

So it's Glenn's song first. Because it's Glenn and Don first, and then it's Glenn and Don and Bernie and Randy, in that order, the last two interchangeable. If the Eagles is anyone's band though, it's Glenn's, which he is happy to share with Don. So now it's Don's band, too. Though still a little bit more Glenn's band, it's unsaid but understood. At least by Glenn. Which Don understands. For now.

This is how it begins, the big bang, and how it will stay, down to the last weary fizz. The same is true for all bands. They are all someone's band more than they are someone else's, even though the "someone else" may be a crucial component of the whole, which in great bands is always bigger than the sum of the parts.

It's not complicated. Asylum Records is David and Elliot's company, but really it is David's company (something he will make crystal clearer by calling his next company Geffen Records). The Stones are Mick and Keef's band. The Who are Pete and Roger. The Beatles were John and Paul. The personalities have to mesh, even if they don't exactly fit, to prosper. If something—someone—has got to give, well, then, they better.

Glenn and Don and the Others are smart enough to know this is their one shot. They are not gonna blow it for the sake of someone's ego. And so they manage to find a way to keep the offstage maneuverings buried beneath the burning creative energy that now comes pouring out unstoppably.

Later, individual personalities will start to matter more, seemingly insignificant things transmogrified into bloody turf battles over who said what and who did what and who played what and who wrote what. Who stands where on the stage, who sleeps where on the Lear, whose crazy-cool girlfriend gets to come on the road and hang and whose groupie slut doesn't.

These are tiny grains of sand that get sucked into the giant force the Eagles are gathering and at first nothing happens, nothing you would notice, but then later, these tiny grains start to erode small pieces of the flesh-machine, and the whole machine runs a little rougher for everybody, not just the principals, but the road hordes propping them up, and the longhaired millionaires writing the checks.

Until, if it goes on for long enough, the important parts begin to erode and rust, the whole thing falls apart and the band splits, rats fleeing a sinking ship.

But this is far in the future when Hell Freezes Over. Right now, back here in 1971, no one knows that these bands—these machines—will keep running for decades. They are not built to. Back here in 1971 things fall apart far more often than they stay together. The industry itself is young and always subject to sudden change, and when you are in the middle of it, you are too close to see it. And you don't give a damn anyway.

As they lie on their backs in the desert, watching the skies and the kings and queens they believe that live there, anything seems possible. There is no definite article. Just the infinite. Just the endless blue. Just . . .

Eagles.

8.

Another Limp-Wristed
LA Country Rock Record

At first they rehearse at the little bungalow behind the Hollywood Bowl that J.D. and Linda rent together. Everything goes quick, easy.

"Wow," J.D. says to himself. "These guys are smooth . . ."

David and Elliot come to hear them rehearse at Bud's, which is way out in the Valley behind a liquor store, and they look at each other and go, "Hmmm . . ."

They tell the frowning band more work is needed. Don agrees. Glenn agrees. Bernie and Randy nod along. David goes one further, a move he thinks more about every time he sees Glenn hitting it at the bar at the Troubadour. Or Jackson swanning out of the kitchen behind the bar, like he owned the place, bringing a couple of cold ones over to sit with Don and J.D. and all the girls and all their other new best friends gathered there with them.

David decides he should get them far out of LA, out of harm's way. Away from the Troubadour, for sure, needy show-off musos and quote-hungry music journos intermingled tight, two sets of people hyper-attuned to whatever bullshit might be going around.

The Canyon scene is good as dead. The bad drugs have taken over. Geffen wants them away from the rising tide of smack and cocaine that is starting to flow through LA in a dark, narcotic river, a sign of the new times, the end of the sixties, the start of the seventies. Maybe it's a reaction to Manson and the Zodiac, a reaction to Altamont, maybe it's the apocalyptic end to America in Vietnam and the carpet-bombing of Cambodia, maybe it's just an end to the fun, fun, fun, two Kennedys down and now Nixon who is nobody's friend. The vibe now is to kill the pain, gouge it with coke, then send it floating away on opium waves, riding out the dark nights.

David Crosby is deep into it after Christine dies in that car smash. So is his drummer, Dallas Taylor. So is Keith Richards. So is Gram Parsons. So, soon, are James Taylor and Mama Cass Elliot and Tim Buckley and Jerry Garcia. So are John Lennon and Eric Clapton and Lou Reed and, oh fuck, just everybody.

But this is not who the Eagles are meant to be, Geffen has decided. The Eagles were what came after the whole world went to shit—the new, stronger, longer-lasting, wiser-time distillation. He does not want their legend enshrined in gothic failure before he has even had a chance to get them to Number 1. With a bullet—if need be.

The Eagles will suck all of this in for their own darkest masterpiece, but for now they are on a plane to Aspen, Colorado, a still-just-about-hippy-enough outpost where Hunter S. Thompson runs for mayor on the "Freak Power" ticket, but that is nonetheless soon to become a glittering and decadent playground for America's super rich. Glenn, Don, Bernie, and Randy find themselves tuning up onstage at the Gallery, an après-ski bar that is often half empty when they play one of their four sets per night, and also a joint in Boulder called Tulagi's. Yay.

"We weren't really a cohesive group as yet," said Randy. "Although we did have that special sound. It was more like an extended, four-way jam . . ."

They play a lot of Chuck Berry, because that is what Glenn likes; they play old blues and R & B, because that's how Glenn and Don hear the band, how they see it going, a lot harder edged than the sappy country rock they know is their calling card with Geffen but are determined not to get tied down to.

They also play a Jackson Browne song called "Take It Easy," which Glenn helps riff up a little and J.D. has added his two cents worth to, and a song of Bernie's called "Witchy Woman," that he started when he was in the Burritos and that he and Don finish off with Don's lyric about Zelda Fitzgerald and the other girls he sees at the Whisky and the Troubadour, a spooky, hooky, slightly hokey little number that has its own kind of burning-the-candle-at-both-ends vibe.

Randy thinks the whole thing is wild, kinda their own "Beatles in Hamburg" period, when things get musically solid through sheer repetition. They stumble into this kind of bar band chic, with the unkempt hair and the faded denim and battered boots, a look that comes from living the life, but because they are young and hungry and don't really have a look, they appear authentic, too, especially Glenn and Don, the kind of guys who'd make you slightly jealous if you walked into the Gallery and saw your girl looking over at them grooving.

A couple of months in Aspen suits them, and it suits Geffen, too, because he can go about finding a producer for the first Eagles record without being encumbered by anything as distracting as the actual band themselves, especially as David has a much clearer idea than they do at this point as to how the Eagles should sound, about the kind of record that will appeal to the American public beyond LA.

He dips a line in the water and tries for a big fish: Glyn Johns, the English studio whiz who has just produced *Who's Next*, already in 1971 regarded as one of the greatest rock albums ever made.

Glyn already lives on the other side of the rainbow, has seen more than one pot of gold, been witness to more than one rock 'n' roll suicide. He'd worked with the holy trinity: Dylan, Beatles, Stones. Also Led Zeppelin, the Band, Traffic. Also Graham Nash, Steve Miller, Rod Stewart . . . *everybody*, man. His last job was *Who's Next*, his next would be *Exile on Main Street*. But between those events he had a gap in his schedule and after Geffen finally let him get a word in on a trip to LA, he agreed to fly up to Boulder to watch the Eagles.

Previously Glyn had never heard of the Eagles. He had never heard of David Geffen. But the Joni and Croz connection intrigued the twenty-nine-year-old Englishman. He took the flight. Then sat there fidgeting in a half-empty joint while the band fumbled their lines.

"They were doing Chuck Berry stuff and they were blatantly bloody awful," he would later recall. "It was a complete cacophony."

What Glyn's expert ears detect are not the silky four-part harmonies he will help create in the studio but the conflict in the band that remains as yet resolved, the way that Glenn and Don drag the sound toward R & B and Detroit while Bernie and Randy pull it back the other way toward country and soft rock.

Glyn tells David thanks, but he's not interested. David is not the kind of guy who likes to hear "no," so he fiends on Glyn hard until Glyn agrees to come see the band again back in LA in "a controlled environment." A professional rehearsal room with a properly kitted-out sound system, not a fucking ski bar in Boulder on a snowy night in hell. David sets it up. Keeps talking fast until Glyn walks through the door.

They spend the morning. They are really trying. Glyn is really trying just being there. As before, however, the Eagles are "awful." They take a break, someone picks up an acoustic guitar and begins to strum a little thing Glenn has written, a very untypical, slushy, and sentimental bit of fluff called "Most of Us Are Sad," which Randy sings in his sweet, wasted-choirboy way, and it happens—they all come together and sing in four-part harmony, and it suddenly becomes clear to Glyn Johns: what the Eagles are and how they should sound. How they *will* sound once he gets to work on them.

Glyn turns to tell David, "This is what the band is all about . . ."

Don still has his doubts, I tell you what. "Now Glyn thought we were a nice, country rock, semi-acoustic band, and every time we wanted to rock 'n' roll, he could name a thousand British bands who could do it better."

Glyn has his doubts, too. He was with the Stones when Gram was on the scene, none of this is new to him, and he doesn't want to make what he calls, "another limp-wristed LA country rock record."

Why should he? This is GLYN JOHNS. You're right and he's wrong? So Glyn stays in town and starts rehearsing them hard, rehearsing them *seriously*. Making them sweat. Making them *earn* it.

That's when they discover the truth. It's hard fucking work trying to sound this free and easy. Glyn takes them to this little rehearsal studio out in the Valley, near Tiny Naylor's coffee shop, aka the local head shop, and therefore not approved of by David Geffen, who is looking to get the band out of LA again as soon as he can.

In the past year, Morrison, Hendrix, and Joplin had all checked out before it was time to leave, and all for the same stupid, selfish fucking reasons. The LA music scene was now awash in coke and smack and everybody was just being cooool about it. David is not going to invest any more of his time and money in that bullshit.

This place, this studio, would be considered way too "social" by Geffen. But Jackson used to crash there when he was between places. Randy used to rehearse there with the Stone Canyon Band.

This place is perfect for the still-young hopefuls working with one of the contemporary greats.

Glyn works them over, pushing harder than they can handle sometimes, because now he hears something he might just be able to do something with. He doesn't hear it all the time, not at first, because the band is fighting it. Even when they hear it too, they cop out with messy R & B and Chuck Berry, still lacking confidence. But it's there. Glyn can almost touch it.

It's there most of all in a song that Jackson starts writing for his first album but can't finish. Glenn hears it a few times around the place in Echo Park and offers to help him out.

Jackson is stuck on the second verse, which starts with him killing time in Winslow, Arizona, something he had actually done, during a road trip along Route 40 in an old army jeep. But Jackson can't find anything to follow it, until Glenn comes out with, an image of a chick "in a flatbed Ford" cruising by "to take a look at me . . ."

It's a very Glenn image—a girl and a car, an archetypal American image—and it blows with the freewheeling cool that this wannabe rock 'n' roll Jimmy Dean works on exuding every hour of every day, with and without the guitar. Why wouldn't this girl in the Ford slow down to take a look at him? Why wouldn't anyone?

Right from the start, Glenn Frey is in the game, baby. Smokes now flipping first time into his grinning oh-yeah cakehole.

Jackson looks on astounded as Glenn finishes the song in "spectacular" fashion. Glenn asks Jackson if he plans to use it on the album he's making for Asylum. "Nah, it's not ready in time," Jackson says, and Glenn acting casual, not wanting to spook him, shrugs and says, "Well, we'll put it on, we'll do it . . ."

Meanwhile, back at the bar, yet another of the Troubadour regulars is Jack Tempchin, who has a song called "Peaceful Easy Feeling" that Glenn hears and asks if he can work on that, too, and the next day—*the next day*—comes back with a demo that Jack later describes as "so good, I can't believe it."

The Eagles play rougher, tougher arrangements of both numbers at Tiny's, neither one quite making it out of the garage, and then Glyn Johns gets across it and identifies what's really there, hiding in plain sight, how it *should* feel, how it *should* sound. Never mind the faders, cool-hand Glyn now knows his most important job will be to convince the band. He tells them straight. I know what I'm talking about. Shut up and listen to me. They do.

He performs the same sonic surgery on "Witchy Woman." Glyn wants those four voices and their close-quarters harmonies to really cut through, not get buried under a bunch of standard R & B licks that make Glenn and Don feel tougher than they really are. Four voices as one celestial cowboy, that's where the special sauce is.

The two voices more equal than the others have to be indulged too, of course. This is Glyn's least favorite part of the gig in the new post-*Pepper* era of album-as-art, artist-as-VIP, producer as acolyte. Glyn only has one way to deal with that shit. You don't like it? Get someone else.

For Glenn and Don, the producer's apparent mission to transform them into a soft-rock chart act is a double-edged sword. They know it's their best chance to turn the Eagles into an act that might just sell a few more records than the Burritos or Gram or whoever the fuck the critics keep saying no one new will ever be as good as.

But they fight Glyn every day, fight him because they don't hear it how he does. Not here . . . Not yet . . . Levels of passive-aggression tipping into overdrive.

Geffen finally decides, "Fuck this," and pulls the trigger. He flies them all to England to make the record there. Glyn lives in London, prefers working out of Olympic Studios, which has the great live room and all the blood on the carpet from Hendrix, the Stones, Led Zep . . . monsters guided to Olympus by Glyn. And no

Troubadour whores hanging at the doors, no Hollyweird hipsters slinging dope.

Nobody in the Eagles takes any of this in. What difference does any of that make when you are in England, in February 1972, where the pubs close at 11 p.m. on weekends and 10:30 p.m. the rest of the week? Where there are just three TV stations! And they all shut down before midnight! Are you fucking SHITTING me, man?

England, where the Maui-wowie and the easy coke connections are six thousand miles away. England, where there is mostly stale, lumpy hash, coke is rarer and more expensive than gold, and they've never heard of Quaaludes. Other uppers and downers aren't impossible to get your sweaty palms on, but you're not going to be stumbling over them on the way to the saloon bar of the Dog & Duck any night this week or next. England is the fuckin' pits, man.

But Geffen is insistent. "Everything is going to be great!"

He flies the Eagles to London, where Glyn meets them and takes them out west, to the stately riverside suburb of Barnes, where the only green leaves are on the tree-lined streets and the sleepy common.

There, at 117 Church Road, is Glyn Johns's place of business—now the Eagles' place of business—Olympic Studios. In the past the building has been a theater and then a cinema but now it is, along with Abbey Road, the prime piece of record-making real estate in the Western world.

Olympic had been there since the beginning of pop time in the late fifties. When it really opened up, though, was when it became known for what future Hendrix producer and collaborator, Eddie Kramer, then working at Olympic as a young tape op, describes as, "the best console in England, possibly the world."

The first valve-based recording console and the first four-track tape recorder in England. That was Olympic Studio One.

Then came Studio Two. Mick Jagger designed the far-out décor in Studio Two. Jimi Hendrix made most of *Are You Experienced* and *Axis Bold as Love* there. The Beatles worked out parts of "All You Need Is Love" and "Get Back" there. Led Zeppelin used Olympic for their first three albums, invoking the kind of thunderhead *Sturm und Drang* that would make their music immortal. Rod and the Faces used Olympic to get drunk and have a real good time in. The kind of rock that Glenn and Don have half an ear on, too, and that Glyn wants them to hurry up and forget.

Half of rock 'n' roll history is coming out of a quiet road in West London, but Glenn, Don, Randy, and Bernie get there and hate it. Glyn has them in there every waking hour, working them hard like always, wearing them down, showing them how real magic is made "with hard fucking graft."

They spend their days and nights shuffling from the tiny flat they're sharing up the road to the studio and back again. By the time Glyn lets them go each evening, the pubs are shut, the TV screens are blank, the neighbors bang on the walls if you play music even at room temperature, and there is nothing to do finally but conk out.

Glyn has banned booze and drugs, he won't entertain them at all, so the first Eagles album, inevitably titled Eagles, is made under the influence of nothing but a tyrannical Brit who has a particular highly polished sound in his head and won't let them stop until he hears it booming out of the studio speakers.

And so they work. There are twenty-nine days in February 1972 and in London it snows on five of them. There is also a national coal miners' strike and power cuts become a regular day-to-day occurrence. "We'd be in the middle of a take," said Don, grinding his teeth, "and the power would go out. It was great."

The only TV they see is when someone at the studio flips on *Top of the Pops* or *The Old Grey Whistle Test*—the only shows in

Britain that feature modern pop and rock. Number 1 in the singles chart that month is "Son of My Father" by Chicory Tip—road builders dressed in chicks' outfits and dipped in glitter, as demanded by the fixation on glam rock in the UK at the time, miming unconvincingly on *Top of The Pops* to their eventual million-selling hit, one of the first pop smashes to feature a Moog synthesizer.

Everything about the Chicory Tip song rubs the Eagles wrong. Men in makeup? Moog what now?

They liked *The Old Grey Whistle Test* better. They were all about albums. Fronted by one of those laid-back, beardy professor types you found on Venice Beach reciting their cool-jazz, sub-Ginsberg poetry. There was some cool shit on that show. Harry Chapin, Zoot Money, and goddamn if they didn't have Poco on one night! They didn't see that; it was just before they got to London, or they could have hooked up. Goddamn the cold and the rain.

But even on *Whistle Test* they still came up against stuff that didn't sit right with them. Glam was okay, maybe, if it was Alice Cooper or Elton John. But David Bowie? Fag rock is now a thing too? Roxy Music? Well, you sure don't rock me, superman. We dig chicks.

Then it was back to work. And they get into it. They have to. They work because they want to get the fuck out of freezing-cold Barnes and onto a plane back to LA, straight from the airport to the Troubadour and the good times they are starting to feel lie ahead once they finally have an album to their name.

They work because at heart, Glenn and Don are pragmatists. Muso credibility is all well and good, but it doesn't pay the rent, as Geffen might have said. Get it right, they both knew, and they'd never have to pay rent again.

Their eyes on the big picture, their ears on the soaring, powerfully affecting harmonies Glyn Johns is wrestling down onto tape for them, they start to see only upside. Accenting the positive, they even allow Glyn to bring Bernie's banjo up in the mix. It's all good, bro. Mama, we're coming home.

Then David Geffen hears the tapes and realizes his big idea for a mainstream country rock act has grown into something no longer fully under his control. That Glyn Johns has discovered another, deeper level of something else in the Eagles. The first touches of the darkness that will bloom in their blood even as they fulfill their heart's desires. It's there even in "Take It Easy," a song that Glenn now says means "you shouldn't get too big, too fast."

A prophesy? A prayer?

It's there in all of the references to deserts and highways and gas-guzzling autos gliding down the highway and the good-time cowgirls that join for the ride.

Apparently simple, innocent daydreams that represent a kind of American *tableau vivant*, a certain freewheeling but well-heeled lifestyle that the sound of the Eagles will quickly come to epitomize.

They make this world sound so loose, so easy, so available that everyone thinks they can have it. Drawing people into their orbit, hoping to carve off a slice of this drive-by paradise for themselves, just a little taste of that honey—buy the ticket take the ride, as Dr. Thompson advised, only it ain't as simple as it sounds.

Now they are yearning for some of those open spaces they sing about. Some of those drugs. Some of those girls. Some of that welcome-back, LA watermelon sugar. They wrap it up, get on a plane, and soar as high into the sky as they can. They don't look down.

They arrive back in LA in spring. Listening to the tapes over and over, David and Elliot decide the record is lacking one thing. They look at each other and say the same words at the same time: "It needs more Don."

They see what's Glyn's done here. Don's the drummer and this ain't the Dave Clark Five. But that voice of his. Roberts identifies the problem immediately. Geffen, less concerned with the magic and more with the method, sees it too. Don's voice, man. It's like no one else's: sweet but not sickly, gently smoky, quivering with emotion one moment, coldly detached the next.

Great for harmony, of course, but maybe even better for the front. Yet Don only has one lead vocal—"Witchy Woman." Come on, guys, get real. We can do better. This ain't Gram grouching out at the mic, this ain't Croz and Stills butting heads with Nash and Young and coming up with burnished, one-off gold. This was the Eagles, and everything had to be Geffen-wrapped perfect.

They put the band back in the studio for a couple of days, and Don cuts Jackson's song about Laura Nyro, "Nightingale." It's easy-catchy on the surface and was originally intended for Jackson's debut album, released a few months before, but somehow Don got to take the ride first with the Eagles. It's a big-wheel-keep-on-turn-ing rocker and Glyn would have known how to record it with his ears closed. But it was Don's voice that really sold it.

It's added to the final master.

9.

The Train Leaving Here
This Morning

Their first official engagement as a band called Eagles is at a tripped-out art gallery show in boho Venice Beach where the gorgeous, arty crowd do their gorgeous, arty thing. It's a private viewing for a new exhibition by West Texan Boyd Elder, who would later create the painted skulls that appear on some of the Eagles' album covers. Boyd, who always dresses in black and wears sunglasses at night, calls the show *El Chingadero*, Spanish-Mex patois for *The Fucker*. Hey, far out, man! Betcha wish you'd thought of that!

Those in attendance include Joni Mitchell, Cass Elliot, Jackson Browne, David Geffen, and Elliot Roberts. Plus the usual extras. The Eagles are set up in a corner of the gallery, right where this keg of beer has started leaking across the floor.

According to Henry Diltz, former banjo-wielding member of the Modern Folk Quartet, now a granite-faced photographer working the room, "They sang 'Witchy Woman' over and over." Even Glenn knew a couple of hot Chuck Berry covers wouldn't cut it here; they simply didn't have any other songs of their own properly prepared. They didn't know what the hell they were doing there anyway. Neither did anybody else—except David Geffen.

You can now find film of it on YouTube, Joni dancing slowly, almost shyly, while the Eagles strum and hum and hope for the best in the background. Doing their best to be unobtrusive, background music, careful not to crash anybody's scene, while doing their best to stick out a mile. If only they'd learned more songs.

Yet it seems to fit right in with the nobody-knows-anything vibe, the 1971 crowd and the 1969 place in mind, and everyone starts to feel it, this thing that Glyn Johns feels, that David Geffen sees, and that Glenn Frey and Don Henley have been reaching for. Their own spot over there by the balcony, away from the brainy boys, surrounded by the brainy chicks, as their collective gaze travels like light toward those Hollywood Hills and the big white sign in the sky.

Meanwhile, back in the lab, David Geffen has turned off the money tap and now it's time for the real work to begin, to bore deep into the ground and strike oil, black gold, then turn the tap back on so that it begins to flow the other way, the right way. That is the kind of LA conversation that David conducts so well, this way of looking into the near future and implicitly understanding what it is that people want just before they realize what it is themselves.

Henry Diltz has a friend called Gary Burden, who is the art director who took Henry's picture of David Crosby, Graham Nash, and Stephen Stills sitting on an old couch outside some shotgun shack in downtown LA and made it into the instantly iconic cover of their debut album.

One of Gary's drinking buddies was Jim Morrison, and so Henry took the shot Gary used on the cover for the Doors' album *Morrison Hotel*. When Joni Mitchell decided not to do the cover art for *Blue* herself, Gary did that, too. Henry didn't get that gig, as Joni already had the pic she wanted.

David Geffen knows that the Eagles is all about catching the right feel, spreading the good word. It must be conveyed not just in how the records sound but in how their albums look. He hires Henry and Gary to do the job. Glenn and Don are told that if they get it right, David will turn the tap back on.

Henry and Gary hear the story of how the band got their name and decide they'll go back out to Joshua Tree and shoot the cover there. They all meet at 1 a.m. at the Troubadour, where they proceed to get as drunk as fuck as fast as they can, before gathering up all of the drugs they can find, loading up Bernie's Jeep and Gary's car and arriving in the desert just before the red dawn.

Bernie leads them "to the secret spot of all the old-time dopers, way out back overlooking Palm Springs" where some kindly hippy has left an old barber's chair for anyone who passes to sit on and behold the majesty before them. They lug all of the photographic gear, several guitars, and all of the dope halfway up the rutted, stony hillside, then make a camp, light a fire, and brew a kettle of peyote tea. Once they are all good and high and the sun is edging its way over the brim of the horizon, Henry and Gary start to shoot.

Once again, the magic happens. Seemingly out of their control but always conspicuously there when it matters in these feeling-lucky early days. For the cover shot, Gary chooses a gorgeous, saturated outline of huge cactus heads, the new desert sol offering a golden burr to the hazed horizon, just starting to turn from Bible black to heavenly blue. Beneath the cactus heads, the band, stoned out of their tiny minds, sit around the hillside campfire trying to be cool.

Gary blows Henry's shot up to four times the size of an album sleeve, and in a clever piece of design, uses the top right quarter of the image as the front of the outer sleeve. The top left quarter becomes the back, while the bottom quarters are designed to be folded upward and inward to place the image of the group themselves on the inner spread.

He puts the band's new logo, which has the word "EAGLES" in an electric-blue outline set on an eagle's back, the bird's giant wings levering it up into the wide blue yonder, at the top of the right-hand quarter. In 1972, in rock, this is high art. Great *2001: A Space Odyssey* energy. The eagle being the advanced alien civilization, the cactus heads below like ignorant apes unaware of the sky.

"It's perfect, man," thinks Geffen, "absolutely perfect." Slightly dreamy, slightly mystical, slightly tough, slightly woozy, a simple but effective slice of Americana that translates exactly the new language this band is going to communicate in. Light, high, beautiful, with the darkness always present and no one quite sure how much longer it will last. The light or the dark.

Geffen hits the button, and the juice begins to flow freely again. He is now ready to make another big bet. This time, on himself. With the Eagles about to hatch, David's ready to go all in with his $100 black poker chips. It's time to put the whole damn roll on the table. Elliot is nervous. But that's normal. David is not nervous, he is hyperactive. High summer, high hopes. *Eagles* is released on June 1, 1972.

With the addition of Jackson's jaunty "Nightingale," each of the Eagles now has at least two lead vocals on the album: Glenn has "Take It Easy," "Chug All Night," and "Peaceful Easy Feeling." Don has "Witchy Woman" and "Nightingale." Bernie has "Train Leaves Here This Morning" and "Earlybird." Randy has "Most of Us Are Sad," "Take the Devil," and "Tryin'."

The album ships. David and Elliot and anyone else they can rope in begin burning the phones, coast to coast. Stores, chains, radio, news, mags, venues, promoters. Geffen rightly guessing that the fourteen seconds it takes to get from the itty-bitty-pretty intro to the foolishly catchy riff of "Take It Easy" would be enough to close anybody. The trick was to get them to take those fourteen seconds and actually listen.

Two hot weeks later, *Eagles* debuts on the *Billboard* chart at Number 102. We're on our way, baby!

David and Elliot hire Paul Ahern as their promotions man-cum-radio-plugger. Paul is a former bass player who knows exactly what end of the business he is now in, and what it is worth. Paul's a fast learner, and the Eagles and their success become his personal mission.

During the remaining months of 1972, Paul gets in his car and visits every AM radio station he can reach, pressing promotional white labels of the record into the hands of programmers, DJs, executives and their secretaries, girlfriends, drug dealers, anybody who even glances his way. He hands out Eagles records and T-shirts, free tickets and after-show passes, any freebie he can think of, with one aim: get the Eagles on AM Top 40 Radio. FM is for the cool kids, but Geffen knows they've got that covered. AM is the goal. That's mainstream mom-and-pop America. That's money.

Paul is fucking unstoppable, racking up the miles, pushing, prodding, emotionally strong-arming, a little toots-sweet, sure why not, I-owe-you-one-buddy—anything to ensure Geffen's huge horde of hundred-buck chips comes up trumps. It's time to send in the cavalry.

The Eagles hit the road for their first proper out-of-state tour. Geffen oversees the hiring of a crew, mostly of friends and Troubadour hangers-on who the band still enjoy having around. It starts well but personal issues soon intrude. They had just come off two nights at the Santa Monica Civic Hall when Don takes a call from his mother begging him to come home. His father is dying.

"He literally worked and worried himself to death," Don reflected. The cardiac arrest that finally proved fatal for his father occurred on July 7, 1972, "after four or five other heart attacks," said Don sadly. As he later put it to Charles M. Young in *Rolling Stone*, you quickly discover what life is really all about when "you see your father in the emergency room heaving and gasping for breath and saying: 'Oh God! Oh God!' Everything else gets real trite after that."

C.J. Henley's death becomes pivotal to his son's increasingly shaded worldview. "I figured out a long time ago, when my father got sick and died, that life wasn't fair," he said grimly. "But I got mad about it. I used to go around and cuss God all the time, because my father died too early, and he suffered. He only lived to see 'Take It Easy' and a couple of weeks of 'Witchy Woman.'"

One week later, with Don's blessing, the Eagles are back on the road. Geffen books them onto two of the major summer tours as a support act, first to Jethro Tull and then to Yes. Neither Jethro Tull nor Yes sounds anything like the Eagles. They are leaders of the British progressive rock scene, mega-muso types whose eccentricities are evident in the unusual music they make, the eccentric way they dress, the funny way they speak, even the weird way they play.

Tull is led by Ian Anderson, who has frizzy, mad-scientist hair and a Jacobean beard. His stage persona is that of an English medieval tramp, and when he's not singing in his nasal gentlemanly way, he plays flute like a peashooter and hops around on one leg, pulling faces and making crazy eyes.

Tull's current album, *Thick as a Brick*, is one long, continuous piece of music split over two sides of the record. It is their first album to go to Number 1 in America. Tull's hard-core American fans don't know what the fuck this Eagles bullshit is, but it ain't cutting the mustard. They want *think* music to lose their minds to, not this easy-listening, smooth harmony shit. Nine hard-knock shows, strictly no encores, down to Texas via Las Vegas and some other stops they never want to think about again.

Yes is fronted by elfin hippy sprite Jon Anderson, who looks and sounds like an over-cherished, ruby-cheeked child-vampire. They have a giant bass player called Chris Squire, whose nickname is the

Fish, because he drinks like a fish, you see, and who towers over Anderson onstage like the shadow of the valley; they have a skittish guitarist with pronounced cheekbones named Steve Howe pretending to be the Young Mozart having great thoughts, and they have a flamboyant to the point of wizardly keyboard player, Rick Wakeman, who wears a long cape and always has at least two pints of strong English ale on the lid of his keys.

Yes also has a new album out, *Close to the Edge*, which is also one continuous piece of music split over both sides of the record, and currently Number 3 in the US charts. And it has a *really* trippy album sleeve by the really *trippy* English artist Roger Dean. Gatefold, natch. Good for rolling joints on.

The Eagles look like they've shown up on the wrong night at the club, in their worn old jeans and dirty sneakers. They don't have fancy lights and props. They all keep both feet firmly on the stage. No capes. They just play and sing, all ten songs from the album, each and every night, in those perfect four-part harmonies. Not that most people are even in their seats, let alone paying attention.

They quickly discover just how big a place America is, and how small a scene there is at the Troubadour or up in the Canyon. Out here in the wilds of Real America they have never heard of the Flying Burrito Brothers or the Dillards or Longbranch Whateverthefuck, don't give two shits what the cool kids are supposed to be up to in LA. In big, ferocious cities like New York and Chicago, no one has even heard of the Eagles. At best the crowds are indifferent, at worst they are raucous and impatient. On a really bad night the band are lucky to get off the stage alive.

Seeing his plan of action failing miserably, Geffen pulls out all the stops for the band's first show in New York, scheduled for September. Gotham is where all the big-hitting music critics live and die, where the main American music business is still centered, where the conversation alone can make or break a new artist's rep.

He pulls them off the Yes tour for the night and puts them on as headliners at the Felt Forum. The Forum is downstairs from its big brother, Madison Square Garden. No balconies, just flat floor seating stretching from the lip of the modest stage to the back of the room. You can squeeze 5,000 people in there if you need to. Or you can move things around, so capacity is limited closer to 2,000.

Knowing the Eagles will be lucky to sell 500 tickets on their own in New York, Geffen turns the show into a showcase evening for Asylum acts. Opening will be J.D. Souther, making his first concert appearance in New York; in the middle will be Jackson Browne, who is better known than any of them in the city and whose debut album has picked up a lot of heat—with the Eagles headlining.

The idea: to "present" both the new label and its latest star signings to the discerning ladies and gentlemen of New York's music elite. As many *Rolling Stone*, *Hit Parader*, *Cashbox*, *Phonograph Record*, and *Creem* snappers and stringers as you can round up. But don't forget the arbiters of good taste at the *Village Voice*, make them feel left out if they don't show up. See if the *New York Times* or *Post* can fill a couple of column inches with it. Like: *LA's coolest new label brings their coolest new artists to the Big Bad Apple for the first time. What's the verdict?*

Geffen leaves all that to Paul Ahern. Paul has already lined up all the radio hacks with their shiny tour jackets and free Rolling Stones tickets, VIP passes, taken care of all the friends of friends—pleased ta meetcha, come on in, the water's fine.

David is more focused on the big beasts of the NY scene. Would it be too much to hope for Ahmet to descend from his throne and make an appearance? The Felt was barely a mile from Atlantic's Paramount Plaza palace. How about Clive? You could see into every window in New York from Clive's penthouse suite at Columbia's Black Rock building on West 52nd: a thirty-eight-story tower of angled granite piers alternating with dark-tinted windows. Clive could see you. You never even knew if he was looking.

It would have been a powerful statement for one of those behemoths to come graze, even briefly, at Geffen's little coming-out party at the Felt. Imagine if he had *both*? Credibility by association. Blood on the dance floor. Live-feed connection.

Geffen has it all worked out long before the band get to town. Then the show begins—and everything falls apart. The Eagles have just completed twenty-nine shows supporting Yes, struggling to make headway with audiences who have little or no interest in them. The feeling is mutual. Glenn Frey in particular is having a hard time trying to understand what the fuck Geffen thinks the band should be doing out there getting slaughtered every night.

The fact that "Take It Easy" has become a Top 20 hit for the band doesn't appear to have made a dent on mainstream perception of the Eagles. In his *Rolling Stone* review of the album, Bud Scoppa described "Take It Easy" as: "simply the best sounding rock single to come out so far this year—danceable rhythm, catchy, winding melody, intelligent, affirmative lyrics, a progressively powerful arrangement mixing electric guitar and banjo, and a crisp vocal, with vibrant four-part harmony at just the right moments for maximum dramatic effect." *Cashbox* likened it favorably to the Byrds and predicted a "sure and rapid-fire smash."

The reviews that really stick in their minds however are all baaad. Robert Christgau, the Big I Am on the *Village Voice*, described the album snidely as, "suave and synthetic—brilliant, but false."

Well, fuck that guy. Likewise, the smug asshole at *Creem* who came on all pious: "None of the tracks is outrightly poor, but a disconcerting proportion just don't demand to be played again and again . . . What's missing most is fire."

Yeah, well, fuck that guy too! You want fire, motherfucker? Smoke this.

Yet the lasting impression among record buyers that summer was of a band cashing in on the country rock shtick to have a novelty hit. A one-off moment of gold, here today gone later today, what else can you show me? Something Glenn and Don see happening but don't know what to do about. Except to get on the phone to David Geffen and bitch.

10.

Celestial Cowboys

There are other bones to pick. When Jackson Browne got his first hit single earlier that year with "Doctor, My Eyes," Geffen had green-lit a promotional film clip—albeit shot cheaply in the recording studio—of him miming to the track, which was sent out to any interested parties on TV. Granted, still not many saw it, and yes it did show Dave Lindley from Jackson's live band miming on a lap steel to session man Jesse Ed Davis's actual guitar solo, but by the time the single climbed into the US Top 10, people at least had an idea of who this nice-looking kid was and what he was about.

Not so the Eagles, where "Take It Easy" got to Number 12 but still felt more Archies "Sugar Sugar" than Byrds "Mr. Tambourine Man." It didn't feel that strange when "Take It Easy" also hit the Top 20 on *Billboard*'s Easy Listening chart. Not like it had when "Doctor, My Eyes" had also appeared in the Easy Listening chart earlier that year. The latter was a song of darkness and despair from an important new artist clearly more focused on humanity; the former a nice singalong everyone could join in on, even your mom and pop.

Jackson also got to tour with artists whose audiences were likely to find his music compatible. While the Eagles were opening for Jethro Tull and Yes, Jackson was opening shows for Laura Nyro, Joni Mitchell, Sandy Denny, and Linda Ronstadt. He appeared at the Mariposa Folk Festival in July, on the same bill as Neil Young, Bonnie Raitt, and Gordon Lightfoot.

Three weeks before he joined the Eagles for their New York debut at the Forum, Jackson had co-headlined a six-night (twelve-show) run at the Bitter End on Bleecker Street in Greenwich Village. The Bitter End held barely 200 people, but it was perfect for sitting listening to what this exciting new singer-songwriter out of LA had to offer. Bolstered by the heavy presence of David Blue, whose first album for Asylum, *Stories*, had also been released that year but contained little of the outward charm of Browne's music and sold nothing like as well. But Blue was a Greenwich Village veteran, one of their own, and his presence on the bill brought another layer of validation for the newbie headliner.

On the final night of their run, David Blue showed up with some strange guy in tow. He said: "Jackson, this is Bruce and . . . Jackson, you gotta hear him . . . can he do a guest set tonight?" Recalling his own early New York coffeehouse gigs as a nobody playing guitar for Nico, Jackson said sure, why not? Then, as he later recalled, David's new pal Bruce "went out there for about an hour and proceeded to do the greatest songs I'd ever heard, with just his guitar and my piano. When he got off stage I said, 'Man, where the hell have you been hiding!'" When Jackson realized he didn't even know Bruce's last name, he asked that too. Bruce replied politely, shyly, "Bruce . . . Springsteen."

These were great feel-good shows, and critics delighted in the intimacy and freshness. Unlike the Eagles who were using up a lot of heart and soul on just trying to stay in the same game as the likes of Tull and Yes. A battle it is impossible for them to win.

Glenn's not allowed to complain. He knows the Eagles represent his only chance at the big time, that he doesn't have what it takes to go out on his own and make it, his soul shrinking at the very prospect of being laid as bare onstage as Jackson always is. Glenn knows that right now the Eagles is about good-time, get-it-on rock 'n' roll, no matter how country it's dressed up, or perfect the vocal harmonies. But, man, right now he is sooo sick of hearing it.

In New York, Glenn finally blows his stack, tells the in-crowd at the Forum exactly what he thinks of their shitty city and its hoity-toity music. It doesn't matter that the evening had been going quite well until then. J.D. came out, unobtrusive, and warmed the unbelievers up nicely. Then Jackson held them in the palm of his hand for an hour. For some reason, the New Yorkers don't see Jackson as LA. His knowing lyrics, his street demeanor, his lack of SoCal swagger, puts him in the same room if not yet at the same table as James Taylor, maybe, or Don McLean, or Todd Rundgren, or Joni. Singer-songwriters with edge. The ones you meet teetering on the ledge, not floating up in the clouds with "seven women on my mind."

Then these Eagles come on and play their album and no one really knows what to make of it, that's the truth. "We're the Eagles, from Southern California," Glenn announces before leading them through an a cappella rendition of "Seven Bridges Road." Then, this new band, with the crowd still waiting, launch immediately into "Take It Easy," hit 'em right away with their biggest shot, and the crowd mainly still just sit and stare.

Hey, man, it's Friday night in New York and instead of feeling some of that slow LA burn, the feeling among the general population at the Felt is one of already having climaxed, now Jackson's gone. What time is it anyway? Can we still make that other thing?

That's when Glenn loses it. Fuck these people! Fuck New York!

New York's response, predictably: fuck you, too.

It is the beginning of what Glenn and Don will come to see as an unbridgeable divide between the Eagles and the East Coast press. Over twenty years later, Joe Smith, former president of Warner Bros. Records, would shrug and say: "Glenn Frey is one of the best friends I have now. But during those years with the coke it was always, '*Those assholes!*' Everyone was an *asshole*."

Or as Jackson Browne put it: "Glenn always went around messing things up, and Don always followed him around cleaning things up."

The Eagles spend the following four nights after the misstep Forum show back on tour with Yes. But the end is now in sight. "Witchy Woman" gets released as their second single and by the time they play their next headline show, at the Bronco Bowl in Dallas in October, again supported by Jackson Browne and J.D. Souther, it's actually becoming a bigger hit than "Take It Easy."

With Don's enticingly smoky vocal and the rest of the band's contagious backing harmonies, and that seductive tribal rhythm, it becomes the must-play radio hit of the fall. "Witchy Woman" beats "Take It Easy" in the charts, too, climbing to Number 9. In less than a year, the only song the Eagles felt confident enough to play in public is now the best-known Eagles hit. They may not be anybody's flavor of the month, but they are building a solid fan base and the *Eagles* album, which contains both their hits, starts its long shelf life in the American charts, only reaching Number 22 on release but destined to sell a million copies over the next few years.

The final weeks of 1972 find the Eagles mixing up occasional hand-picked headline shows—usually supported by Jackson and J.D. or just Jackson—with more enormodome openers for Ten Years After and the J. Geils Band. They end the year back in LA with an all-friends-united show in December opening for Linda Ronstadt at the 1,800-capacity UCLA Royce Hall.

If things had ended there not even Glenn Frey would have much to complain about. But then Geffen signed off on a third single release from the album, plumping for "Peaceful Easy Feeling."

Paul Ahern frantically does the rounds of the major radio stations again, but he's suddenly pushing at a swinging door. With both FM and AM radio now primed to playlist anything Eagles, "Peaceful Easy Feeling" becomes another hum-along Fun Forty hit, cresting at Number 22. Jack Tempchin may have written it, but Glenn sings it and the boys sweet harmonize as though it were one of their own. Cinematic lyrics and luminous guitar breaks. Fresh, breezy feeling with a tang of something else in the air. Something extra-cool coming your way sooner than you think.

It's becoming a giant machine that feeds itself, a machine that digs into that pipeline of money that Ahmet gave David and turns it right around, pumping even more money back in the other direction—the right direction—to David Geffen and Asylum Records.

By the start of 1973 it becomes clear the Eagles have done what Poco and the Flying Burritos and the rest never could: synthesized the sound of country rock into something much more mainstream and acceptable to the mindset of Middle America.

America hears what Glyn Johns hears, this witchy SoCal sound that has you dreaming of packing up the car and hitting the highway, heading west, taking it easy. Suddenly it doesn't matter that none of the Eagles are actually from California. That Joni Mitchell and Neil Young are Canadian. That J.D. Souther is from Detroit, Linda Ronstadt from Arizona, David Geffen and Elliot Roberts from New York, because LA is a town built on the exceptional demands of its cultural immigrants. California the destination for all those in search of more. America the country founded on its traveling adventurers, explorers of new frontiers, where it is all about dreams, American dreams, which are about freedom, about making life what you want it to be.

That's what Glenn and Don feel they are about too.

As soon as they come back off tour both men immediately get the fuck out of Echo Park. Those days are already gone. They head for the hills, not yet rich but on the way. Glenn has scored big with his 50 percent of "Take It Easy." Don has scored big with his 50 percent of "Witchy Woman." Jack Tempchin has won the lottery with his 100 percent of "Peaceful Easy Feeling." Everyone is doing well off the album, everyone is on the same royalties.

Right now, however, they are temporarily marooned in that weird time lag between making it big and the actual money finding its way into your bank account, because that money has a long journey from the pockets of the fans at the shows and in the record stores, through the cash registers and the promoters, back down the pipe that David has drilled, to the record company and its accountants, the IRS, everybody taking their slice, earning their cut . . . So yeah, it's coming, but right now, it's still more of a trickle than the mighty geyser they pray it will soon become.

For now they are feeling cautiously righteous. Glenn finds a pad in Laurel Canyon, on Kirkwood and Ridpath. His housemate is Paul Ahern. The house has its own set of gates, and like most snazzy places in the Hills, it has a large, open-plan living area on the top deck for the soft breeze and the stoned mountain view, the bedrooms down below kept cool in the shadows. It's the perfect bachelor pad, furnished with a poker table, decorated with empty beer bottles and full ashtrays, the driveway doubling up as a basketball court.

Don takes a place a little higher up, a crazy house on stilts that once belonged to Roger McGuinn that, when the wind blows, seems to sway a little, and almost as soon as he has it, he and Glenn write a new song there which they call "Desperado." They don't have any lush musical vistas planned as yet, but they have the rich melodic drift of the song, and it feels like it sums up exactly where they are now. As a band. As people. As Eagles.

In time, "Desperado" will become the "Ave Maria" of 1970s rock, an epic musical Hail Mary. But then Don decides he doesn't like the whole weird stilts in the wind thing—"it makes me nervous"—and takes a new place just up the street from Glenn on Ridpath.

In these heady months, the first few real, do-what-you-want months of freedom and bliss, they create a little scene around them, a scene that begins, inevitably, at the Troubadour for drinks and weed and maybe a little coke, then drifts upward, as upwardly mobile as Glenn and Don themselves now are, up and up to Glenn's cool new pad, where there are marathon poker sessions that go on for two or three days, crew people heading back down to Sunset to gather food and booze and more weed. And coke. Goddamn, don't forget the coke! There's a Sunday afternoon basketball game "where everyone got so fucked up the score at the end of an hour might only be ten to four . . ."

There are barefoot girls, getting prettier and happier to hang out, get high, get laid. "We had a great time," Don told Marc Eliot matter-of-factly. "Girls, drugs, booze, cards, and songwriting— what more could you want?" What indeed, in the city of willfully lost angels?

It's now that Don really gets to know J.D. It's now that Glenn and Don forge a true songwriting partnership. It's now that Glenn's place takes over from the Troubadour as the real center of things in LA. The new number-one hangout for J.D., Jackson Browne, Paul Ahern, Ned Doheny, Boyd Elder . . . It's here and now that the central power base of the Eagles becomes Glenn Frey and Don Henley, here that they follow the first new song of their partnership, "Desperado," with the second, "Tequila Sunrise."

It's here and now that the Eagles, the *real* Eagles, learn to fly.

11.

You Only Want the Ones That You Can't Get

S o one night they drift down to the Troub to see Tim Hardin do his thing. *Afterward, Glenn, Don, Jackson, and J.D. get a jam going, and after a few shots of Jack Daniel's and a few shots from the hip of Charlie and a few tokes of the grass spokes that keep the whole deal turning, turning, this wiggy idea begins to take shape. A concept album . . . A concept album about the bad guys, the outlaws, the outsiders . . . about America's lost innocence and its wild past . . . about the mythic America of which the Eagles are already a part . . . They can take the mood from "Desperado," which already sounds like it's a part of something bigger . . .*

Jackson tells them about this book he has been reading given to him by Ned Doheny, about gunfighters. It was the era of Butch Cassidy and the Sundance Kid, *of* McCabe & Mrs. Miller, *when Clint Eastwood was the Man with No Name and Bob Dylan was Alias in* Pat Garrett and Billy the Kid. *Gritty westerns with a counterculture sensibility. Woodstock with loaded guns. What if you set that shit to music—man, that would sell itself! They used to read about the Doolin-Dalton gang back in the Echo Park days . . .*

Glenn loves the idea of a rock 'n' roll band being like an outlaw gang . . . He loves James Dean too, of course, rebel music with claws, it's like the stars are finally aligned. When Jackson shows Glenn a song he's begun writing about James Dean, Glenn immediately co-opts it for his idea about an album of songs about outlaws and agitators. J.D. and Henley jump on board, firing off ideas until they have an upbeat rocker that might even make a good single, it's so catchy.

The ideas rattle around, percolate, start to connect. The lines blur. The lines converge. One big snowplow, hit straight to the sky.

MANY YEARS LATER, kicking back with one of the only *Rolling Stone* writers the Eagles would even let through the door, Don Henley told Cameron Crowe how "Desperado" came from "a song fragment that I'd had since the late sixties." He didn't have the title "Desperado" for it yet, but it bore "the same melody, same chords. I think it had something to do with astrology." It was Jackson Browne who originally suggested the Wild West analogy: "Something to do with playing cards," said Don.

Then, after they got back from England and Don and Glenn had moved into their own hip little wooden pads in Laurel Canyon, Don showed Glenn his old unfinished song idea, playing a rough and ready version on the piano. He told Glenn, "When I play it and sing it, I think of Ray Charles—Ray Charles and Stephen Foster. It's really a Southern Gothic thing, but we can easily make it more Western."

Hugely turned on by the idea, Glenn got straight on it. Adding words, tightening the chords. "That's when we became a team," said Don. Glenn told Cameron Crowe, "Originally, it was written for a friend of [Don's] whose name was Leo. And so the song started out, 'Leo, my God, why don't you come to your senses . . .'"

By the time it was finished, Glenn had renamed the song "Desperado." It was the first fully realized song the two had written together. "I brought him ideas and a lot of opinions; he brought me poetry," said Frey, "we were a good team."

The idea of building a whole album around the theme of what Glenn called "angst-*meisters*—antiheroes" came directly from the lyrics. "James Dean was going to be one song, and the Doolin-Dalton gang was going to be another." Overnight the Eagles went from being an easy-listening west coast groove outfit to a fully-fledged gang of musical outlaws.

Glenn saw it as a gang—his gang—right from the start. Not just the Eagles. The gang that hangs out at his place in Laurel Canyon, playing poker and basketball and getting loaded. The new writing partnership with Don solidifies everything, fuses into the core of the band. Despite Glenn's brotherly pronouncements, Randy Meisner and Bernie Leadon aren't in the gang. They are free to do their own thing.

As Don sees it, "Glenn is not a great guitar player, and I am not a great drummer. On the other hand, Randy and Bernie are incredible on their instruments. We've just taken it upon ourselves that writing is our department."

It was all good, brother, at least according to Glenn and Don.

But bands are complex organisms. Relationships within them are always fragile and easily altered, constantly evolving, mutating. The Eagles' dynamic changed with the blossoming of Glenn and Don as the main songwriters and lead voices on the band's singles. Hit singles were everything: even if most people couldn't usually remember or even care what you looked like, the songs would carry your career.

"Art for art's sake. Hit singles for fuck's sake!"

Like all classic fifty-fifty front-man relationships, from Lennon and McCartney to Jagger and Richards, Gilmour and Waters to Page and Plant, their personalities are very different, but like many great songwriting pairs, together they make a whole. Opposites attract. For Don, the serious, quiet, only child, Glenn moves into the role of big brother that Richard Bowden held in Don's early life. Glenn is the same outgoing, cocksure alpha male figure that Don works so well with.

Exhibiting the same work ethic that his father had instilled in him becomes the cog that moves the wheel for Don, the grit that makes the pearl. And when Don joins Glenn's gang it brings him into an orbit where hedonism reigns, where the pursuit of a good time comes guilt-free and strictly part of the deal. The quiet, well-read, good-hearted country boy can begin to indulge his deeper, darker desires.

As Don was the first to admit: "We could be cocky at times," but it was "really just a front." They tried to appear sophisticated but really all they wanted, Don said, was for "the girls to like us, but we had all the immature emotions that young men have—jealousy, envy, frustration, lust, insecurity—the lot." That cockiness could also play in reverse. "I want that girl over there who couldn't care less if I live or die.' Hence the line in 'Desperado': 'You only want the ones that you can't get.'"

At the same time, Bernie, who can be spiky and has a temper, plucky like his banjo, and Randy, who is shy and insecure, married with kids but drawn to the life that Glenn and Don can freely lead, both get that they are not quite on the inside, however good they are on their instruments, however well they sing.

They put up with it because, frankly, what else are they gonna do? But they don't like it. When Randy talks about the nicknames the band begin giving one another, the passive aggression is visible from outer space: Glenn is "Sportacus" because he loves basketball and baseball. Bernie is "Marty Martian" because, "we'd think of him with little antennae sticking out his head like *My*

Favorite Martian." Don is "Lobster Bat Ears" because "he got sun-burned a lot and his ears really stuck out." Randy is "Chipmunk" because of his teeth, or "China Doll" because his eyes slant when he smiles.

Glenn and Don are solid. No one fucks with Bernie. Behind his back, Bernie calls Don "Stone Face." But Randy . . . he feels deeply his differences with Don. He wishes Don would loosen the fuck up. "He was always uptight about most things," said Randy. He can't help but reflect on the obvious contradiction between the cooler-than-thou image the Eagles are selling and the way Randy sees things. Randy looks at Glenn and Don and sees "two guys who are so completely different and yet they somehow fill in each other's personalities."

THE DOOLIN-DALTON GANG—*aka the* Wild Bunch, *aka the* Oklahombres, *aka the* Oklahoma Long Riders—*are stick-up art-ists, and throughout the 1890s they rob banks, hold up trains, pil-lage stores, and kill lawmen across Kansas, Missouri, Arkansas, and Oklahoma Territory.*

The gang, led by Bill Doolin and Bill Dalton, and including Emmett Dalton, William "Tulsa Jack" Blake, George "Bitter Creek" Newcomb (aka "The Slaughter Kid"), Dan "Dynamite Dick" Clifton, George "Red Buck" Waightman, William "Little Bill" Raidler, Roy Daugherty (aka "Arkansas Tom Jones"), Richard "Little Dick" West, Ol Yantis, and Charley Pierce, were seen as folk heroes and Robin Hoods because they only plundered and attacked large institutions.

All eleven members of the gang would meet bloody ends, killed in various gun fights, and only two members made it into the new century. Their nemesis was US Marshall E.D. Nix, who appointed over one hundred deputies and gave them orders to hunt down the

Doolin-Dalton gang and do "whatever is necessary" to bring law and order to the wild Oklahoma Territory.

What a fuckin' story that would be set to music! Tales of the Wild West, of America's mythic past, young outlaw gangs living by their own rules outside society.

J.D. gives Glenn a picture of the gang as a birthday present that Glenn keeps with him for inspiration. He looks at it, turns it over in his hands, and sees it. An American rock opera about the young daredevils who gave a nation its rebellious spirit and love of freedom.

"It definitely draws some parallels between rock 'n' roll and being an outlaw," says Glenn. "Outside the laws of normality, I guess. I mean, I feel like I'm breaking a law all the time. What we live and what we do is kind of a fantasy . . ."

Before he tries selling it to Don, Glenn gens up J.D., Jackson, and Ned Doheny, who all fall for the Doolin-Daltons in the same way—hey, that could be us, only we have guitars instead of guns—and start to write songs inspired by their story. Jackson comes up with a snippet that later, fleshed out, will become "Doolin-Dalton."

Now Don is coming to a realization: "When we formed the band, it was supposed to be one of those 'everybody's equal' affairs," he told Robert Hilburn in 1982. "But the fact is people aren't all going to be able to do everything the same. It's just like on a football team. Some people quarterback and some people block."

Randy and Bernie are unsure that really needed stating—again—and see it for what it us: Don underlining that this is his and Glenn's masterpiece.

While Don plays quarterback in his mind, Glenn says he thinks they can do a whole record about outlaws, about the Doolin-Dalton Gang and others. He tells them about the different characters in the gang that they could write songs about.

He says that a concept album could be the band's grand artistic statement. It was the era of progressive rock, glam rock; even jazz and soul now came with cool concepts and heavy ideas, allegory, and intention.

As Bernie remembers: "Glenn sat everybody down and mapped out which characters in the gang could have songs written about them or encouraged us to write songs about this concept."

Bernie goes along with it. At least he's got something important to do. He writes "Twenty-One" and "Bitter Creek." "Twenty-One" is a reference to the age of Emmett Dalton when he was shot twenty-three times during a botched raid in Coffeyville, Kansas, in October 1892, then thrown in prison for fourteen years. Randy starts "Certain Kind of Fool" and "Saturday Night" and hands them over to Glenn and Don and they finish them together. The concept tightens during long sessions around the piano at Glenn's house. Glenn and Don, J.D., and Ned, "eating, breathing, and sleeping music."

Glenn and Don naturally take charge. They are Doolin and Dalton. The axis of the Eagles shifts, and everyone is fine with it at first. Until the album fails, and both sides blame the other.

Then, just as the battle lines are drawn, David Geffen sells Asylum Records.

12.

Geffen Sells Out

D avid Geffen never stuck at anything for long. He's never had to. He's too clever, too hungry, too good at seeing into the future. Hanging on and hoping for the best is a sucker play.

David's business ambitions are as wide and far-reaching as Glenn's and Don's artistic ones. He's always in a hurry to embrace the next opportunity, the next deal, the next killing. He was never going to wait around while his little roster of artists made record after record, getting harder and harder to deal with as the money and the fame kicked in and they started wanting to make concept albums about how tough it is to be a rock star.

Meanwhile, in just a couple of years, Asylum has done something remarkable. It's transformed a strictly niche genre into something mainstream, helping to coin a new sound for the new decade. Call it country rock, call it California music, call it AOR or soft rock or the SoCal sound of the seventies, call it whatever you like, Asylum has it. David understands instinctively that these moments are fleeting, once in a lifetime. Nothing is ever as good as the first time. You don't wait for things to plateau before making your move. You read the signs, cash in while the dice are still running hot, don't wait for the bell to ring for the last round.

"What happens," explained Ron Stone, who came to LA and opened a hippy-clothes store next to the Troubadour before snaring a job as a junior executive with David and Elliot, "is the next wave of artists comes into the system, and they are not your compadres. It becomes more businesslike. Even with the Eagles, half a generation behind Crosby, Stills & Nash, and Joni, I think David cared less."

David needs distance, space away from the day-to-day bullshit and nannying that running a record label and managing artists involves. "Many times I felt I had become too close to my artists," he said. "It had become too personal." As Jimmy Webb, perhaps the most underrated songwriter in America and author of "Wichita Lineman," "Galveston," and "MacArthur Park," pointed out, "When he first started out, David dealt almost entirely from the heart . . . But to be honest, I believe he became so wealthy that it became more about the money than the artists."

Doesn't it always, though?

Jimmy went on, "Once money has accumulated to a certain amount, people have a tendency to go into alternate realities."

This is never truer than in LA. Once you have more than you can spend, money takes on another dimension. It's less about what the money can *do* and more about what it *means*. It becomes a way of competing, a method of keeping score with other very wealthy, successful people. David Geffen got very rich very early in his life and he will never be poor, and he knows it. He has the golden touch. If he were a songwriter or a rock star, his outlet would be the creation of timeless masterpieces. But in his line of work, the outlet, the expression of his genius, is through the businesses he generates, the wealth that he creates. It's not about how much. It's about how much more.

This is the world David Geffen is moving into in the final months of 1972.

The big unrefusable offer shows up in the form of Steve Ross, the CEO of Warner Communications, which has under its umbrella the company's music, film, and TV arms. He offers David $2 million in cash for Asylum, another $5 million in Warners stock—a total package worth in purchasing power today around $46 million. Along with the title of label president. Steve has already bought Jac Holzman's Elektra label and he wants to create a new division called WEA: Warner Bros.-Elektra-Asylum, with Geffen at its head.

David doesn't have to think it over for more than a minute. As soon as he says yes, he and Elliot become two of the company's largest shareholders. More even than money, Geffen hears the magical sound of doors opening, the gateway into film as well as music and wherever else that might take him. Privately, he wonders whether Asylum might already have peaked. David Geffen shakes Steve Ross's hand and walks away with his head held high and his pockets stuffed with bundles of cash.

The move blindsides the Eagles like a twenty-four-ton truck sideswiping them on a two-lane highway. Just as they were gearing up for their make-or-break second album. Don Henley would bitterly recall the sauna they took with Geffen when David spoke excitedly and earnestly of his vision for Asylum as an enclave for serious artists, where the music would always come first: "Asylum was an artist label for about a minute," Don sneered, "until the big money showed up."

The sale means that David must unravel the conflicting interests he has in Asylum, the Geffen-Roberts management agency, and their music publishing arm. He transfers all of the company's assets over to Elliot, who soon gives the company back its original name, Lookout Management. "I've always thought it was the right decision to make," Geffen will say.

The band, meanwhile, like all bands, doesn't give a shit what corporate moves might be afoot, only in how it directly affects them. They knew Geffen had his nimble fingers into a number of juicy pies but had contented themselves with the notion that the Eagles, of all Geffen's artists, was always his first priority. Now that feeling is gone. David tries to sell the move to Glenn and Don as a good one for the Eagles. Whereas they had been part of an independent label, they now have some real corporate muscle behind them—and they have their old friend and trusted mentor sitting pretty at the top of the pyramid, directing traffic.

Geffen prays that message will be enough for Don and Glenn to price into their own lofty ambitions of marrying artistic acclaim with huge sales and truckloads of cash. But as David knows, so much of business, as with so much of life, is about timing. The sale comes just as Glenn and Don are deep into their *Desperado* outlaw fantasy. They feel even more like outlaws now, and the songs they are writing take on a new, more heartfelt meaning.

As a result, *Desperado* becomes a concept album not just about the America of old, but the America of now, where the cowboys use guitars and not guns to make their money and leave their mark. WEA becomes the bank they must rob, the train they must blow the doors off, the hostile town on the other side of the border where the sheriff and his men need to be dealt with mercilessly.

People miss the big picture. The Eagles aren't trying to emulate anybody, certainly not hipster commercial flops like Gram or Gene, or musical elitists like Crosby, Stills & Nash. The Eagles came from the same suburban pool of white hipster rock that would flourish in America in the mid-seventies with heavy-brow fellow-travelers like Steely Dan and Fleetwood Mac, Elton John and the Doobie Brothers. Rock sophisticates with edge, but with only Donald Fagen and Walter Becker matching Henley and Frey for the most vividly detailed depictions of the world as is, toxins in full view, scars on display, not the world of innocents those cats in the sixties sang about. Backed by supreme musical chops and cinematic production.

They see themselves, justifiably more so as time passes, in the same cerebral musical universe as Steely Dan, a cool convergence of styles coming from a certain fixed point—Steely Dan as New York jazz, Eagles as country rock LA—immediately blossoming like blood sucked up inside a syringe into something far more . . . heightened. More *elevated*. Visceral, like hit you with a flower. But smooth, too, so that you don't feel the burn or even notice the tiny razor cuts until later.

There were a lot of variations on the theme circulating. Fleetwood Mac blues, Little Feat Dixie, the Stones, pirating country cool and setting it down among the rose thorns of rock 'n' roll savagery. The Average White Band, supreme copyists, ultimate showboaters, dripping white rock privilege while using up all Brother Brown's tightest riffs.

The Eagles had it down better than all of them. While contemporaries looked to country for their credentials, Eagles couldn't wait to ditch the whole shtick and take flight from it. Next stop: Pink Floyd.

13.
Guitarschlonger

Early in the new year, Geffen sends the Eagles back to London to record *Desperado* with Glyn Johns. Winter-deep, London is even colder than last time. There's one improvement. They are not in back-of-beyond Barnes this time, but more fashionable Notting Hill, at Chris Blackwell's newly minted Island Studios, located in a deconsecrated church and equipped with a purpose-built studio console that had already been used for two of the biggest albums of 1971: Led Zeppelin's officially untitled fourth album and Jethro Tull's good vs. evil concept album and all-time best-seller, *Aqualung*.

They arrived, to stories of Jimmy Page leaning back on the console, a cigarette dangling from his girlish lips as he rang out the rapturous solo on "Stairway to Heaven" on a guitar borrowed from the devil. On weekends, they wander Portobello market, digging the scene. They discover Kensington market, where Freddie Mercury worked before Queen, picking up stuff you won't find anywhere else, like newly minted illegal bootlegs, just ask the guy at the counter, "Got any new . . . *live* albums?"

Island is also the occasional studio drop-in and green-vibe-yard for Bob Marley and the Wailers, bringing their authentic brand of Jamaican reggae for the first time to the white rock world, but who neither Glenn nor Don have heard of. The suggestion that they would one day create one of the classic rock anthems of all time, based on a gently chugging reggae rhythm, would have been greeted with slightly appalled laughter.

It was still too damn cold everywhere, but Island studios was pretty cool, man. Notting Hill had it going on too.

Except it might as well be fucking Barnes.

Once again, Glyn Johns insists on a no-drugs policy inside the studio. He records fast, on a four-week schedule that only allows for four or five takes of each passage of music before zooming onto the next. The band feel like they're constantly being rounded up. They get stir crazy—again. They manage to sneak in the odd joint when Glyn's out of the room, but that's about all the fun they have at work. It's not even grass but that stodgy brown or black hash the English roll with tobacco—believe that shit, man?

Glyn notices the change, starts to see what has happened to them since that first record blew up.

"My major problem with the Eagles was the desire of Glenn Frey to be the leader of the band," Johns later told Bill Flanagan in *Musician*. While the producer saw it as his responsibility to keep the band on track in the studio, Glenn and Don "became so insecure about the end result they weren't going to have anything that they didn't think was up to their quality of writing on the record."

He added: "I could see it cause a hell of a cleft in the band."

With their first album Johns had followed his ear and found a way to capture the Eagles as he thought the world should hear them. Deciding how to repeat the trick with *Desperado* would be another kettle of fish. It was bogged down by the concept from the start. A musical horse opera about rock star outlaws riding the prairie had to sound a certain way: more country, much folksier, more true grit in the saddle-sore keester, rather than less—something that was paramount on songs like the elegiac "Doolin-Dalton" and Bernie Leadon's self-consciously down-home "Twenty-One."

The whole thing felt counterintuitive to the practical-minded producer. While it was understood that the first album should underline their country rock fundaments, Glenn and Don had emphasized that they did not want to be fenced in by them. Hence, feel-good soft rock anthems like "Take It Easy" and "Peaceful Easy Feeling," pure pop in country rock clothing.

Now in what appeared to be a reversal of that direction, Johns was presented with narrative-driven ditties like Bernie's lo-fi "Bitter Creek," a hymn to peyote and that place "where the desert meets the sky"; and Randy Meisner's "Certain Kind of Fool," about how a certain kind of man becomes a cowboy roaming the plains. These were good songs, Glenn felt, but too dependent on the overarching story to have true universal appeal. You needed too much background to get it first hit.

It was a similar story throughout. The only exceptions, the unexceptional, "Out of Control," which tried to do what it said on the tin and only sounded feebler for it. And David Blue's ruefully rowdy "Outlaw Man," chosen because it fit the story so perfectly, but cooking all the same, Frey offering up his best cowpoke twang as he rocked his careworn heart out for a lady not to love him, not to "understand" because road life "is the life of an outlaw man . . ." The band getting late-Beatles heavy. Hurricane harmonies. Bernie's burning guitars.

Glyn did his best with the available material and made sure all the hallmarks of the earlier album were still in place—cool-breeze harmonies, cinematic choruses, tight, flawless performances—but the whole king-of-the-rodeo theme drained the color from the songs, turning them into turn-of-the-century sepia.

The only true stand-alone musical triumphs were "Desperado" and "Tequila Sunrise," neither of which needed the unnecessary prop of a conceptual context to stand out. The former a lush, yearning ballad; the latter a pure slice of aspirational soft rock. Both stood head and shoulders above the rest.

Inevitably, the album the Eagles fly back to America with is symptomatic of the conflicting forces surrounding its creation, and of the fundamental questions—still unanswered—about what the Eagles are actually supposed to be, who they think they really are. It's a dilemma summed up by the reaction of Jerry Greenberg, the president of Asylum's parent company Atlantic, the first time he sat and listened to the tapes: "Jeez. They've made a fucking cowboy album . . ."

They go all in for the album sleeve, rehiring the team of Henry Diltz and Gary Burden and saddling up for a trip to the Paramount Ranch in Malibu County, a former movie location where the one-time owner William Hertz had constructed a faux Wild West frontier town for tourists in Stetsons and tin stars to visit.

"We got them dressed up in real movie cowboy clothes that you can rent in LA," Diltz recalled. "We got a bunch of guns, blank ammunition, and some horses . . . All the guys just wanted to shoot their guns all day. They played cowboys like kids would, clutching their chests and falling in the dirt, 'Bang, bang, bang!' We did it so much that a big cloud of smoke began to rise above the Malibu hills and the fire department came. People thought the hills were on fire."

It's one hell of a jolly for sure: the whole band, plus Glyn Johns, Boyd Elder, Eagles road manager Tommy Nixon, soon-to-be for- mer manager John Hartmann, J.D. Souther, and Jackson Browne, spend the day messing around with fake guns and real horses, holding shoot-outs, playing cowboys, and posing for the pictures that become the cover of *Desperado*—the band on the front replete with loaded gun belts, leather waistcoats, and, in Don's case, a ten-gallon hat.

Maybe they were trying to extend their metaphor about the music business, because the sheriff's posse in the image is made up of Johns, Nixon, and Hartmann, while the slain gang before them is made up of the band, plus Jackson and J.D. To try to claw back some of the expense of the shoot, Burden and Diltz also make a Super 8 film to promote the album, which Don describes as "a commentary on our loss of innocence with regard to how the music business really worked." Serious stuff.

Desperado is released on April 17, 1973. Reviewing for *Rolling Stone*, Paul Gambaccini writes: "The beautiful thing about it is that although it is a unified set of songs, it is not a rock opera, a concept album, or anything pretending to be much more than a set of good tunes that just happen to fit together."

Concluding: "*Desperado* won't cure your hangover or revalue the dollar, but it will give you many good times. With their second consecutive job well done, the Eagles are on a winning streak."

In the UK, the influential *NME* tastemaker Charles Shaar Murray goes even further, describing *Desperado* as "an album of exceptionally beautiful songs, sung, played, arranged, and produced with an exquisite blend of technical precision and emotional involvement. Nothing on it communicates as instantly or as perfectly as 'Take It Easy' on the first album, but it's far more satisfying as a whole."

Those aren't the reviews, though, that Glenn and Don pore over. It's that damn Robert Christgau again that gets their goat. Reviewing in the *Village Voice*, Robert, true to form, does not hold back.

"With its barstool-macho equation of gunslinger and guitar-schlonger, its on-the-road misogyny, its playing-card metaphors, and its paucity of decent songs, this soundtrack to an imaginary Sam Peckinpah movie is 'concept' at its most mindless."

Even more perturbing, the Great American Public appear to agree. They don't seem to give a shit about the Eagles' conceptual metaphors or cowboy allegories. They want California music, free-wheeling hits like "Take It Easy," not mournful songs about long-dead gunslingers. The result: *Desperado* is a flopperoo, a turkey rather than an eagle, squawking its way to Number 145 on the *Billboard* chart in the week of release, slowly crawling to a peak of Number 41.

More unexpectedly, both of the singles released from the album flop too, don't even sniff the Top 40. The first, "Tequila Sunrise," too maudlin a pun, perhaps, on the then Cali-fash cocktail, only got as far as Number 64. The other, "Outlaw Man," an odd choice on paper, fared only slightly better, stalling at Number 59. The album's other immortal moment, "Desperado," is not even released as a single.

This time, Paul Ahern can work no magic. Firing blanks when he sends two Asylum employees dressed in full cowpoke regalia to the stations. Rock radio ignores the record because it's too country, too obtuse. And has no hits. Country stations won't play it because the Eagles are not a country act. And it has no hits.

The Eagles barely tour the record—just twenty shows spread across seven months, featuring just five songs from the new album, though not the title track, which seems insane—and *Desperado* slips away unloved, as dead as the Doolin-Daltons were once their brief time had passed.

"Glenn was enamored of this analogy between outlaw groups and rock 'n' roll," said Bernie Leadon, as laconic as any cowboy worth his jangly spurs, "and some of the first reviewers for the album said this was a bit of a stretch."

"The metaphor was probably a little bit bullshit," Henley would later grudgingly concede when speaking to Marc Eliot. "We were in LA, staying up all night, smoking dope, living the California life and I suppose we thought it was as radical as cowboys in the Old West. We were really rebelling against the music business."

Were they, though? Or was that just the coke and weed and wine and pussy talking? As he later admitted to Eliot: "Suddenly we were getting famous and making all this money, and it just turned our little heads around." They were, he tried to explain, "living outside the laws of normality." That much was true. "We just decided to write something about it to try to justify it to ourselves."

14.

Already Gone

When they thought about it, which they did, a lot, Glenn and Don alone together, snufflin' it up, it was fuckin' staggering how quickly everything had come apart. Three hit singles, the biggest debut album in America that year, staples on FM radio, easy-listening crossovers to AM, signed to a fast-moving, innovative independent label, managed by LA's shit-hottest up-and-comers, produced by one of the world's most respected and successful soundmen.

After *Desperado*, that is all gone.

No hits, lame sales figures, just as Asylum becomes part of Atlantic, which is part of WEA, which is part of Warner Communications. David splits, Elliot too. Irving Azoff happily jumps in, casting himself as savior. Truthfully, Glenn and Don have no clue what to do. Irving knows that. Makes his move.

Yet by the time the Eagles have finished another album there will be a new producer *in situ* and a new band member bringing his own fire to the line-up; the band will never again be the same, never again contain the original four voices. Never again leave so much to chance.

All of this ends and begins with *Desperado*. The end of one era and the start of another. This is what happens:

On a purely practical level, Elliot Roberts was managing Neil Young and Joni Mitchell, and though he was officially responsible for the Eagles, too, a lot of the day-to-day stuff was dealt with by John and Harlan. Nobody was really going in to bat for them after Geffen departed the scene—until Irving Azoff came charging over the horizon like the cavalry. As Paul Ahern told Marc Eliot: "When Geffen left, Elliot was in no position to handle it all. He was never going to do the Geffen eighty-hour week number. He couldn't. So he just walked away from everything and everyone except Joni, Neil, and J.D., everyone including the Eagles."

Jackson Browne's career path follows the same unflattering trajectory as the Eagles. His first album, self-titled, produces a genuine, dyed-in-the-wool Top 10 single in "Doctor, My Eyes" that pulls the album into the Top 50.

Having co-written "Take It Easy" and been at the epicenter of the Troubadour scene, Atlantic are expecting his second album, *For Everyman*, to blow through the roof, to take Jackson from scenester to superstar. It's certainly starry enough. Joni, Bonnie Raitt, and Elton John have cameo roles. David Crosby duets with Jackson on the title track, Glenn on "Redneck Friend," and Don on "Colors of the Sun."

Taking no chances, Jackson even cuts his own version of "Take It Easy," along with "These Days," a song he'd written at sixteen and has since been recorded at various times by Nico, Gregg Allman, and Tom Rush.

The album also marks the start of his long-running partnership with multi-instrumentalist David Lindley. It has an atmospheric cover shot of the courtyard of Jackson's family home in Highland Park, built by his grandfather. The album is rave-reviewed in *Rolling Stone*, with Janet Maslin acknowledging Jackson's "genius."

But just like *Desperado*, the album is a flop. "Redneck Friend," the lead-off single, refuses to fly, even with Eagle Glenn on it, and

Jackson's unsatisfactorily vanilla version of "Take It Easy" doesn't even make the Top 200. "Why play the poor man's version when you can spin the original," as one radio programmer put it.

As a result, *For Everyman* only gets as high as Number 43.

The only diamond still sparkling in the dirt is Linda Ronstadt, whose debut album for Asylum, *Don't Cry Now*, is her first to go gold, for over $500,000 worth of sales. Still the barefoot, doe-eyed queen of the Canyon—complex, artistic, as wholesomely beautiful as Jackson Browne is dreamily handsome—Linda has the reputation of a man-eater (entirely unfair and a product of the double standards of the day). The truth is she likes creative men, songwriters. Guys with heart and soul.

As David Jackson, who played bass in Dillard & Clark, observed, "Linda would hear a song and fall in love with the writer through the song . . . what a joy she was, so beautiful and so effervescent."

The producer David Geffen suggests for Linda is J.D. Souther, who he knows she is already in love with. The title of the album is after one of J.D.'s beautiful life-worn ballads, "Don't Cry Now," which of course Linda sings in a voice full of heartbreak while still smiling that wholesome, golden-child smile. There are also heartfelt renderings of more challenging material like Randy Newman's anti-slavery anthem "Sail Away" and Neil Young's profoundly conflicted "I Believe in You."

The record's truly transcendent moment, however, comes with Ronstadt's version of "Desperado," a sublime remake that will bring the song its first real recognition as the classic it is now recognized as. Faithful to the original, but with the enchanted touch of Linda's soaring, compassionate voice, the dripping cynicism of the Eagles' original transformed into something yearning and hopeful.

Everything is groovy, baby, while the red light is on in the studio. But the record takes a long time to make, partly because J.D. is not the kind of no-artsy-bullshit, technically brilliant producer that, say, Glyn Johns is, and partly because J.D. and Linda are now living together.

"We were like kids in the studio, just inept, and we took a lot of time," Linda recalled wistfully.

"Tough situation, eight to ten hours in the studio, then home for another ten hours. It was real tense," J.D. agreed.

As the pair burn through Asylum's money with no end in sight, David Geffen finally steps in. John Boylan produces three songs and then, in a moment of kismet, J.D. and Linda's friend, twenty-eight-year-old Peter Asher, is suggested. Peter is a brilliant everyman from London. The "Peter" in Peter and Gordon, whose 1964 UK Number 1, "World Without Love" was written for them by Peter's sister Jane's boyfriend, Paul McCartney. Peter would move on to become a producer/A & R exec at the Beatles' Apple label, where he signed James Taylor, became James's manager and producer, zipped across to LA, moved into the canyons, and started a golden run of production jobs that would include some of the decade's biggest records.

Peter finishes off the rest of *Don't Cry Now* and begins a working relationship with Linda that will turn her into a major international star.

"Pete was different," Linda explained. "He was prepared to validate my musical whims." Linda taught Peter things he didn't know before, too: "Linda was my educator in that world," he said. "All I knew about country music really was that it was old guys in hats singing songs that had nothing to do with me."

Finally released in October 1973, propelled by her jaunty soft-rock revamp of "Silver Threads and Golden Needles," which becomes a Top 20 hit on the country charts, *Don't Cry Now* is Linda Ronstadt's first meaningful hit.

FM radio got hold of her version of "Desperado" and put it on nonstop rotation. Repeat requests and critical plaudits followed. Any other label would have released it as a single in a hot minute. Not Asylum. Why? Some suggested it was because Geffen didn't want to embarrass the Eagles, still trying to regroup after the commercial setback of *Desperado*, the doomed cowboy concept album, where the gorgeous title track was also mysteriously not considered a single. Another mistake.

Meanwhile, US radio just loved playing Linda's version. If some kindly soul on late-night radio did occasionally rotate the Eagles original, they would invariably get calls from irate listeners insisting they play only the Linda Ronstadt "original." Crazy business, rock 'n' roll.

More gallingly for Geffen, at least, it is Linda's previous label, Capitol, that will reap the benefits of Ronstadt's breakthrough. Part of the get-out-of-jail-free deal Geffen made with Capitol to release Linda from her contract, it was agreed she would make one last album for them.

The result: the Grammy-winning *Heart Like a Wheel*, which she completed in 1974—then watched awestruck as it danced all the way to Number 1. The key was two massive hit singles: "You're No Good," a minor hit for Betty Everett back in 1963, and "When Will I Be Loved," a Top 10 hit for the Everly Brothers in 1960. Both elegantly reconfigured for an up-to-date soft-rock LA sound *in excelsis*, tasteful guitars and funkalicious rhythm marinated in star-kissed vocals and celestial harmonies, angels with whiskey wings.

Asylum may have shit the bed with *Heart Like a Wheel*, but it just made Geffen absolutely determined to cash in on such lottery-winning success. Then J.D. began an affair with Joni Mitchell, one that almost destroyed Linda and took her two years to recover from, by which time Geffen's head was entirely elsewhere.

"There's not a girl singer who ever set foot in Los Angeles in that era that John David did not have a relationship with," observed Peter Asher. "There was a famous moment when Joni and Linda met on his doorstep—one leaving and the other arriving."

Ned Doheny, whose own debut record for Asylum had taken so long and cost so much that Geffen eventually told him that if he wanted it finished, he'd have to pay for the rest of it himself, recalls the scene: "J.D. unfortunately had a tendency to shit where he ate. His reputation as a ladies' man was more important to him than his friendships."

So what? The Eagles need to get their own shit together, even as Linda makes "Desperado" the radio hit they coulda, shoulda had. The band are still split down the middle: Glenn and Don vs. Bernie and Randy. The division of labor becomes more evident when their songwriting royalties are readdressed.

Don and Glenn's bid to take creative control has a financial impact as well as an artistic one. Up until *Desperado* the band had an arrangement to split all of their royalties four ways. Geffen's departure now sees each member of the band establish their own publishing company, with royalties now allocated by writing credits rather than split equally regardless of who wrote what when.

Because song publishing is where the real action is, the division of credits has been contested since the music business began. Colonel Tom Parker, manager of Elvis Presley, was notorious for insisting his boy have a writing credit on almost every song he recorded. It didn't matter that Elvis couldn't write a hit song if his life depended on it. The Colonel's reasoning was that the actual writers were better off with 50 percent of something rather than 100 percent of nothing, which is what they would get if Elvis decided not to record their song.

With album-oriented artists like the Eagles, the situation was more volatile and more subtle. On a huge-selling album, even the songs that might be categorized as "fillers" could generate large amounts of royalties for their composers, while a credit on a song like "Desperado" or "Take It Easy," played endlessly for half a century—well, do the math, baby. In that regard, Jackson Browne and J.D. Souther might be—must be—making as much or more out of the Eagles than some of the band members.

So Glenn's and Don's decision to appoint themselves as lead writers for the Eagles has heavy long-term implications. Randy Meisner sees the irony in the anti-corporate "outlaw" ethos of *Desperado* when weighed against Glenn's and Don's financial acuity. "It was always about the money," said Randy resignedly. "That's what fucked everything up."

With no new songs to speak of, Glenn and Don decide that the next Eagles album—which they know in their blood is a make-or-break deal—needs to follow their original vision of more hard rock, less country. Nonetheless, as 1973 plays out, they troop onto a plane and head back for England, where they know Glyn Johns will be waiting to pour a bucket of cold shit on that idea and insist they go back to catchy country rock songs layered in marmalade harmonies and yet more of Bernie's dueling banjos.

J.D. comes along too this time, as they return reluctantly to Olympic Studios, back to backwoods Barnes, and to the Spartan regime of the domineering Johns. Only these are no longer the naive kids that Glyn coaxed through the first record, or the fervent would-be conceptualists of *Desperado*. The Eagles are more worldly but also divided, adrift, angry—badly in need of a hit record.

They still hate London. They still hate Olympic and Glyn's bullshit no-drugs policy. They're not sure what they want, but they're pretty clear about what they don't. They last six weeks, which Glyn Johns later describes as "a disaster area."

Glyn was "pissed off because they wouldn't grab the situation by the balls and get on with it. There were a lot of hang-ups, individually and with each other. But what it boils down to is they weren't ready to make another record."

Nothing if not astute, the producer hit the nail on the head. Instead, they play cards, high-stakes "Eagle poker" that sometimes gets heated, and they chase girls. Anything to distract from getting down to the job in hand.

Elliot Roberts and Neil Young stop by as Neil arrives in London for his first UK tour. Registering the bad vibes between Glenn and Glyn in particular, Elliot suggests the band take a break and come and support Neil. They can't get out of Olympic fast enough and rent a tour bus to head out for a blissful week of just playing and having a good time.

"There had always been disagreement with Glyn," Bernie shrugged. "Randy had wanted to fire him over the first album and record the whole thing again. When *Desperado* didn't sell, we were all like, 'It's Glyn's fault!'"

As soon as the shows with Neil are completed, they fly straight home to California, do not pass Olympic, do not collect Glyn's thoughts.

In the end, all the Eagles have to show for their six weeks in England are two songs, one that Glenn had begun way before the trip to London. The genesis for what would become their first Number One hit song had begun one afternoon in Laurel Canyon, when Glenn was fooling around with a particular guitar tuning that Joni Mitchell had shown him. "I got lost and ended up with the guitar tuning we used."

He, Don, and J.D. had worked it up in London—"we were on deadline to get it finished," recalled J.D.—and used a lyric of Don's that he had written about his breakup with a girl called Suzannah Martin. They get a version of the song, called "Best of My Love," down with Glyn, along with another ballad, this one a joint effort between J.D. and Don entitled "You Never Cry Like a Lover," which might just be the best, certainly the most real, thing they've done together.

Nineteen seventy-four is at the door before you know it and none of them are sure of their next move. Luckily for the Eagles, Irving Azoff knows just what to do.

15.

Gram Burns Up

He likes to go out to the desert and space out. To the place that's been calling him back since he first crash-landed there in 1969. Joshua Tree National Park, in the southeast of sun-smeared California. Where he and his many good friends drop acid in the dead of night and wait for the UFOs to come and put on a show—which they nearly always do. Big ones, small ones, flying in formation.

Everything's fucked now, though. Everything's fucking fucked.

Poor little rich kid, Ingram Cecil Connor III—Gram to his less privileged dime-store cowboy friends—is the son of a citrus fruit heiress and a Second World War flying ace. Beautiful and damned, talented and tortured, one of those born-cool guys everything comes easy to. Except the one thing he really wants.

Poor little trust-fund baby.

Gram Parsons in his cream nudie suit adorned by creeping marijuana leaves and splashed with red poppies, a half-stoned smirk on his privileged, pretty-boy face. Gram now looking at the Eagles like Elvis Presley once looked at the Beatles. No, that's not it. Try this: Gram now looking at the Eagles like Arthur "Big Boy" Crudup once looked at Elvis.

Or as the King himself once sagely observed: "The colored folks been singing it and playing it just like I'm doin' now, man,

for more years than I know. They played it like that in their shan-
ties and in their juke joints and nobody paid it no mind 'til I
goosed it up."

Nobody's paying Gram no mind, neither. Nobody beyond his
small coterie of stoned acolytes, dedicated flunkies, and other
wannabe-wannados in the hip media.

In 1972, right after Gram is kicked out of his own band by the
other Burritos—some "brothers" they turned out to be, he'll tell
ya straight—"Take It Easy," "Witchy Woman," and "Peaceful
Easy Feeling" begin riding the American airwaves hard. Asked
what he thinks of the Eagles, Gram wrinkles his nose: "Bubblegum,"
he says, smiling like the sun just came out, but inside seething with
junkie malice and envy.

Gram watches through uptight glassy eyes as the Eagles soar
high above him, and suddenly everything he's done with the Byrds,
the Flying Burrito Brothers, on his own as a solo act, or as a musical consigliere to the Stones, don't mean shit, honey.

Gram sees it and hates on it, and for good reason. Gram makes
what he calls "cosmic American music"—an intoxicating mélange
of new country, old gospel, trad blues, and rocking rock—and
those Eagles assholes take it and just "goose it up." Making beaucoup bucks along the way.

Meanwhile, Gram the Great Original is still a complete
unknown to the people in America who listen to the radio and
watch TV, the people who run to the record store and buy the
records or wait in line for tickets to the show. While Gram is still
relying on fat monthly checks from the family to make a difference,
the goddamn Eagles come along and make faking it look easy.

Fucking assholes.

What else rubs Gram wrong: the Eagles have former Burrito
Brother Bernie Leadon on guitar and banjo and highly polished
harmony vocals. On top of that, the Eagles album features Bernie's

song "Train Leaves Here This Morning," which gives a co-writer credit to former Byrd, Gene Clark, who watches the publishing checks roll in while Gram's fortunes flounder, reading all this in Rolling Stone and making like who gives a shit about that shit anyway, shithead?

But Gram got kicked out of the Burritos for being too fucked up to work, for flirting too heavily with Keith Richards and heroin, for being right all the time even when he knew he was wrong. So Gram moves in with golden-boy Byrds producer Terry Melcher, son of Doris Day, best buds with Dennis Wilson of the Beach Boys.

Gram tells Terry he wants to make a solo album and asks Terry to produce it. Terry gets it and says, hell yeah. But Gram is everlastingly high in the city and Terry grows bored and takes a rain check.

Gram splits for the South of France where the Stones are deep in the devil's hole trying to make what will become their last truly astonishing album, Exile on Main Street, and gets so fucked up that he once again takes off after being warned off by some Corsican drug smugglers.

Gram cools it. Marries his sweetheart Gretchen Burrell, heads to London, gets clean for a bit, then returns home and recruits some of Elvis Presley's Taking Care of Business Band: guitarist James Burton and drummer Ron Tutt. Then adds this beautiful twenty-five-year-old chick singer named Emmylou Harris to the mix. Emmylou has a holy-water voice—not as full-strength and valley-wide as Linda's, but much more haloed and night-like.

Gram stays off the nod long enough to see what he has stumbled on and quickly makes a solo record with these people before it all goes to hell again, which he calls GP. Released in January 1973, it's a good album, now regarded as possibly one of the greats. At the time it had Bud Scoppa in Rolling Stone gushing, "Gram Parsons is an artist with a vision as unique and personal as those of Jagger/Richards, Ray Davies or any other of the celebrated figures."

But it doesn't sell. At all. Neither the album nor the single, "She," ever sees the inside of the Top 200. Bad scene, which Gram deals with, in the usual fashion.

The good news: Gram now has enough of a name with the right crowd that he is able to take the band, including Emmylou, out on the road, jamming flea-heaven clubs and weed-and-wine colleges, beer-sticky dancehalls, and no-home-to-go-to bars. Everyone getting paid and having a fine time. Ignoring the scenery and just grooving on the gigs.

But there's trouble in paradise. While stoned, immaculate, rich-kid Gram and midnight-incandescent, po' girl Emmylou make insane magic together onstage each night, pretty little beach-blonde Gretchen with nothing better to do than watch gets jealous of raven-eyed Emmylou consuming all her husband's attention and decides fuck this and bails.

Gram doesn't care or says he doesn't care, not while he's got Emmylou and this kick-ass band.. Gram is fortunate to have a great tour manager in Phil Kaufman, a thirty-eight-year-old Vietnam vet who served time in the mid-sixties for wielding major weed, banged up at Terminal Island Federal Correctional Institute in San Pedro, California, where he became friends with fellow inmate, Charlie Manson.

Later, after they both got out, Kaufman lived with Manson and his followers for a couple of months. A believer in Charlie's head-fuck music, Kaufman formed his own company to release a Manson album after the cult leader had been rejected by all the major record labels—and abandoned by Terry Melcher, who said he wanted to sign the psycho and make a movie about him, then reneged on the deal and vanished from sight, triggering the horrifying Manson murders of August 1969, specifically the killing of Leno and Rosemary LaBianca two days after the murder of movie star Sharon Tate and several other people in Benedict Canyon.

It was while Manson was in jail awaiting trial for the Tate–LaBianca killings that he begged Kaufman to find a way to "please put out my music," phoning him five days a week. Manson was "very anxious for his music to be heard," said Phil. No shit.

Eventually, Kaufman raised $3,000 (over $20,000 today) and pressed 2,000 copies of an album entitled LIE: The Love and Terror Cult. *Each of the original copies came with a poster that bore the signatures of many prisoners and inmates, all supporting Manson and the Family. Not an obvious floor-filler, the album did contain two songs that would become famous in different ways: "Cease to Exist," which had already morphed into a Beach Boys song, "Never Learn Not to Love," and "Look at Your Game, Girl," which Guns N' Roses would release a deliberately "controversial" version of nearly twenty-five years later.*

Phil's real break in the music biz came when he was hired to chauffeur Mick Jagger and Marianne Faithfull around Los Angeles when the Stones were in town mixing their album Beggars Banquet. *Mick began referring to Phil as "my executive nanny." He was a cool guy, said Mick. A guy who got it.*

It was Keith Richards who really became a friend to Phil, recommending him to his pal Gram Parsons as a likely tour manager for the Flying Burrito Brothers. Since then Phil and Gram had rarely been apart.

Things go from bad to beyond between Gram and Gretchen in the summer of 1973 when their house in Topanga Canyon burns to the ground. The house going up in flames is a sign, Gram decides. For how bad things had gotten between them. And a message from the music gods: don't fuck this next album up.

Gram splits, holing up in the spare room at Phil's pad. He fills the time by hanging out again with his high school sweetheart, Margaret Fisher. He starts working on another record. He's still got a lot of great songs he's writing.

Things start to look up again. Gram, Margaret, and Phil often spend a few days out at Joshua Tree, searching for easy meaning in the great desert skies. Getting loaded and letting it all come down for a spell. At one with the rattlesnakes and coyotes. Chowing down on moon-size stars.

Gram is no fan of the so-called real world. That place where right now his attorney in LA is preparing divorce papers to serve to Gretchen. So one bright and early afternoon in September 1973, Gram, Phil, Margaret, Gram's assistant Michael Martin, and Michael's girlfriend Dale McElroy, drive out for a two-night stay at the Joshua Tree Inn, a secluded desert hideaway at 29 Palms Highway, 140 miles east of Los Angeles.

"He was always anxious to go there," recalled Parsons's manager Ed Tichner. "I visited him there once. It was nothing exciting—but he knew every bar and saloon in the area."

He's off the hard stuff, no horse galloping through his veins for weeks. Gram just wants to drink and smoke dope. They hit some bars in a small nearby town named Yucca Valley. Gram scores some 'ludes and "reds" (the barbiturate, Seconal) and adds them to the mix. All fall down.

By the morning of the second day they have already run out of weed, so Gram sends Martin back to LA, pronto, to score more. That night, after failing to persuade Fisher and McElroy to drink with him (Margaret doesn't really like alcohol and Dale is recovering from a bout of hepatitis), Gram cheerfully announces, "I'll drink for the three of us," and sinks six double tequilas. Just like that.

By the time night falls at the Joshua Tree Inn, Gram is out of control on tequila and reds. Somehow, using his junkie antennae, he scores a speedball from some chick in room number one—coke and smack dissolved together in a hot black spoon. As Old Bill Burroughs, another renowned Southern gentleman and trust-funded freak of nature with a taste for H, once intoned in the voice *of a sheep-killing dog: "If God invented something better, he must've kept it for himself."*

Gram shoots up by the light of the TV and immediately keels over, his face turning yellow and blue. Gram has fallen for the classic recovering junkie's sucker punch—taking the same amount he did before he got clean when his body's tolerance was still huge. Cleaned-up it's enough to kill him if immediate action is not taken. But as everyone knows, strong heroin mixed with a flood of alcohol also invariably results in massive overdose. Throw in the 'ludes and the reds and you've got a double whammy of what the fuck did he do now?

Margaret unbuckles his belt and drags down his pants so she can push ice cubes up his ass—the word-of-mouth remedy as prescribed by fellow junkies. Gram is not out cold quite yet, but he can't speak for drooling, can't hold his head straight without help. Is no longer in control of his limbs. Margaret with the help of the others somehow manages to drag him into a cold shower then, still in his soaked clothes, onto the big double bed in their room, number eight, and leaves Dale McElroy to watch over him while she runs out to fetch strong black coffee from somewhere.

It doesn't occur to any of them to try and keep him awake, maybe force him to walk around a bit. Anything but put him to sleep.

Lying there comatose, Gram has put away so much booze, eaten so many downers, and shot up so much smack that his breathing slows and slows until it just stops, and no one can make it start again. Dale attempts mouth-to-mouth resuscitation, but it's not working.

Margaret Barbary, who owns the motel, later recalls how Gram had "looked a little pale," that day. But she had no idea what was about to happen next. When members of the party come pounding on her doors and windows just after midnight, saying Gram is unconscious and that they can't wake him, Barbary calls for an ambulance. Her son, Al Barbary, who saw action in 'Nam, also tries giving mouth-to-mouth but it's too late. According to Al, Gram was already "dead as a doornail. His body was so full of poison that I about died myself." By Al's reckoning, "He'd been dead about a half hour."

Paramedics arrive and Gram's cold, wet body is rushed to Hi-Desert Memorial Hospital in Yucca Valley, where he is offi-cially pronounced dead.

"He was clean and took a strong shot," Keith Richards would shrug when he got the news. "That's the one mistake you don't want to make . . ."

Gram makes that one mistake and pays the heavy price. He is twenty-six years old.

The San Bernardino County coroner's office duly reports that Parsons died of heart failure due to natural causes, but that the exact nature of those causes would not be known until after a toxicology report is received. Upon which they release the body to the family.

Gram's stepfather, Bob, immediately organizes for the body to be flown "home" to New Orleans, where the family intends to hold a private funeral ceremony, to which none of Gram's actual friends will be invited.

Word around the dealer's table is that Bob will inherit Gram's share of his grandfather's estate if his stepfather can prove that Gram was a resident of Louisiana. Fuck that shit, decides Kaufman. Gram has already told Phil that when he dies, he wants his remains cremated and his ashes scattered in the desert at Joshua Tree, on the steps of Cap Rock.

So Phil and Michael Martin come up with their own plan. They rent a hearse and drive it out to LAX, where, posing as mor-tuary workers, they persuade a baggage handler to release the body to them.

Then they drive Gram's dead body back out to Joshua Tree, carry the coffin to the foot of Cap Rock and, as darkness falls, Phil pours five gallons of gasoline into the open casket then throws a lit match into it, causing an enormous fireball to explode that can be seen for miles in every direction.

Later accounts claim the cops showed up and chased the two men, who according to the official report "were unencumbered by sobriety" but who somehow escaped. Other accounts suggest there was no chase, that they had simply been pulled over by traffic cops and arrested for an "open-container/motor-vehicle violation" and/or suspected DUIs.

Nobody knows where the hell these stories come from.

What is clear both Kaufman and Martin are arrested at home in LA a few days later. But since there is no law against stealing a dead body, they are each fined $750—for stealing the coffin. Nor are they prosecuted for leaving 35 pounds of Gram's charred remains in the desert. What's left of Parsons's body will now be buried in the Garden of Memories Cemetery in Metairie, Louisiana. Bob makes rootin' tootin' sure of it.

The album Gram was working on when he died is titled Grievous Angel *and when it is issued four months later, it becomes accepted as his masterpiece. The preeminent British music paper* Melody Maker *writes: "There are no words to describe the sense of desperation and the haunting quality of these last works."*

According to the crazy cat in Crawdaddy: *"Though it might seem that Gram indeed succeeded in throwing his life away, it's worth noting that—like Hemingway, Rimbaud, Nathanael West and other truncated geniuses before them—he ended it with style." Huh?*

The album still barely broke the Top 200, but the legend was already congealing nicely.

Bernie Leadon—as many writers feel obliged to underline, now of the Eagles, but once of the Burrito Brothers—guests on three of the nine songs on Grievous Angel. Bernie knew all about Gram, uptown and downtown. Feels burdened by his death. But forgives him because his music cured the heart.

Bernie writes his best-ever song, "My Man," in tribute. An exquisitely delivered, heart-clutching piece of high-pop balladry up there with the best. Bernie plays it, Bernie sings it, Bernie speaks the truth as he gives his best vocal performance on an Eagles record.

No man's got it made, till he's far beyond the pain
And we who must remain go on living just the same ...

It's a fantastic track that will appear on the next Eagles album. Many years later, Bernie tells the makers of the acclaimed Parsons documentary Fallen Angel: "In the first place, it wasn't a proper cremation. It was a partial burning. And they left him; that's what's so stupid. If you're going to cremate someone, do a little research, you know, and like, do it properly. But don't go leave him in the desert by the side of the road half-burnt. That's not cool."

Nevertheless, Gram Parsons in death becomes so cool no one is ever allowed to say anything bad about his music again. Keith Richards claims that Parsons's "effect on country music is enormous," but actually that's not really so. Gram was never going to be a welcome son of Nashville. His influence, however, on a certain kind of knowingly earthy Americana remains undisputed.

Emmylou Harris, flattened by the news, would continue to keep Parsons's work alive throughout her career, covering a number of his best songs, including nailed-on Gram classics like

"Hickory Wind," "Sin City," and "Ooh Las Vegas." While Harris's own songs, "Boulder to Birmingham" from her 1975 album Pieces of the Sky and "The Road" from her 2011 album, Hard Bargain, are personal tributes to her mentor.

Gram was so highly regarded among his peers the tributes were being paid even before he'd died. Poco's album, Crazy Eyes, released just four days before Gram shot himself on the highway to honky-tonk hell, was now said to be a kind of prophetic "homage" to their fallen friend, after Richie Furay revealed the title track was written "in honor of him."

A nine-minutes-plus rock opera featuring impossibly lush orchestration and cathedral-like production, it was based, said Richie, on the days when he and Gram had "lived across the street from each other in Greenwich Village in 1964."

Richie had actually begun the song, he said, in 1969, when he and Gram were in the Burrito Brothers. There was also a cover on the album of an as-yet unreleased Gram ballad, the shimmering "Brass Buttons."

Furay and Poco had endured their own kind of death when Richie's departure from the band was announced four days before Crazy Eyes was released. It was Poco's last Top 40 album for five years.

But that was just collateral damage. David Geffen had already signed Richie to what he was talking up around town as "the first country rock supergroup"—the Souther-Hillman-Furay Band.

Yeah, baby. J.D.'s musical cred was sky-high from his work with Linda, the Eagles, and Jackson, but there was no real public profile fully in focus yet. He needed help the same way Glenn did. He needed other guys standing around making him look good.

Meanwhile Chris Hillman's rep was unassailable. Still wearing his Sweetheart of the Rodeo halo, his Dillard & Clark–Flying Burritos–Stephen Stills pedigree dragging behind, leaving a trail *for others to not even dare try follow. All this belied the fact no one even knew what he looked like anymore.*

With Elliot there to handle the guys, Geffen lit up the phones as he thrilled to the idea of teaming up Chris the Elder Visionary and J.D. the New Fastest Gun with Richie Furay—another hugely talented guy with all the right connections, and another perpetual second banana. Play these cards well, Geffen and Roberts must have calculated, you could have another Eagles on your hands. One with built-in critical fawn. Win-win. The only kind of win David Geffen ever settled for.

Only snag: J.D. just didn't dig Richie's music at all *and didn't try to hide it.*

"Fuck him!" J.D. was heard to scream. "I ain't singing on his song!"

J.D. just didn't do compromise. Otherwise he'd have been in the Eagles, right?

The subsequent album, The Souther-Hillman-Furay-Band, *was good enough to ride its badass rep all the way to Number 11 in 1974. To J.D.'s immense displeasure the only single they had that hit the Top 30 and buzzed the car radio was the feel-good funk of the insanely catchy "Fallin' in Love"—written and sung by Richie Furay.*

There was a quickie follow-up that no one really talked about, but by then J.D. was already out.

The "country rock's first supergroup" tag was a stroke of genius, though. None of these guys were stars. But Geffen now knew how you could change that.

Just a shame Gram didn't stick around long enough to meet David. This book might have been about him, not the Eagles.

16.

Irving Makes His Move

Irving Azoff may have been small in stature—just five foot three inches in his tube socks—but he had the mind of a stone-cold corporate assassin. Never one to pass up an opportunity, as David Geffen waved his unhappy Eagles off into the sunset, Irving decided what the gang needed was a new cutthroat leader.

He was from Danville, Illinois, just like Gene Hackman, star of *The French Connection*, one of his favorite movies, except Irving Azoff was no movie star. Instead he would become the most powerful star maker and breaker in America across six decades. To look at him, you'd never have guessed. Short, squat, glasses, pleasantly nebbish even as a young college grad, he looked like Spencer Tracy's lost younger brother. With a Martin Scorsese beard.

His father was a pharmacist and his mother a bookkeeper, and right from high school, Irving had been a productive promoter, a spot-on talent spotter, a brainiac mega-mogul in waiting. He had booked his first shows in high school to pay for college, then dropped out of college to run a small Midwestern concert-booking agency. His first clients were a band from Champaign, Illinois, called REO Speedwagon, a bunch of guys he was at university with.

Named after the 1915 truck, they immediately did well in the Midwest markets, where early, hairy-chest anthems like "Prison

Women" went down a treat. Irving officially took the band on for management while getting them signed to Epic Records in 1971.

Irving's second client was a singer-songwriter named Dan Fogelberg, from Peoria, Illinois. Irving discovered Dan when he opened at a show for REO and noted a cool young artist somewhat in the James Taylor/Jackson Browne mode. So they head for California, where Irving has read all the young, cool singer-songwriters go to hang out and score. Fogelberg is not of the same caliber as his other big signings back then, yet Irving Azoff is able to persuade Clive Davis into signing his boy Dan to Columbia Records.

That night Azoff phoned his pal and business partner in Illinois, John Baruck, and told him: "Okay, get your ass out here. We can take this town." Baruck did as he was told and still remains Azoff's right-hand man to this day. "I never felt the music business was that competitive," shrugged Irving. "It's just not that fucking hard. I don't think there's that many smart people in our business."

Getting a load of this and wondering who in fuck this wise-ass newbie is, David Geffen and Elliot Roberts investigate further and discover a guy cut from the same cloth as them. They immediately decide they could use a guy like Irving on their team and sign him up for Geffen-Roberts, where he joins the bear pit of hungry, edgy juniors scrapping their way toward the top table, or as close as they can get.

Just as Irving arrives, John Hartmann moves sideways. John has, along with Harlan Goodman, been looking after another addition to the Geffen-Roberts roster, a band formed in London by the kids of US service personnel called, ambitiously, America. America were already starting to irk Glenn and Don by having a couple of big, fat hit singles in "Horse with No Name" and "Ventura Highway," songs tuned into a more contemporary musical reflection of America, and printing money, honey.

Hartmann has been angling to take the Eagles on as a client of his own but leaves Geffen-Roberts soon after his plan becomes known to David (according to Hartmann, David threatens to "bury" the Eagles if Hartmann takes them from Geffen-Roberts). John doesn't need that in his life.

Irving Azoff sees all this, breathes it in with satisfaction, and decides to use the Eagles as the vehicle to make his own indelible mark: "I immediately made them my business," he explained years later. Then, more disingenuously, "We were all just a bunch of punk kids who were the same age."

Around the same age, sure. But *punk kids*? Living high in Laurel Canyon, snorting Peruvian flake and fucking models with only one name?

Irving's first encounter with the Eagles becomes the stuff of legend. The band are at LAX airport waiting for a limo to glide them home to Hollywood. The limo doesn't show. An irate Glenn Frey calls the office, and Elliot, who simply cannot be fucked anymore to listen to Glenn's *endless fucking complaining*, not today, hands the phone to Irving with a message for Glenn to "take a hippy taxi."

Wow. But Irving does as he's told and in response gets a thundering rant down the phone from Glenn. Glenn is screaming about how rivals like America "get limos because they record for Warners, but the Eagles don't! They get hippies in taxies because they record for fuckin' cheap shots Asylum!"

Irving listens courteously as Glenn explains about the motherfuckers and assholes he is fucking furious with at that precise moment, Irv making sympathetic noises. He sweet-talks Glenn like a mother does an errant infant, shushing him and making him smile again by arranging for the longest, sleekest black limousine money can buy to be sent straight out to LAX to collect "Glenn and the boys."

From that day onward, whenever Glenn calls the office about *any*thing, he only asks for Irving—no one else. Ever. Irving adapts to his new role effortlessly, adding a helmet of curly hair to his thick black beard, dark magpie eyes camouflaged behind permanent-midnight shades.

With John Hartmann and Harlan Goodman now moved over to one side—and with Geffen playing God in his luxurious new office and, as he liked to tell you "now a very rich man"—a power vacuum emerges around the Eagles, one that will be ruthlessly exploited by Azoff.

When Azoff calls Roberts to say that he has officially assumed management of the Eagles, Elliot, only half joking, replies, "The who?" Irving can't wait to tell Don and Glenn what Elliot said. Elliot can't wait to yuck it up with David.

Geffen however is not in the mood to make nice. He may be richer than Irving, better connected than Irving, but don't be fooled. David Geffen's new gig as head of WEA ain't all wine and blow jobs. To his abject dismay, the value of his stock slumps almost as soon as he takes office.

"I got completely fucked on that deal," he complains. "I was very unhappy."

David's grand plan is to run Elektra/Asylum alongside Atlantic, with himself and Ahmet as co-chairmen, brothers in arms, sorcerer-and-apprentice. But Jerry Wexler, who has been a senior partner at Atlantic since 1953 and who, side by side with Ahmet, built Atlantic into a giant, rejects the idea and rants to Ahmet, "One day, you'll cry tears of blood from this wonder boy of yours..."

But David has signed a five-year deal and makes a plush new home for himself at the Elektra/Asylum offices on La Cienega, where he begins his tenure as he intends to go on: carving his way through the existing Elektra roster, which he sees as mostly dead wood.

"What made Elektra/Asylum exciting," he glittered, straight faced, "was that there were all of these fabulous artists on Asylum."

It's bad news for the critically feted Paul Butterfield, who's never seen one of his six Elektra albums crack the Top 40, same for Delaney & Bonnie, another cool critics' choice that doesn't sell bupkes. And it's bad news for Brit-signed Elektra follies like the Incredible String Band and the New Seekers.

"The only ones that really have a future," announces Geffen, are "Queen and Carly Simon." Overnight, the Elektra roster is cut to just thirteen acts. David makes it clear that these aren't musical choices, but decisions based purely on business.

"We were suddenly in a different era," says Mel Posner, a future president of the label. "Asylum was Jackson Browne and Linda Ronstadt and the Eagles. Everything broke loose, everything that David had envisioned as part of this thing. It was Laurel Canyon. It was California rock. It was a golden time."

Meanwhile, Irving Azoff is thinking about how he can follow in Geffen's footsteps. Irving knows how pissed off the Eagles are about the failure of *Desperado*. He knows they need to make a change, up the ante. He knows that he is the man to lead that change.

Speaking years later, Irving will insist: "I got my swagger from Glenn Frey and Don Henley. No doubt about it." But he was already way ahead of them.

Irving is part David Geffen, part Colonel Tom Parker. He's a street fighter, sharp-minded, verbally dexterous, not a man you would ever wish to cross, nor one who will ever forgive a slight, but absolutely the man you want defending your corner, because like all true back-alley dogfighters, there is no quit in Irving Azoff.

As one music biz insider described him at the time, Irving is, "the shortest kid in school who dreams of making the basketball team."

Now, at last, here come that team. Here come the Eagles and here comes the main chance, the big show, the on-the-buzzer, three-point jump shot that all the great ones need to make. Irving knows that Don and Glenn think the Glyn Johns sessions are a fucking disaster. The way they see it, Glyn has nothing on the line here. If the next Eagles album tanks, Glyn will just go on to his next project, already lined up: a new Stones album, *It's Only Rock 'n' Roll*.

But this could be it for the Eagles. Elliot Roberts has tried to salve the wound by giving Don and Glenn higher percentiles of the publishing before it is split equally. But they know that Elliot is pulling back, and David is making Hollywood mogul power plays. They know it's shit or bust time and they know that Irving Azoff is as ambitious as they are. Glenn and Don go and see Irving, plead for him to make his move.

"Henley and I got [Irving] in a room together. There was something about it. We started telling him our problems with the band, how we wanted our records not to be so clean and glassy and how we were getting the royal fuckin' screw job."

Irving offered what the more experienced, better resourced David Geffen never could: his undivided attention. His personal 24/7 care. His love. He would take care of Glyn Johns, forget about it.

"Here was a guy our own age," Glenn reasoned, "catching his rising star the same time we were. We decided that night Irving could manage us."

It isn't that simple, of course. Nothing ever is. Elliot downsizes and Harlan Goodman and John Hartmann look like they're going to leave then stay then leave again. Then when they do finally go—taking America and Poco with them—Don Henley gets hold of the financials and realizes that most of the money the Eagles have earned has gone back to pay advances, commissions, and production fees to Asylum and Lookout. Once upon a time in show business, baby.

The band, coached by Irving, meet with Elliot and David, lay out their grievances in forensic detail, and listen to Elliot say that he will release them from their management contract immediately. They leave the meeting alone. Then when they leave the company, Irving leaves with them.

Many years later, Don Henley tells Marc Eliot: "Both Roberts and Geffen, with their combination management/record company, had a huge conflict of interest and we decided to call them on it.

"Suddenly the management company downsized, and we were out on the street. We could have sued both of them right there, because there were conflicts all up and down the line, but we were young and didn't know the ropes well enough." He added: "Fortunately Irving was there."

But that is the older, wiser Don talking. Back in the early seventies, when the right number of people to fit into a Jacuzzi was considered more important than contracts and lawyers, this felt like a betrayal of the band's soul.

It worked well enough and long enough to get them to here, which is where they needed to be. But how is it supposed to work now that Mommy and Daddy have split up?

Fortunately, Irving Azoff assures them, he knows exactly what to do. He scraps the Glyn Johns sessions. Then plays them *The Smoker You Drink, the Player You Get*—the new hit album by ex–James Gang singer-guitarist Joe Walsh, who Irving has also just taken on for management. It also contains a solid-gold hit single in Joe's song, "Rocky Mountain Way."

The album has already gone Top 10 by the time Irving plays it for Glenn and Don. But they haven't been paying attention, except to the single, which American radio had been sinking its teeth into all summer and was therefore impossible to ignore.

Irving wants to demonstrate to them the work of Walsh's long-time producer, Bill Szymczyk.

Both Glenn and Don put their serious listening faces on and agree. The record kicks ass. Not only that, it seems to contain a better mix of rootsy Americana and straight-ahead rock than anything achieved so far by the Eagles.

Plus blues, folk, jazz, even a Caribbean lilt on one track. But it doesn't sound cheesy or overproduced, the way they feel Glyn Johns wants them to sound. It's not country rock corny, it's just rock cool.

Joe Walsh is a cool guy, a wild spirit—like Glenn, he knows what he's got and how to use it. He comes from Wichita, Kansas, where he was born Joseph Fidler, the son of a US Air Force pilot who died in a plane crash in Okinawa, Japan, before Joe was two years old. Joe's mom remarried and he took the surname of his stepfather. The family moved to Columbus, Ohio, and then New York and then New Jersey.

Joe's mom was a classical pianist so that's where the music comes from. He began strumming his first guitar at age ten. He did the usual local band thing, and then minored in music while majoring in English at Kent State University.

Joe was there on May 4, 1970, when the Ohio National Guard shot and killed four students during a protest against the Nixon government's expansion of the Vietnam War into Cambodia. The bloody hell that Neil Young turned into a classic rock song.

Joe is "affected profoundly" by what comes to be known as the Kent State Massacre. He decides life is too short and drops out.

He's already in a band: the James Gang, formed at Kent State with two other students.

They support Cream on tour; Joe gets to talk guitar with Eric Clapton. They get a manager, get a deal, put out an album called *Yer Album* that is produced by Bill Szymczyk, and overnight Joe becomes the breakout star of the James Gang.

Quickly becoming well known for his pyrotechnic riffs and the sharp, meaty attack of his playing, brought about in part by the way he hot-wires the pickups on his guitars, for most people Joe is the James of the Gang.

He sells one of his special hot-wired axes to Jimmy Page of Led Zeppelin, another band the James Gang ride with on tour.

The James Gang support the Who, and Pete Townshend, who doesn't get on well with his own band, gets on so well with Joe he invites the band to tour Europe with them.

The Gang release a second album, *James Gang Rides Again*, and score a sizeable radio hit with "Funk #49"—two verses about sleeping all day and partying all night and Joe blasting out his baby on his ferociously funky lead guitar.

A third album, imaginatively titled *Thirds*, follows in early '71, again with Bill in the producer's chair, and features another break-out radio hit in "Walk Away"—an even groovier funk-rock classic about a chick leaving.

Joe is well on his way now. A star in waiting. But he is also a restless, rangy kind of guy, sensitive to the volatility of the times in which he lives, alert to the vibes. Joe learns quickly that bands form, deform, crash like cars, turn into black holes from which you can't escape, fuck you up bad if you let 'em.

Joe plots his vamoose before the bad stuff really hits, and by the start of 1972 he's no longer leader of the Gang.

Former Small Faces main man Steve Marriott thinks enough of Joe to ask him to move to London and replace Peter Frampton in

Humble Pie, who have just hit the US Top 20 with their way-cool live double album, *Rockin' the Filmore*.

Joe always got on well with Townshend, Page, all those cats Marriott calls friends. But Joe turns Steve down, can't tell you why exactly, just not feeling it. Instead he moves to Colorado, to a farm-house at the foot of the snow-lidded Rocky Mountains, and forms his own outfit, Barnstorm. Only no one ever calls it that. This is Joe Walsh's band, dig? Only a rookie would think otherwise.

All the while there is Bill Szymczyk by Joe's side in the studio. At the same time he was helping make Joe's James Gang and Barnstorm albums, Bill was also in the studio making miracles with B.B. King, Edgar and Johnny Winter, J. Geils Band, and some other talented cats that history no longer recalls with any color.

Bill Szymczyk is a thirty-year-old studio god in the making, never on the clock, never off the case. Bill has almost no back-ground in music, he's all about the moment, the lightning in a bot-tle. The sound of the air in a room.

He'd come to the newfound art of sound sculpture when he was a sonar operator for the US Navy and attended audio production classes as part of his training.

Born in Muskegon, a modest river-port city in Michigan, Mom was a nurse, Dad was a factory worker. As a kid he assembled his own crystal radio from a store-bought kit and found himself glued to a Nashville station he couldn't believe at all. Blues and R & B, a little rockabilly, country blues, maybe. Some really good stuff, folks.

At seventeen he joined the navy, where he learned enough about "production" to snag himself a place at New York University's Media Arts School when he left the service in 1964.

For pin money he began working in various studios, quickly moving up from tape-op to producing demos for aspiring new art-ists. It was the mid-sixties; records were no longer being made in mono. It was no longer about just hitting the record button and letting the acts blow.

He learned about where to place the microphones, about using more than one track, about baffles and wedges and amps and how to coax a good performance out of guys that were sometimes so nervous they couldn't get their brains in gear.

Bill grasped early that it was a combo of technical knowhow and personal relationships and trust that produced the best results. Soon he found himself working inside the Brill Building for hit songwriting teams like Carole King and Jerry Goffin. He worked on sessions night and day, learning all the time, absorbing the sights as well as the sounds. He got to work at the right hand of Quincy Jones.

Bill dropped out of college and took a job as producer for ABC Records. His first gig: bringing blues legend B.B. King back from the commercial dead. Bill felt for sure he knew just what to do. ABC said, "Naw, we need a name."

Bill fought his corner. No dice. So he appealed directly to B.B. Showed his obvious love and empathy for the music and, even more, the man. But also kept it simple: Bill would lift B.B. King's career to a new level if he would let him produce.

Fifteen albums, only one of which ever made the *Billboard* Top 200 (*Lucille*—Number 192, in 1969). Four live albums, four chart stiffs.

Since then: crickets.

B.B. was open to offers. Any offers.

Bill persuaded him. The result: four of the finest, most successful albums B.B. King had ever made—all produced by Bill Szymczyk.

Still most people didn't know his name.

Then came the James Gang and Joe Walsh and Irving Azoff. Bill took it all in his stride, never any drama—certainly not from Bill— and always there ready with the goods at the end of it. Reliable, relatable, an easy hang but with an acute focus that always keeps things rolling along, even when they're not.

Irving saw to it that Joe and Bill made *The Smoker You Drink, the Player You Get* in their own time, at the Record Plant in LA. Now he books the Eagles into the Record Plant too. Irving feeding on the kinetic energy of the move.

It pulls the Eagles out of the ditch into which they have fallen and are now in danger of becoming trapped in. Elliot managed them but he never had a *vision* for them, Irving explains. That old one. They always fall for that one.

17.

Borderline

David Geffen has "the vision thing," Irving will concede, but it was now mostly a vision of himself as one of the most powerful men in Hollywood. Irving is the only one with the hand-built radio that tunes directly into Glenn and Don's high-frequency mental waveband. Irving is the only guy in the room who understands their deepest desires, their worst fears, their need to be something more than another easy-breezy country rock band. Their true-blood belief.

Their need to succeed.

And make money.

Lots of money.

The vision Irving is selling is also very much Glenn and Don's vision of the Eagles. It is not Bernie Leadon's vision. Bernie has a place up in Topanga Canyon where the breezes blow cool. He's in no hurry to get to the top. Bernie is already right where he wants to be, making good music and getting paid well for it. Really well.

He doesn't need a fucking Learjet. He's already on the couch, he's home and he's high. Bernie's a pot guy, not a coke guy. He's a girlfriend guy, not a groupie guy.

When Elliot checked out, Bernie says later, "I was like, 'shit, this changes everything.' I remember going to Elliot and saying, 'Dude, you're on top of the world. Why are you doing this?' And he said,

'Dude, when you've got enough, you've got enough.' He just wanted a quieter lifestyle."

Bernie digs that. He listens back to that message. But after Dillard & Clark, after the Flying Burritos, after Gram and all that, it ain't his first go-around at the rodeo, as the badass cowboys say on TV.

He's seen his friend Gram Parsons nearly blow up and only half burn out. No body, no ashes, just what's left of the carcass on top of the bonfire. Bernie Leadon looks at Glenn Frey and sees trouble coming around again. He knows how this song goes, and he is reluctant to play it again.

So is Randy Meisner, who leaves town every chance he gets to go home to Nebraska and be with his family. There's already a distance between Randy and Glenn. Glenn and Don's vision, Irving's vision, is not Randy Meisner's vision, either.

Bernie's old friend from his time at Gainesville High School, in Florida, Don Felder, becomes his new sounding board. Felder is twenty-six and has nothing whatsoever to do with country music, though he can play it because Don can play anything on guitar.

Never formally trained, Felder picked up a guitar after seeing Elvis Presley doing "Hound Dog" on *The Ed Sullivan Show* in 1956, swiveling his hips and swinging an acoustic around like a girl. When he was thirteen, he formed his first high school hop outfit, the Continentals, which also featured fifteen-year-old Stephen Stills on guitar. When Stills left for New York City, Bernie Leadon took his spot.

The same age, Don and Bernie became best buds, trading licks. But where Bernie had studiously learned music from the page, Don picked everything up by ear, playing along to tape recordings he made at half-speed so he could figure it out. He would get anyone he met who could play to show him what they got, until he could play it too. There was Bernie, and there was the music grad from

Berklee who started his own music school, who showed Bernie a little music theory and notation. Then there was Duane Allman, who walked into a music store Don was temporarily working at one day and showed him how to play slide.

Don Felder got so good at everything so fast he began giving lessons of his own, including, he later claimed, to an eager teenager named Tom Petty—something the late singer always denied but which Don swears is true. Although it might have been the piano.

After that Don Felder followed the familiar trail of short-lived, no-luck bands. The Continentals morphed into the Maundy Quintet, signed a deal with the Tampa-based indie label Paris Tower and throughout 1967 released a couple of records typical for the wear-some-flowers-in-your-hair times, the best of which, "2's Better Than 3," was written by Bernie and augmented by Don's colorful guitar licks and some superior Mamas & Papas energy four-part harmonies.

When that went south, Don hooked up some guys from another local outfit named the Incidentals and headed for New York, where they began working as a quartet called Flow. Don recalled: "Flow was, without any doubt, what my father would have called a hippy band. They specialized in free-form jazz-rock and were heavily into pot."

Hey, man, it was 1970, nobody wanted that glossy, flowerpot, puff-pop any more. They wanted to go deep now. Flow, with their improvisational flair and gift for longer, thought-bubble numbers like the seven-minute-plus "Here We Are Again," more than lived up to their name. Signed to the newly independent CTI Records, home to other hip, jazz-rock, black-white-same-diff acts like George Benson, Eumir Deodato, and Freddie Hubbard, their only album, *Flow*, was released into the ether in 1970—and promptly sank without a trace.

Tom Petty recalled seeing Flow play "at some hippy house party, and it blew my mind how good they were. No more covers. Everything was original. I talked to Don after, and he said, 'We're not going to get anywhere if we don't get record deals, and we are not going to get record deals playing other people's hits all the time.'"

For twenty-three-year-old Don Felder it was also another opportunity to pick up new skills as a guitarist, to experiment freely with different music, learning how to *fuse* musical space and time. None of which paid the rent. When Flow went down the plughole Don found himself a job working out of a recording studio in Boston. The pay was good, but times sure were slow. So Don saved up a few bucks then quit his job and headed for the West Coast, where Bernie had finally made a name for himself in his new band, Eagles.

Felder comes to town toward the end of '73, playing with another old Geffen-Roberts act, David Blue. He and Bernie have kept in touch down the years. Don jammed with the Eagles backstage in Boston during that godforsaken support slot with Yes, where he played so well that Glenn nicknamed him "Fingers."

"With every take he just blew us all away," Frey said. "If he isn't Duane Allman reincarnate, I don't know who the fuck is."

Bernie is there hanging out with Don when David Blue completes a run of dates supporting David Crosby and Graham Nash with some solo shows at the newly opened Roxy Theatre on Sunset Strip, co-owned by Geffen and Roberts, along with fellow music biz alumni Lou Adler, Elmer Valentine, and Peter Asher. David Blue may be a little too dirty-fingernailed to fit easily into the Hollyweird vibe of the Strip in 1973, but Don Felder shines in his new surrounds.

When Crosby and Nash's guitarist David Lindley falls ill, Don deputizes. He plays a studio session for Joni Mitchell. He moves his pregnant wife, Susan, to LA, finding a cheap place near Bernie in Topanga Canyon. Don's on the scene, official.

Now that they are neighbors, Bernie and Don share all their secrets. Talking about the other Eagles, Bernie confesses: "These guys never stop arguing. Glenn and Don. Talk about creative tension. They think they're the new Lennon and McCartney."

Don Felder listens, rapt.

"Nothing Randy or I write is good enough, and now Irving's in charge, he and Don seem to be very thick. I'm seriously beginning to wonder what I've got into . . ."

Don Felder listens and takes it all in. Usual band bitching, heard it a thousand times before, he tells Susan. When, one morning a month later, he picks up the phone and hears Glenn Frey's voice on the end of the line, he is caught off guard. Glenn asks Don to come out to the Record Plant. "We're looking for someone who can play some real dirty slide," he says.

"Sure," says Don, "I can do that."

The Record Plant is located at the junction of 3rd Street and La Cienega Boulevard in West LA, where it's been open for four years and has already assumed the reputation as being the only place to play while you play. The first recording studio to offer a spa, bedrooms and lounges, everyone from Black Sabbath (who ride the waves of cocaine flowing freely through the city to make the ultra-druggy *Vol. 4*), to the Bee Gees, Billy Joel, the Isley Brothers, and America have all recorded some pretty fucking cool records there.

Joe Walsh and Bill Szymczyk love it there, too, Irving tells Don and Glenn. And as soon as they walk in and smell the weed in reception, they know Irving is right. Everything smells and looks and feels different working with Bill at the Record Plant than it ever did working with Glyn Johns.

Hanging out between takes has never been such fun. There are pool tables and ping-pong to play, bedrooms to crash in (one of them S&M-themed), nooks and crannies to get stoned in, a Jacuzzi known as "the scum pond" that only the very brave or the totally wasted venture into.

Glenn's new place in Coldwater Canyon isn't too far away either, and there are all-night parties there, too: "Copious amounts of Acapulco Gold or lime-green Maui Wowee were smoked, and cocaine became the best way of pushing on through the night," Felder recalls. Then there are the girls. Bernie shook his head as he recalled, "These girls just come crawling out of the woodwork, and they'll do anything to please you . . ."

At Bill's suggestion, they retain two of the songs recorded in London with Glyn: Glenn, Don, and J.D.'s lush ballad, "Best of My Love," inspired by an old Fred Neil album Glenn had become enamored with, with lyrics by Don about his recent split from his girlfriend. And Don and J.D.'s "You Never Cry Like a Lover," Henley's honeysuckle-blues voice laced over Glenn's shiny, hard-ass blues guitar.

Bill may not have the same rep as Johns as a producer of giant hits, but he is comfortable enough in his own skin to admit those two songs work really well with Glyn's production. Working with Bill, it quickly becomes clear, is about more than just capturing the right sound. Glyn Johns's "no drugs" rule is also history, the band are in their home city, not stuck in some backwater of London where the pubs close at 11 p.m. and nothing's open on Sundays. Glenn and Don love their new studio abode. Really start to appreciate their new producer.

"Bill and Glyn are similar to each other in their own elements, but Szymczyk is a premier *American* rock 'n' roll producer/engineer," Glenn said, reflecting on the classic guitar sounds that he is starting to hear. "We just wanted to sound American instead of English," echoes Don.

Speaking to a journalist just two days after the separation from the Eagles was made official, Glyn for his part insists the problems were never his.

"The six weeks in the studio [in London] were a disaster area," he told David Rensin in *Crawdaddy*. But he insisted, "it had nothing at all to do with me." Glyn did not "believe in kid-gloving artists." But he even noted a new restlessness about the band: "They weren't comfortable physically or mentally in England. There were a lot of hang-ups, individually and with each other. But what it boils down to is they weren't ready to make another record."

Now they are. One of the first things they work on arrives in the post when Jack Tempchin, who'd written "Peaceful Easy Feeling," sends Glenn a tape of a new song he's co-authored alongside Robb Strandlund, called "Already Gone." It's exactly the sort of playing-to-the-balconies rock track Glenn and Don have been talking about, packed with the tight melodies and bright harmonies they excel in singing but with a much tougher, guitar-led edge.

When they start work on another tough-sounding Glenn and Don track, "Good Day in Hell" (one of two songs on the record that touch on the death of Gram Parsons), Bill wants a harder-edged guitarist than Glenn or Bernie to play some slide, and Bernie suggests Don Felder. Glenn picks up the phone . . .

Don Felder rocks up to the Record Plant the very next day carrying a newly repaired Les Paul, feeling happy and confident. He's starting to think that maybe he can get somewhere in this business. If he can fit in onstage with the recalcitrant David Crosby and good cop Graham Nash, if he can play sessions for the meticulously minded Joni Mitchell and stay upbeat while touring with the permanently hangdog David Blue, he can sure as shit handle the Eagles, who he knows from Bernie are at a crossroads.

He's relaxed and loose, as he later writes: "I was there primarily to play some music, take the money, and meet up with some old buddies."

He nails his chunky slide parts for "Good Day in Hell" inside six takes, each as good as the other. Encouraged, they ask if Felder can do something similar on Tempchin and Strandlund's "Already Gone." Don says you bet and happily goes toe to toe with Glenn, dueling guitars, all of the band gathering around and laughing as they play the session back in the control room.

Felder is taken by how self-consciously cool Frey is, wearing shades even in the windowless perma-gloom of the studio, chewing his cocaine-dried lips, and chain-smoking. Don Henley is quieter, like Randy, and Bernie just seems to weave musical magic every time he goes near an instrument.

Felder has a blast, packs away his Les Paul, shakes everyone by the hand, and heads home, unaware that his life has just changed.

As soon as he's gone, the band have a conference along with J.D. and Bill, right there in the studio. The next morning, Don Felder is having breakfast with his pregnant wife Susan when the phone goes. It's Glenn Frey once again. This time he asks Don Felder if he would like to join the Eagles.

Don holds the phone away from his ear so that Susan can listen too. He plays it as cool as he can.

"Sure," he tells Glenn, like no big thing.

"Great," Glenn says. "Well, come to the studio at two o'clock tomorrow so that we can start work on recording the rest of the album."

"No problem," says Don while Susan hops up and down trying not to scream.

Before the Eagles can officially become a five-piece, however, Felder has to go and tell Graham Nash that he's quitting. Word spreads fast in LA.

When Don meets Graham, Graham says, "I heard something from Elliot. What's come up?"

"The Eagles. They've asked me to join them, and I've agreed."

Graham Nash, who found his own future right here in LA, shakes Don Felder's hand.

"Smart move," he says.

SIDE TWO

Heavenly Bills

18.

Limp Handshakes and Tense Backslaps

When Don Felder arrives back at the Record Plant for the first time as a fully-fledged member of the Eagles, his new bandmates greet him one by one. As he hugs him, Bernie pulls Don close and whispers in his ear: "Don't say I didn't warn you . . ."

Felder asks if Susan can come and watch his first session. She sits in the control room, staring through the glass. Don Felder soon sees what Bernie means. "Not a day passed during the recording of that album when someone didn't blow his top, or stalk out, slamming the door behind him," Felder recalls in his memoir, *Heaven and Hell: My Life in the Eagles*. Glenn and Don were fighting tooth and claw "for control of the band and the musical direction it was taking." Bernie was also sticking his oar in: "Glenn wanted to speed things up and Bernie wanted to slow them down." Felder, meanwhile, steered clear of confrontations, but would go home at the end of every session, wondering "how long it would be before the fuse reached the keg." The answer was: not long.

While Susan gets freaked out and wonders whether it's too late for Don to rejoin Crosby and Nash, the guitarist sits in the corner tuning up or changing his strings or whatever, thinking, how long can this thing last? And yet, like Burton and Taylor, when the

Eagles are good together, they are really good—the soaring harmonies and synthesis of musicians that comes along maybe once in a generation.

The new vibe at the Record Plant makes a difference. They cut eight more songs to add to the two from the aborted Johns sessions, for the album they decide to title *On the Border*, after one of the best of the ten. One of only three Eagles songs Leadon would share a co-credit with Henley and Frey on, "On the Border" was very much next-gen Eagles in terms of its more contemporary feel, combining slashing guitar rock with hard-hat funk and blue-eyed soul vocals—along with some of Henley's darkest lyrics to date, a precursor to the more paranoid, blood-pooled directions he would take in the coming years.

Don explained the song had been inspired by the Watergate hearings then taking place in Washington—and the increasing belief that government had completely overstepped the mark when it came to people's privacy, from illegal phone-tapping to office-bugging, break-ins, mail interception, and all the other tricks of the spy trade President Nixon's government were now accused of routinely employing against anybody they perceived to be "the enemy."

At the very end of the track, if you listened closely, you could just about hear Glenn whispering, "Say goodnight, Dick." One of the catchphrases from the hip TV comedy show, *Rowan and Martin's Laugh-In*—repurposed here as a pissed-off kiss-off to Nixon, who would eventually be forced to resign within a few months of the album's release.

In retrospect, it's hard not to see "On the Border" as a breakthrough moment in the band's musical development—one that actually placed them at the front of the curve of white rock bands incorporating a modern black sound into their music, from the low-slung Bobby Womack guitars to the Temptations-style backing vocals.

By summer's end, the Average White Band—who took the new hybrid form to unparalleled lengths by omitting as much of the white rock influence as possible—would have an American Number 1 single and album with "Pick Up the Pieces" and *AWB*, respectively. Within a year everyone from the Rolling Stones and Elton John to Rod Stewart and David Bowie were overtly parading their funk soul brother credentials.

In 1974, black artists had never sounded so intentionally rock. At the same time that Stevie Wonder was having his fourth Number 1 hit with "You Haven't Done Nothin'," his politically charged funk-rock attack on Nixon, Motown producer Norman Whitfield was flying his freak power flag high, writing and producing two psychedelic rock 'n' soul classics for the Temptations in *Masterpiece* and *1990*.

That summer also saw the arrival into the charts of a new black-and-white band out of Chicago called Rufus, who hit Number 3 with the Stevie Wonder–penned, "Tell Me Something Good": rock-god guitar and a heavy-breathing funk groove fronted by a ballsy chick singer in hot pants and hippy beads named Chaka Khan.

For once, the Eagles aren't the last ones to the party, although Henley later dismisses "On the Border" as a "clumsy, incoherent attempt" to write "an R & B–type song" but which, for perfectionist Don anyway, completely missed the target.

Musically, the tectonic shifts in the band are there for all to see throughout the album. Glenn sings lead on the first two singles, "Already Gone" and its similarly pop-rocking near-twin, "James Dean"—the latter revived after being discarded for *Desperado*. Don sings the album's big ballad "Best of My Love." Randy sings lead on his own "Is It True?" and Nashville songwriter Paul Craft's "Midnight Flyer." Bernie sings the lush "My Man." Glenn and Don share lead vocals on "Good Day in Hell" and their country-syrup version of "Ol' '55," a charming ditty from new Asylum signing, Tom Waits.

Twenty-four-year-old Waits is a Skid Row, Charles Bukowksi–type figure who becomes the latest graduate of the Troubadour school of hard knocks to attract Geffen's attention. A million miles from the usual Lookout Mountain minstrel Asylum backed, Waits was more jazz and desperation than country and good times. David figures he'll be giving the kid a break by engineering a cover of one of his songs on the next Eagles album.

However, in what will soon become recognizable as his typically contrarian style, Waits lets it be known that he is appalled by the result. As far as he was concerned, the Eagles version of his tribute to a vintage automobile was "about as exciting as watching paint dry." Adding, with a sneer: "[The Eagles] don't have cowshit on their boots—just dogshit from Laurel Canyon."

When Glenn and Don heard what the upstart Waits had been saying they immediately dropped "Ol' '55" from their live set and refused to talk about it again.

The writing credits eventually split: one for Bernie, one for Randy, three cover versions, and the rest to Don and Glenn, along with J.D., who has three co-writes, and Jackson Browne, who has one. The new dynamic is clear. Randy and Bernie are being pushed even farther to the sidelines. The arrival of Don Felder—Glenn's new favorite—further impacts Bernie's role.

Bernie sees this and shrugs. He's beginning to take a step back anyway, viewing everything that's going on with an increasingly jaundiced eye. He's pretty much done with the groupies and the drugs. Fuck that shit—just look at what happened to Gram. Look at David Crosby and James Taylor—both now hopelessly hooked on H. Look at all the other bombed-out casualties with the thousand-yard stares now littering Sunset Boulevard. How long before the next one joins Janis, Jimi, and Jim Morrison in an early rock 'n' roll grave?

Instead, Bernie's latching on to the new SoCal trend for health foods and exercise, fresh air, and daylight. The others don't get it, especially Glenn and Don, who now live mostly by night. One band insider reveals, "It was almost as if [Bernie] was held in suspicion for not doing drugs. You have to wonder what kind of mindset that was, but I'll tell you this: Glenn and Don took it as a personal indictment of their lifestyles . . ."

But when *On the Border* comes out on March 22, 1974, it rips it up, going gold after a month or so, reaching Number 17 on the *Billboard* Hot 100, powered by the Eagles' first Top 40 single for two years with "Already Gone." When the follow-up, "James Dean," comes out later that summer it doesn't match the high chart placing of its predecessor, but it does get blasted out on radio seemingly day and night.

As a result, all of the commercial ground lost because of *Desperado* is quickly regained, even though Glenn is still sitting on the bomb and refusing to release "Best of My Love" as a single, wondering if it might have everyone thinking the Eagles are a sappy country ballads band after all. Plus, it was one of the two Glyn Johns–produced tracks on the record, and you know what, fuck that guy.

That aside, Glenn is flying high when he tells the music press all about the rejigged, refueled Eagles, comparing Bernie to the influential bluegrass and country rock guitarist Clarence White, who died in 1973 after being run over by a drunk driver, and claiming Don Felder was a spectacular player in the mold of Duane Allman, the young Allman Brothers guitarist who'd died in 1971 after a motorcycle crash.

Glenn tells *Crawdaddy* that "Don Henley is like a rock, besides the fact that he's the best singer I've ever worked with. Randy is the perfect ribbon for the package." Leaving Henley to return the compliment in the same article. "Glenn adds the grease," Henley chimes in. "He's all action and he moves around more than any of us trying to get people off. Maybe that's why he's called the Teen King." The what?

When he reads this, Bernie looks at Randy and asks: "When did Frey start calling himself the Teen King?"

Randy shrugs. They've heard it all now.

Irving now goes everywhere on the road with the Eagles, working every angle he can come up with, the phone permanently glued to the side of his head. The success of the records and tour drag both *Eagles* and *Desperado* past 500,000 sales as new fans discover the back catalog. It's the virtuous circle of tour–album–tour, but you have to be hard, you have to be tough to survive this life. It's not for everyone. Bernie Leadon and Don Felder both have nice homes to go to. Randy Meisner too.

Irving, Don, and Glenn, however, thrive on the road. Feed off the adrenaline and put it all back in the tank so they can keep going and going. As the serious money finally begins rolling in, they start flying private rather than luxury-tour bussing. The women and the drugs come too, only there is now more of everything.

Irving calls a band meeting.

"His Shortness has summoned us," says Bernie, deadpan.

The five Eagles troop into Irving's hotel suite. Irving tells them they are now joint and equal owners of a corporation called Eagles Limited and that all non-publishing band income will be received by the new company before being split five ways. Bernie gets straight to the point. Reminding everyone that when he joined everything was a four-way split, and now Don Felder is taking a slice, and "didn't put in the hard time like the rest of us."

Felder feels a bit sideways about the fact it's his old friend who brings this up, but the point is fair, he can see that. Glenn says that they've all been sidemen before and there will be no sidemen in this band. Irving pitches a solution. He will give Don Felder a fifth of the revenue from the two tracks he has played on, on the album, and from then onward a fifth of everything else.

It's finally agreed on with limp handshakes and tense backslaps. The company needs a president and a secretary, so Glenn is appointed president and Don Henley is appointed secretary. They sign the papers that bring the new company into life. Felder soon has enough money to buy a house. Glenn and Don soon have enough to buy anything they damn well please.

They tour through the summer of 1974, headlining mostly, but also appearing second on the bill at various festivals, or sandwiched between the Beach Boys and Kansas, or the Doobie Brothers and the Ozark Mountain Daredevils. It beats the hell out of touring with Yes and Jethro Tull, but it's still just a little too fields-and-streams for Glenn's taste.

America in 1974, however, is not the place to complain too much about the view. Darkness keeps poking through the sunshine. Flying in a helicopter to the Ontario Speedway on an unseasonably hot April afternoon to earn $12,500 as a down-the-bill act at the California Jam, lit up by the news that things are finally getting too hot to handle for Tricky Dicky, Glenn and Don take their crooked president's impending downfall as another sign they were right all along. As if they personally—and their fellow post-Woodstock, don't-believe-the-hype hippies—have made this happen; willed Nixon's sorry fate into being. That's what it feels like anyway, man.

The California Jam '74 was the greatest stand-alone rock festival of the year. The best sound system, the best facilities, the best security, the best vibe. And they paid better too. Word of mouth anoints it "the Woodstock of the West," and nearly 300,000 flock to the Jam to see Emerson, Lake & Palmer, Deep Purple, and Black

Sabbath, plus five lesser-known bands. The Eagles come in sixth on a bill of eight. It's still nice and sunny out there when they hit the stage.

Just for this show they are back to being the original four-piece. Don Felder was there for the TV recording of their appearance on the Don Kirshner *Rock Concert* show, which aired in April. But he and Susan's first baby was about to be born and Don needed to be home, so the Jam was just the four originals.

It's a neat show. They look and sound really confident, they look and sound young and cool. Take a look for yourself, online.

At the end of their set, Deep Purple smash their instruments and set off explosions through the 50,000-watt sound system. It sounds like the end of the earth. Meantime, the presidency of Richard Nixon is rumbling volcanically to its twisted climax. Looked at the right way, it's like everything fits, man.

Sitting in his trailer, Glenn Frey can't take his eyes off the endless parade of beautiful young women gliding through the backstage area. Every time Glenn sees a girl he likes, he shouts: "I want one!"

Jackson Browne tries to make him cool it, but Glenn is on a roll. The journalist Barbara Charone, there to report on California cool for London's hip *Sounds* magazine, writes of him: "Glenn Frey sat in the Eagles trailer radiating a cocky confidence that perfectly complemented his punky rock star personality . . ."

When Charone asks Frey about his look, his mood, his band, his life right at that moment, he tells her: "You have to exaggerate what you do without prostituting how you feel about yourself. I'm trying to eliminate schizophrenia from my life. I wanna relate to myself as a rock 'n' roll star, a struggling songwriter, and a regular guy all in one frame of reference."

By late July, around the time the Eagles go onstage at the Boston Garden, where 15,000 recently reminded and/or recently converted fans are waiting to "Take It Easy," the Judiciary Committee of the

House of Representatives recommend three articles of impeachment against President Richard Milhous Nixon: Obstruction of Justice, Abuse of Power, and Contempt of Congress.

On August 5 the White House releases the "Smoking Gun" tape recording that finally drives the stake through Nixon's cold heart. He resigns a few nights later. On September 15, twenty-year-old Patty Hearst, kidnapped by left-wing extremist movement the Symbionese Liberation Army, before joining the gang as a full-time machine-gun carrying member, is arrested in San Francisco. She lists her occupation as "urban guerrilla." The Eagles only have one more show until New Year's Eve. It feels like providence. Especially with an ounce of blow at your elbow.

As Barbara Charone reported in *Sounds*, the tour finally ended at yet another Ramada Inn, where Bernie Leadon "collapsed on the Formica tabletop at breakfast the morning after the very last show."

Glenn and Don spend the rest of 1974 snorting coke, smoking weed, drinking breakfast beer, and drowning their sunsets in tequila while making sweet love to one very special lady after another—or not, depending on the mood and what the signs only they can see tell them. Mainly, whenever they aren't doing whatever the fuck they want, they dwell on what felt to both men like the rapidly darkening side of American life, even now Nixon's gone, even with the big bucks. On or off the snow.

Nineteen seventy-four going into 1975 is a time of growing cynicism in America. The sight on the TV news each night of miles-long lines of cars queuing at gas stations around the country, due to the oil crisis, had been almost as shocking as the earlier pictures of hundreds of body bags of dead American soldiers returning from Vietnam. As for the war itself, with Gerald Ford there to pardon Nixon and hold the fort until the next election in '76, Vietnam is rapidly folding in on itself. The war is lost. It's just about what happens now.

The biggest movie of '74 was freaky William Friedkin's *The Exorcist*, about the demonic possession of an innocent child. Like your worst acid trip, replete with flashbacks that will last for years. The hippest movie of '74 was rocking Roman Polanski's *Chinatown*, which traced the maniacal roots of real-life LA noir, with double-cross and unbridled paranoia the defining motif.

The biggest date-movie of the year was *The Great Gatsby*, a Southern Gothic rom-dram highlighting the rottenness at the heart of the Beautiful People that exemplified America's Jazz Age, offering sage future-echoes of America's Rock Age.

Even American TV had become more knowing, more below-ground. Comedies like *M*A*S*H*, which brought a wry Woodstock filter to the Korean War, and the *Mary Tyler Moore Show*—thirty-something, single white feminist with comic edge takes on world—were ostensibly upbeat, but beneath the joking there was an easily detectable heart of darkness, a reappraisal of societal norms. Same with *The Rockford Files*—wrongly convicted ex-con turns trailer-home PI—and other "rumpled" seen-too-much detectives like *Barney Miller* and *Harry O*.

When *Godfather II* opened to thunderous acclaim in New York that Christmas, it felt zeitgeisty. The American family's moral defeat at the hands of its own blood-fate. Whatever idealistic tics still lingered from the sixties counterculture blancmange now firmly dispelled as America confronted its first national psychic nightmare. Everything was connected. The fix was in. No one here gets out alive.

New Year's Day 1975 in Los Angeles. Looking ahead and feeling gooood.

You just had to know how to make it work for you. Had to know how to roll on down the highway. This was a time when *Rolling Stone* (sex and drugs and Hunter S. Thompson) ran ads for roach clips and coke spoon necklaces. When the *National Lampoon* (with cover pic of a topless Minnie Mouse wearing flower pasties) was selling over a million copies a month.

Dylan was back, baby—and signed to Asylum! Touring with the Band for the first time in years and getting a standing ovation each night for that line in "It's Alright, Ma (I'm Only Bleeding)" about "even the president of the United States must sometimes have to stand naked."

It was the end of innocence—and Don and Glenn badly wanted the Eagles to reflect that. With the cringey musical cosplay of *Desperado* now off in the cool distance, Glenn and Don are tired of what they see as greasy kids' stuff. They want to go deeper. Darker. Everyone did. David Bowie was also now living in LA, drawing pentagrams and holding occult rituals. "Rock has always been the devil's music," a fully coked-and-loaded Bowie bragged to Cameron Crowe in *Rolling Stone*. "You can't convince me that it isn't."

After the Manson nightmare everyone in LA carried a gun in the car. And at home. Behind the front door. By the bed. Throw a few bowls of sparkly pharmaceutical cocaine on top of those after-midnight, before-dawn thoughts and you've got yourself a musical death trip.

Glenn and Don sit there inhaling all this, soaking up the rays. Then begin to write. Henley later recalled this period without irony as his and Glenn's "satanic country rock period."

As Eagles, they entered 1975 on a triumphant note with a sold-out, bring-all-your-friends show to 6,000 people at the Shrine Auditorium in LA, supported by Irving's boy, Dan Fogelberg, and J.D.'s girl, Linda Ronstadt, whose *Heart Like a Wheel* album has just come out and already overtaken *On the Border* in the charts.

Then, just as sales seem to have plateaued, "Best of My Love" finally comes out as a single and the Eagles have their first Number 1 hit. Not that Glenn and Don are entirely thrilled. Glenn, in particular, has never wanted it released as a single. It's only after the track began to be rotated at a Michigan-based radio station, WKMI-AM in Kalamazoo, that Geffen gave the go-ahead for Asylum to issue a limited edition of 1,000 copies of the track as a 7-inch single specifically for the Kalamazoo area.

When demand in local stores outstripped supply, Asylum did as they always knew they should and went ahead and gave "Best of My Love" a full nationwide release. First though, they edited out a minute and nine seconds to bring the single version down to a radio-friendly three minutes twenty-five seconds.

With the record now flying up the charts you can't say Asylum really got it wrong, but Frey is furious at them for unilaterally editing the track without his or the band's permission. Henley, who is secretly ecstatic that a song with his honeysuckle lead vocal on it has gone to Number 1, makes a big show in front of Glenn of telling Irving the single should be pulled from the racks and destroyed.

Irving played along, tut-tutting and banging phones, but privately couldn't stop rubbing his hands with glee—Number 1, baby, with a bullet! Later, after the single had sold a million, Irving sent over a Gold record to Asylum with a corner piece missing, mounted on a plaque with the inscription: The Golden Hacksaw Award.

It takes three months for "Best of My Love" to eventually climb to the top of the *Billboard* Hot 100, getting there at last in the week of March 1, 1975. Tellingly, it also tops the American Easy Listening chart. It's a sign of the times—the seedlings of Dad Rock—where the acts that have preceded the Eagles at Number 1 since the year began are Elton John, Barry Manilow, the Carpenters, Neil Sedaka—and Linda Ronstadt, who beats her friends to the top of the singles chart by a couple of weeks with "You're No Good."

Soon to come in 1975, fresh easy-listening-with-edge hits from Fleetwood Mac, Peter Frampton, the Doobie Brothers, America,

Wings—and, in August, a second Number 1 record for the Eagles. The era of soft rock is upon us. Or adult-oriented rock, to give it its newly minted American radio name.

When Glyn Johns hears the news, he is delighted. "I must say it put a large grin on my face when 'Best of My Love' hit," he tells anyone who asks. "That was the record that really put them on the map, after they had turned themselves into what they thought was a rock 'n' roll band." Then he adds, unable to resist one last jibe: "A pretty lame one, in my view."

19.

The Million-Dollar View

I n 1949, the actress Nancy Davis signs a seven-year contract with Metro-Goldwyn-Mayer. She has dated Clark Gable and Peter Lawford but on November 15, 1949, she meets Ronald Reagan, when, in his capacity as president of the Screen Actors Guild, he helps Nancy get her name removed from the Hollywood Blacklist. She has been confused by the House Un-American Activities Committee with another actress with a similar name and been written off as some kind of commie sympathizer.

Ronald Reagan plays lead roles in action movies and romantic comedies and acts off-screen as an FBI informant on suspected Communist sympathizers in the film business. He has just divorced Jane Wyman, and he and Nancy fall for one another right away: "I don't know if it was love at first sight," Nancy confides, "but it was pretty close."

In 1952, they marry, and their daughter, Patricia Ann Reagan, is born later that year. Patti—as everyone knows her—is fourteen years old when, in January 1967, her father is sworn in as the Republican governor of California, and Nancy becomes first lady of California.

By 1974, now using her mother's maiden name, Patti Davis is trying to forge a career as an actor and writer. Unlike her parents, Patti is politically liberal and vocally anti-Republican, a stance *that will cause a rift with her parents that widens further when she begins dating Bernie Leadon, who is five years older than Patti, and a hairy-faced, dope-smoking, hippy musician in some rock band Ron and Nancy have never heard of.*

When Patti moves in with Bernie, Nancy throws a shit fit. The very idea that the Reagans' daughter would live as an unmarried couple with some banjo player is simply beyond the pale and Nancy publicly "disowns" her wayward daughter.

Patti's arrival into the Eagles' story also has the other, more considerable side effect of the band disowning Bernie.

IN NOVEMBER 1974 the Eagles head back to the Record Plant. Somehow, despite all the unease, a record begins to emerge, a special record, one that has none of the creative drag of *Desperado* or the confused outside influences and cover versions of *On the Border*. They are about to take what Glenn calls, "A quantum leap."

To make writing together easier, Don and Glenn rent a place together, a big far-out spread on the exclusive Trousdale Estates on Briarcrest Lane, Beverly Hills, where neighbors include Frank Sinatra, Elvis Presley, and Howard Hughes, and an average house costs over $3 million (around $20 million today). This is no average house, though, with its spectacular night-time view of the Santa Monica Mountains that Glenn and Don proudly dub: "the Million-Dollar View."

"It was built in 1942 by the actress Dorothy Lamour," Henley proudly tells Cameron Crowe. "Glenn and I lived at opposite ends of the house, and we actually converted a music room to a full-on recording studio." Don further explains that the house is located at the highest point of the hill, rewarding viewers with "a 360-degree panorama." He waxed lyrical about peering out in the daytime over snow-topped mountain ranges. Then, at night, absorbing the neon ooze of the pulsing LA cityscape below. Don and Glenn gave the place its own name: the House with the Million-Dollar View. To everyone who worked for them, from Irving to the chick who made coffee, it was known simply as the Eagles' Nest. "We had some great times up there," chuckled Don. Yeah, baby.

The bare bones of the new, more "satanic," Eagles songs emerge quickly enough but takes weeks and months to flesh out, the pair spending days sometimes wrangling over a single line in a song, agonizing over the right word.

New numbers with titles like "Lyin' Eyes" and "After the Thrill Is Gone" quickly bubble to the surface. Plus one titled "When a Bad Boy Meets a Bad Girl in the Night," a number Glenn actually co-wrote with Joni Mitchell during the brief period on Lookout Mountain when they were together. According to Cameron Crowe, "It's classic Eagles kind of harmonies and it's really the crossroads between Glenn Frey and Joni Mitchell." It ends up on the "maybe" pile.

Glenn and Don aren't interested in what used to be. They are taking this new aesthetic, these things they see and feel all around them, and with strange alchemy, turning them into gold, hopefully platinum.

"We wanted to capture the spirit of the times," explained Glenn. "So, perched up there on top of that hill, almost all night, every night, we had a big, phantasmagorical scene which included song-writing and, uh—research. Lots of research."

You holding?

Speaking forty years later to David Browne for a *Rolling Stone* piece doing a deep-dive on the Eagles' back catalog, Don painted a fairly prim picture of his and Glenn's writing routine at the House with the Million-Dollar View. "We needed quiet, private space, usually a room with a coffee table, a couple of acoustic guitars, and a piano," said Don. "Maybe some beer or maybe just soft drinks or water."

Hmm. *Maybe some beer? Soft drinks and water?* Maybe.

Don enlarged on his *Waltons*-esque depiction of he and Glenn chewing pencils, strumming lonely guitars and slurping sodas together. "Lots of legal pads and pens. We both contributed music and lyrics. Sometimes Glenn would lead the way; other times I would." Trailblazing stuff. It was a process that required "time, thought, perseverance, elbow grease; revisions, rewrites."

And a seemingly endless supply of co-co-co-cocaine.

Charlie. Blow. Flake. Snow. Toot. Dancing with the ice queen.

The good shit. Quality uncut from Bolivia, Colombia, Mexico. Top-shelf pharmaceutical, bought straight from the lab shelves. Wherever whenever whatever.

This was the period when people would proudly show-off their little gold spoons on a chain around their neck.

Wanna bump?

One night in Dan Tana's on Santa Monica Boulevard, the two men are eating a steak dinner together while eyeing up a corpulent, rich executive and his dinner date at the next table—a woman young enough to be his daughter—and Glenn turns to Don and observes, "She just can't hide her lyin' eyes." A line they sketch into verses on the back of a menu then turn into a new song when they return later that night to the Eagles' Nest.

"'Lyin' Eyes'—the story had always been there," Glenn reflected. "I don't want to say it wrote itself, but once we started working on it, there were no sticking points. Lyrics just kept coming out, and that's not always the way songs get written. I think songwriting is a lot like pushing a boulder up a hill. I'd love to get the legal pad for 'Lyin' Eyes' again, because I think there were verses we didn't use."

Inspiration just kept hitting. As Don described, "We'd started to explore our love of rhythm & blues and the Gamble & Huff records that came out of Philadelphia. We were also huge fans of Al Green." Something made glacially clear by the easy-grace funk groove and sweet little guitar lick that became the intro to one of the greatest Eagles songs of all time, "One of These Nights."

"Glenn, I think he sat down with a guitar and started playing that rhythm part," said Don. "I just went over to the piano, and I started playing this little minor descending progression, and he comes over and goes, "One of these nights . . .""

Goddamn, but Glenn had struck gold again.

He explained: "We've all said, 'One of these nights I'm gonna do something—get that girl, make that money, find that house.' We all have our dreams—a vision we hope will come true someday. When that 'someday' will come is up to each of us."

"All our records have the same theme," said Don, "and that is *the search*. It doesn't matter if it's romance, money, or security; it's the act of looking for it. Your whole life is one long journey, getting there is more important than the journey's end."

They also start working together on a song that Randy had begun to write one night after the Troubadour but that he was struggling to finish. "I'd get a verse or two done," he remembered, "and they would help fill in the blanks."

Randy had the payoff line: "Take it to the limit," but the rest was still a blank. It was a song, he said, about how important it was "to keep trying before you reach a point in your life where you feel you've done everything and seen everything, sort of feeling, you know, part of getting old. And just to take it to the limit one more time, like every day just keep, you know, punching away at it." He continued, "That was the line, and from there the song took a different course."

That is certainly one way of putting it. The course "Take It to the Limit" takes is set solely by Don and Glenn, because this is the course the Eagles are going to take, and "the limit" will become an apt metaphor for everything from their new, more grandiose sense of musical artistry to their new, million-dollar-view lifestyle.

Glenn speaks of the "dramatic improvement" in his and Don's writing together. He calls it "fluid and painless," the only pain coming through the lyrics that increasingly explore the haunted psychic state of living and loving in Southern California in the mid-seventies, the wildness and uncertainty extending from limitless sex, drugs, and rock 'n' roll, to the depthless, paranoid heart of the government.

Glenn and Don may hate Richard Nixon and all he stands for, but like him, they do what the fuck they want, when they want, how they want. They take it to the limit. A prophetic metaphor for the way the me-generation would forge a more drastically conservative direction in the eighties, sneering at the very mention of such antiquated ideas as peace and love.

Henley will later reflect on how he and Glenn as songwriting partners "were really beginning to come into our own." The decision had already been made between them. Whatever difficulties they might encounter from the other three members of the Eagles, "Glenn and I now wanted to take advantage of the momentum we had going; we wanted to write more songs that would be played on the radio . . ."

Into this elephant trap blunders Bernie Leadon, hand in hand with his new right-on girlfriend, twenty-one-year-old Patti Davis. Patti is one of those California-dreaming girls that guys who join bands fantasize will one day come tumbling eagerly into their arms after they've made it and all the other girls want them too. Patti is brown smiling eyes, long dark shiny hair, lush carmine lips, heart full of hope.

But Patti hasn't just blown into town from Winslow, Arizona. Patti also happens to be the daughter of the current Republican governor of California, Ronald Reagan. She is the rebel of the family. As a teenager, she recalled, "I was wearing white lipstick and black around my eyes and I'd put my hair down over one eye and tightened all my skirts. They were so tight I couldn't walk. I thought I looked great."

In 1974, she had ceased being Patricia Ann Reagan and become Patti Davis. "I wanted my own name, something of my own." Dropping out of college, living with a rock musician, smoking marijuana, speaking out in favor of those issues her father was implacably opposed to—the Equal Rights Amendment, abortion, nuclear disarmament—Patti is nothing if not her own person.

On the surface, Bernie and Patti make something of an odd couple, but it's good while it lasts. It certainly feels real. An almost unheard-of commodity on the road. But the relationship pulls Bernie a little further away from the band—a direction he was already moving in, even if he wasn't quite ready to acknowledge it.

One morning he hears Patti messing around with a tune she has written. He helps her to finish it, coming up with the second verse and making the arrangement. They call it "I Wish You Peace." It's a simple, pretty song with a universal sentiment ("I wish you peace / When the cold winds blow" . . . yadda yadda) and Bernie takes it to the band. He isn't writing too much of his own stuff, and, hell, he really likes "I Wish You Peace." It's a cool song and it doesn't sound too much like anything else the others are writing.

He takes it in and plays it for the guys—and they hate it. How will a song called "I Wish You Peace" fit into their new "satanic country rock" record?

Bernie is nonplussed. Don and Glenn don't want it? But it's a beautiful song. What will he tell Patti? Later, Henley will dismiss the song entirely as, "smarmy cocktail music." He added: "Nobody else wanted it. We didn't feel it was up to the band's standards . . ."

When Glenn and Don insist it isn't for the album, and can't even be polite about it, Bernie decides to draw a line and decides he isn't going to take anymore shit from these fucking guys.

The Eagles ain't just their concern, Bernie complains to Patti. It ain't just about their songs, he insists. "I basically let it be known that if they didn't record that song, that I was gonna break [Glenn's] arm, or something like that," Bernie will later let rip. "It's absurd, right? The song is 'I Wish You Peace,' but I'm gonna break your fucking arm if you don't record it . . ."

Yet that's how it is as the Eagles prepare to enter the numinous darkness of their mid-seventies "satanic country rock" period, an era that they will come to define and that will come to define them. They enter it with violence and rancor. With division and argument. With dreams and visions and a haunted Californian grandeur that borders on the gothic.

In the end they do record "I Wish You Peace"—just to shut Bernie up. But stick it on as the last track on side two. A place they hope no one ever gets to. They needn't have worried. No one does, lifting the needle off the record so they don't have to swallow its sugar more than once. But Patti gets her co-writing credit, and all is well at her and Bernie's unmarried home—for now.

They get to thinking about what comes after. Glenn loves the old B.B. King song, "The Thrill Is Gone." It gives Don an idea. "It was a straightforward statement," said Don. "But we wanted to explore the aftermath. We know that the thrill is gone—so, now what?" It becomes a metaphor for what the core of the Eagles—their music, their perspective, their place in post-sixties American music—is actually all about.

The seventies are what has happened now the thrill of the sixties has gone. And Don is right, it's about the aftermath. America no longer feels like a young country reaching for the stars. Post-Vietnam, post-Nixon, post-two Kennedys, Dr. King, Jimi Hendrix, and

Charles Manson, America is now a hawk-faced old dowager with lyin' eyes.

For Beverly Hills-born, longtime scenester and future Doors biographer Danny Sugerman, LA circa '74 "conjured up images of decaying mansions . . . an uncleaned pool, palm fronds afloat . . . sunlight was out, nightlife was in."

"After the Thrill Is Gone" was about exactly that. "That record is a lot of self-examination, hopefully not too much," said Glenn. "There was a lot of double-meaning and a lot of irony."

He quoted Don's lyric: "'Any kind of love without passion— well, that ain't no kind of lovin' at all . . .'" He smiled. "Pure Henley."

But also pure Frey. Glenn writes most of the verses "with a little help" from Don. They are the only people left they can talk to who have any idea what they're going through. "As exciting as the whole Eagles thing was at times, some of the luster was beginning to wear off," Don admitted. "We were combining our personal and professional lives in song."

Ah, the luster. Everyone thinks it's a breeze being in one of the best new bands in America, finding yourself at the forefront of something big and important. But Glenn and Don don't think that way. The fact that they have assumed leadership of the Eagles is no longer questioned by the rest of the band. There are lingering resentments, not least from Bernie Leadon, but the war over who's boss is now officially over.

Glenn Frey and Don Henley simply want it the most, and they are prepared to get down in the trenches where the real graft is done to get it. They don't half-finish songs. They don't write with their girlfriends. They don't detach from the process. They engage with the muse, which is a hard thing to do. And when the muse doesn't show up, they go looking for it. Night after night. Day in, day out. Music *and* business. You holding?

Everyone else thinks it's a breeze, the tunes appearing out of the ether up in the music room of your beautiful house on Zillionaire's Row in Beverly Hills. But songwriting is like any other artistic discipline—99 percent perspiration, hard work, grinding it out, learning the craft as well as fine-tuning the raw talent.

Even the fastest, natural-born runners need to train—to get the best from themselves, scoop out the guts and use it. This is what Frey and Henley have been doing, running hard for five years. And now the training is paying off, the apprenticeship is complete. They are running their own show.

At last, just like Jackson Browne had shown them in that dive of a place in Echo Park, they have learned how to work it. These songs they have been writing holed up at the Eagles' Nest are the fullest expression yet of their talent, the songs that will take them to places very few people ever get to go.

First, though, they have to record them.

From Don Felder's memoir *Heaven and Hell: My Life in the Eagles*:

"I wasn't looking forward to a return to the pressure cooker atmosphere of the studio, especially with the added burden of bettering the last Gold-selling product." He explains: "Bernie meanwhile had become increasingly dissatisfied with how [Glenn and Don] treated him and Randy. He didn't like them taking rough mixes back to their house to decide which tracks would stay or go, nor did he and Randy like Glenn's ability to 'change a word and gain a third'—coming to a song that was in their minds substantially done, lyrics and music, making what to them seemed modest contributions and suddenly becoming entitled to a third of the songwriting royalties."

From Marc Eliot's book, *Take It to the Limit*:

"Henley claimed all the pressure from the record company was affecting his creative process. Long days in the studio dissolved into weeks, with, for the most part, nothing to show for them. Every so often, Henley and Frey would simply throw their hands up, escape to Aspen, and cool out for a while before returning to the discipline of the recording studio."

From "Eagles: The Earthpeople's Band," a feature by Steven Rosen in *Sounds* magazine, in 1975:

"The creative process does tend to work in groups, though. Usually, a single lyric line or chord change is enough to spark the magic which begins in groups of two and three members. Don Henley and Glenn Frey usually concentrate on the lyric end while Bernie Leadon and [Don] Felder handle musical responsibilities. While the actual composing takes place in small gatherings, the recordings are done as live as possible with all five members playing simultaneously."

Contributing to the album liner notes for *The Very Best of the Eagles* by Cameron Crowe, Glenn Frey said:

"There's no doubt in my mind that *One of These Nights* was the most fluid and 'painless' album we ever made. A lot of things came together on *One of These Nights*—our love of the studio, the dramatic improvement in Don's and my songwriting. We made a quantum leap with [the title song] 'One of These Nights.' It was a breakthrough song. It is my favorite Eagles record. If I ever had to pick one, it wouldn't be 'Hotel California'; it wouldn't be 'Take It Easy.' For me, it would be 'One of These Nights.'"

Where does the truth live? Not merely in *facts*, anyone can google those. But the deeper, underlying truth(s). The sizzle, the shtick, the inside line that tells you what was really going on while the magic was being made.

For that, you must lean back into the times.

20.

The Dark and the Light

It's about the visions that come in the day and stay throughout the night.

It's about the aesthetics of being in a big commercial band. About what that band sounds like, what it looks like, what it creates in the feverish imaginations of its most ardent followers.

It's about the visions it gives them, the trip it takes them on. They can smell it, see the blood flower into bloom as the delicious fix goes in.

The Eagles are now ready to take you on that trip. Tell you the real story they've been reaching toward but only just now finally arrived at.

It starts right here, in 1975, with the arrival of anti-rock disco music; with the attempted assassination of President Gerald Ford by Manson Family hit-chick Squeaky Fromme; with Bernie's old lady's dad, Ronald Reagan, announcing a run for president; with the Thrilla in Manila, the brutal third clash between Muhammad Ali and Joe Frazier, which leaves both men so badly beaten neither will ever recover.

With the arrival on NBC of *Saturday Night Live*. With movies so perfectly attuned to the zeitgeist they could be titles of Eagles songs: *The Day of the Locust, Dog Day Afternoon, Nashville, Shampoo, Chinatown*.

With all the mad energy and dark matter that in the mid-seventies sucks everyone down like quicksand to a new subterranean level of disbelief.

Don and Glenn know how this should sound, how this should feel. What their own place in all this should be. They take the trip and start to lay it all down in the studio with Bill Szymczyk.

They use Don Felder and his hard-edge guitars. They use the divine voice of Don Henley. They use the high harmonies of Randy Meisner. They go to Miami's Criteria studios, stop-start, then shag it back to the Record Plant in LA, keep plugging until the mood leaves again. Slowly, slowly, over three months and a few hundred thousand dollars, they hear and see and feel their vision emerge into a record that finally, conclusively, at the fourth time of trying, actually captures the sounds Glenn and Don have heard in their heads for so long, that matches the visions they had in the house overlooking the mountain on Briarcrest Lane, the vision that has united Glenn and Don and had them take over the Eagles until they *are* the Eagles and the Eagles are them: Don and Glenn. Glenn and Don. The Eagles, no matter what the contracts say. The others can piss and moan all they want about the record. These are the songs that will change their lives.

Bernie is fading fast now anyway. His vision of an all-men-are-equal, hippy-happy country band full of dedicated minstrels unconcerned with money has never been what Glenn and Don thought of as the Eagles, certainly not now. Bernie knows it. He feels it as much as anyone. Has benefited as much as anyone, with a large swatch of his songs across all their albums now earning him mega bucks.

But Bernie has fallen hard for Patti Davis. Under threat of having their arms broken, the Eagles record "I Wish You Peace," plus a six-minute instrumental, a piece of bluegrass psychedelia Bernie has written entitled "Journey of the Sorcerer." Again, neither Glenn nor Don sees the point; there aren't even lyrics to give it meaning and meaning on this album is what everything is about.

Nevertheless, it's a haunting piece, the banjos lifted into cinematic infinity by the addition of orchestra and occasional mad-fiddler parts, and the title fits right in with the darker theme of the album.

And there is a song written by Bernie's brother Tom, "Hollywood Waltz," on which Bernie, Don, and Glenn also get co-writing credits. It doesn't stop the track sounding like a low-tide stroll about someone's baby. But when you scan the lyrics, you see what Don and Glenn were up to when they came up with the verses. This waltz is for Hollywood, where you: "Learn how to love her with all of her faults."

Bernie brings Patti to the studio for the recording of "I Wish You Peace," which gets Don's back up. Bernie also insists on Patti's co-writing credit for the song, which none of the band are thrilled about. Bad Yoko vibes, man. Whatever happened to the rule: no chicks in the studio?

But Bernie is not about to start eating anyone's shit. He operates on a short fuse now. One night, the band want him to listen to some playback and he walks out for three days. He doesn't see the difference between that and Glenn's and Don's trips to Aspen to "get their heads together," but Glenn and Don do. Don Felder tries to mediate between his old friend and jamming partner and his thorny new bandmates, but all of the stress and the obvious futility of it drives him further and further into piles of cocaine.

Bernie gets just one lead vocal on the album—"I Wish You Peace." Don Felder tries to talk him down, persuade him the band is merely evolving, that Glenn and Don have written the best new songs this time, but next time . . . who knows? Bernie doesn't buy it, can't shake his original vision of the Eagles as four equal partners in a simple country rock band.

Randy is almost as distant, at one point stranded back in Nebraska by illness, so it's left for Don Felder to write the bass part for "One of These Nights." Don nails it. It's sick disco, strolling bones, full-moon fun. A song about demons and desires, and about being caught "between the dark and the light."

In the end, none of it matters, because when Glenn and Don finally pronounce the new Eagles record finished they know they have finally done it, finally realized a vision that fits perfectly with the times. Their times.

They choose "*El Chingadero*," Boyd Elder, to produce the cover. Boyd shows them two paintings of cow skulls, they pick one and Gary Burdon designs it, debossing parts of the image to make the skull and the wings and feathers that embroider it stand out more.

According to Burdon, the cover represents where the band has come from and where it is going: "The cow skull is pure cowboy, folk, the decorations are American Indian inspired, and the future is represented by the more polished reflective glass beaded surfaces covering the skull. All set against the dark eagle feather wings that speak of mysterious powers."

Perhaps they remember those trips to the desert long ago, lying on their backs, looking up into the great beyond and wishing, searching, hoping . . . for that which is about to arrive.

The title track, the instantly appealing "One of These Nights," comes out as a single in May 1975 and immediately causes a sensation. Apart from Henley's honeyed vocals, there is absolutely no trace left of the "country rock" sound that was supposed to have defined the quintessential Eagles sound. In its place a form of laid-back, white boy's disco, slo-mo funk, until you get to the searing guitar break, where Felder's solo is diamond-cut lightning. The harmony vocals are sumptuous, the arrangements and production immaculate, to the point you can feel the Hollywood neon lights pulsing beneath the ooze.

Like "Best of My Love," it's an edited-for-radio version—down from four minutes fifty-five seconds on the album to three minutes twenty-eight seconds on the 7-inch 45. Only this time Glenn and Don are in on it, both agreeing that if that's what it takes to top the American Top 40 again then that's perfectly fine with them. And it works. Not only does "One of These Nights" become the second Eagles single to hit Number 1 in America, it also becomes a hit around the world, their first Top 10 single in the Netherlands, their first Top 5 in New Zealand, their first single to hit anywhere on the prestigious UK charts, reaching Number 23 and earning the Eagles their first appearance on *Top of the Pops*, whose regular fifteen million viewers made it the most influential music show then on British TV.

The band themselves were unable to appear as they were now breaking box-office records on tour in America. So the BBC producers did what they always did back then in the pre-video age, and had the show's dance troupe, Pan's People, gyrate to the track.

Pan's People were known for their skimpy stage attire and obvious sex appeal. Yet for "One of These Nights" they were dressed in a curiously low-key way. Baggy jeans with big turn-ups, white cowgirl boots, and frilly off-the-shoulder, buxom-barmaid tops. You could read the BBC producers' thought bubbles: Ah yes, the Eagles. Country rock. We will need the girls to give it some yeehaw. For the biting guitar solo they can toss their long hair around a bit. It synced into the metro street-funk and lonely city yearning of the song not even a tiny bit.

The *One of These Nights* album is released worldwide in June. A month later it becomes the Eagles first American Number 1 album, taking over from Wings' *Venus and Mars* and holding the top position for five weeks, until it is supplanted by Elton John with *Captain Fantastic and the Brown Dirt Cowboy*, which is Elton's fifth American chart-topping album in a row. Even Glenn and Don can't argue with that.

The "One of These Nights" single takes ten weeks to climb to Number 1, reaching the summit on the week ending August 2, 1975. The *One of These Nights* album is already sitting pretty at Number 1. The Eagles are the hottest American band in the world.

Bernie Leadon is still not convinced by success, that it can be a thing in itself, more important than almost anything else. "Like anything, some people like it. Some people don't . . ." Bernie is burning out, dude. Wow.

No one wins 'em all. Take this guy Stephen Holden, who reviews the album for *Rolling Stone*. He says the Eagles "lack an outstanding singer."

Don is like this asshole Holder, Holden, Holdup, whatever, has shit for brains. Glenn is like, fuck him, what does he know?

But when Don reads on, he sees that Holden does at least partially get where the band are coming from, beholds the aesthetic: "A major reason I like *One of These Nights* more than its forerunners," he writes, "is its relative lack of conceptual pretension. The best songs portray LA culture fairly straightforwardly, using occult eroticism ('One of These Nights,' 'Too Many Hands' and 'Visions') and sexual duplicity and malaise ('Hollywood Waltz,' 'Lyin' Eyes,' 'After the Thrill Is Gone') as metaphors for the city's transient, hedonistic ambience."

He concludes: "The Eagles' music reflects the Hollywood ethos of glamorous, narcissistic ennui, exhibiting the contradiction between the city's atmosphere of 'laid-back' machismo and its desperate rootlessness of spirit."

And that is *exactly* it, that is *exactly* right. Glenn and Don are ecstatic, though they are goddamned if they are going to admit it in public. Fuck the press, man. And especially fuck *Rolling Stone*.

Not everyone gets it though. More typical is the comment in *Let It Rock* by esteemed British writer Mick Houghton, who begins his review: "I can't think of anything good to say about 'One of These Nights.'" Gee, thanks, pal.

Lester Bangs, American music's most fearless writer, savant seer, clown prince, also decides this is the right time to pass judgment on the Eagles. His piece in *Music Gig* begins: "I have a friend who is the most depersonalized individual I know—her love life is all mixed up . . . She seems to live in some kind of half-fantasy world from which she exploits people by using her charm and telling absolutely everybody 'You're my best friend!' The Eagles are her favorite group, and one day her younger sister said to her: 'You know that song "Lyin' Eyes" is about you.' 'I know,' said my friend, deep in suddenly tapped melancholy."

Bangs isn't going out of his way to do the band any favors, yet he captures something of what it is about the Eagles' music that connects with the public soul: it's not just *about* them, it's about their secrets and lies, their fantasies, enough to enable them to project themselves onto the musical narrative, to see a romantic version of their own lives, even as they slink off into penthouses or drop down into cellars.

That's the trick. That's what Eagles' music represents.

"The music is macho but wholesome," he adds, "not like those dirty hoodlums Aerosmith and Bad Company. If [the Eagles] wrote a song about gang-raping a twelve-year-old convent girl, it would come out smooth as silk, sung by angels' choirs."

Bangs drives at the same question of authenticity that has plagued the Eagles since they first learned to fly. Yet it's the question they know they really don't have to answer. Hell, these guys aren't real cowboys. They're not from Southern California. They're not country musicians. They're not even a rock 'n' roll band.

But they don't have to answer to any of that because unlike the other bands that Lester Bangs champions, the scuzzy, New York street acts that glory in living in the three-chord squalor their ripped and torn music describes, the Eagles have set out to become their own ideal—a stadium rock act with universal songs that sells a vision of life and love—complicated by the inevitable accompanying darkness.

No songs about gang-raping twelve-year-old convent girls. But plenty of real horror if you know the real Hollywood and know where not to look. That's the trick, Lester seems to suggest, if you want to conquer American hearts. Feed them their own poison dipped in candy cane. As the wicked wind whispers and moans . . .

21.

"Ooo"s for Bucks

The 1975 *One of These Nights* tour had begun in New Zealand back at the start of the year. Followed by high-profile first tours of Australia and Japan, followed by a one-off show in Hawaii. Then it was back to LA to finish off the album.

By early summer, the Eagles had begun their biggest US tour yet: a marathon seventy-four-date trek that will take them all the way through to October. From the get-go they are headlining arenas, like the 9,500 capacity Municipal Auditorium in Nashville. They are also still obliged to lower the bar in places where the new album hasn't hit yet, like the 4,000-capacity drag-racing park in Cincinnati and the 2,700-capacity Music Hall in Boston.

By the end of May, however, with the "One of These Nights" single now on nonstop rotation on American radio and bulleting unstoppably to Number 1, they headline the 65,000-capacity Tampa Stadium in Florida, on a four-band bill featuring the Charlie Daniels Band, followed by Linda Ronstadt, then Seals & Crofts. A week later, with the album still awaiting release, the Eagles headline the 58,000-capacity Jeppesen Stadium in Memphis.

Then on June 21, eleven days after the album is finally released, they fly into London for the biggest, most high-profile stadium show the Eagles have ever done, though they are not headlining this one.

Billed as Midsummer Music at Wembley Stadium, the Eagles are third on a six-act bill headlined by Elton John, then at the very peak of his commercial success. It was a huge show for Elton, who was premiering an all-new backing band by performing the entirety of the new ten-track *Captain Fantastic* album. A novel idea for the times that appeared unmatchable—at least, on paper. The whole dream turned into a nightmare for Elton, however, when the two acts immediately preceding him on the bill—the Eagles followed by the Beach Boys—took the opposite approach and simply stuck to the hits and obvious crowd-pleasers.

While Elton is swanning around backstage having pictures taken, hanging out with a seemingly endless parade of his latest celeb best friends (Jimmy Connors, Candice Bergen, Paul and Linda McCartney, Billie Jean King, and Harry Nilsson, among others, are all guests in Elton's personal VIP lounge) the Eagles go on in mid-afternoon and simply kill. Seven numbers from their fifteen-song set are recognizable hits. Elton had recently gone on record predicting the Eagles would become "the cult band" of the late seventies and his audience was not disappointed.

Hot from the road in America, buoyed by *One of These Nights* becoming their first Top 10 hit album in the UK, the band go down a treat. Acutely aware of the criticism they had faced in England from critics more used to rock stars who "jumped up and down in dresses and makeup," as Frank Zappa put it, Henley had been particularly stung by one critic who had accused the Eagles of "loitering on stage."

For the Wembley Stadium show, they are joined onstage, to much fanfare, by Jackson Browne, who plays piano on opening number "Take It Easy," while Joe Walsh, who Irving had wangled onto the bill one rung below the Eagles, joins them onstage for encores of "Carol" and "Best of My Love."

They make it look effortless, playing California-toasted songs to kids from Harrow and New Malden, from Rickmansworth and Ealing. "Time and only time earns recognition," says Don Henley, being interviewed backstage by *Sounds*. "In the beginning we'd open for Tull, Yes, Cocker and people would be yelling 'boogie!' during a ballad. We paid some heavy dues and got paranoid. Now it works only because we've been around long enough for people to know who we are."

Deal sealed.

The Beach Boys, who followed, put on an even more commanding performance, stuffing their set with more than a dozen of their coolly carefree hits, all performed in brilliant sunshine. By the time Elton finally came onstage it was dark and hundreds of fans were starting to leave, utterly satiated by the two goliath American acts that had already entertained them that afternoon. The headline of the review that followed in *Melody Maker* said it all:

[EAGLES'] CUP RUNNETH OVER.
ELTON LEFT TO PICK UP THE EMPTIES.

While the review in the *Guardian* described the Eagles as "the epitome of easy-listening, quality country rock . . . with chugging rhythms and fine harmonies they were perfect at what they did." A week later the band were second on the bill on day two of the annual Day on the Green Festival in Oakland, California, where Elton joined them before the 50,000 sell-out crowd for the encores.

Along with the trip to England, they go to Germany, Holland, France, Canada, Japan, Australia, and New Zealand. They "special guest" at shows with Tina Turner and the Rolling Stones. The first Stones show is in Kansas City. Don Felder is keen to meet one of his heroes. The Stones take the top two floors of the Holiday Inn.

Don is escorted up. They search for Keef. They catch a glimpse of his leg sticking out of a bathroom door. They check him out: motionless, gray skin. "Doing," as Don says later, "a very good impression of a corpse." Next day, there's Keef, shirt slashed to the navel and mad devil grin on his face, cranking out the riff to "Jumpin' Jack Flash" like nothing just happened.

Official entry into the global superstars' club is made official when, in September, *Rolling Stone* runs its first Eagles front cover. Written by Cameron Crowe, the piece begins with an amusing anecdote from the road that summer, while the band were still out doing promo interviews with radio stations to promote the "One of These Nights' single. In town for two concerts at the Arie Crown Theater, the band find themselves in the studio with Chicago's self-styled "Superjock" Larry Lujack.

"Say, I remember reading somewhere that the Eagles do the best 'ooo's in the business," says Larry. "What do you say to that?"

"Ooo's for bucks, Larry, that's our motto," snaps Glenn quick as a flash. "The only difference between boring and laid back is a million dollars."

The article addresses the claim Bernie had already left twice— and returned twice. Shrugging it off. That's just Bernie. More revealing is to read Glenn Frey talking about worrying sometimes about the inter-band fighting. "There's a keg of dynamite that's always sitting there," he freely admits. But for Glenn it's all about success. The kind you can't argue with. "I just figure we can't lose . . . I thought we'd break up after our first album."

Released the same month as the *Rolling Stone* cover is the next Eagles single, "Lyin' Eyes." Again, edited down from its six-minute-plus album version, to a more radio-friendly four-minutes-just, "Lyin' Eyes" begins an eight-week climb up the US charts to Number 2, only kept from Number 1 by their new pal, Elton John, and his single, "Island Girl."

In Britain it gets to Number 12, the band's biggest hit there to date. More astoundingly from the band's point of view, "Lyin' Eyes" also gets to Number 8 on the *Billboard* Country chart—the first Eagles record ever to make it onto there.

More top-shelf brand burnishing takes place the same month when the Eagles are profiled in *Time* magazine—and elevated to just the right level of pretentiousness for that magazine's more poker-faced audience. The piece, by an unnamed staffer, begins, rather magnificently:

"The Eagles were conceived in the teachings of Carlos Castaneda and his ephemeral medicine man, Don Juan. The Mojave Desert was their classroom, and they named themselves after one of the major spirits in the Indian cosmos: the eagle. During long sleepless nights on raw tequila and peyote, the young musicians studied.

"'There is a scene in Castaneda in which Don Juan tells him to walk until he finds his power spot,' says guitarist Glenn Frey. 'After searching for hours, he collapses. He wakes up to find Don Juan, who laughs and tells him that he has found his spot. We all wandered around with different bands, but as the Eagles we have found our power spot.'"

Frey is a "nocturnal playboy," the piece elegantly notes. Henley "reads Rimbaud," doncha know. Leadon and Felder are "almost recluses." While Meisner "is a family man." You see, simple really.

In November comes the pure limitless pop sunshine of the "Take It to the Limit" single, with Randy singing that beautiful, heartfelt, almost yodeling lead vocal, while earthbound angels consort on the chorus. It's like John Denver at his most patriotic and hopeful, but with just a hint of seventies despair, which sullies it just enough to make it achingly meaningful. It only gets as high in the US as Number 4, but it outsells every other Eagles single to date.

Glenn said he remembered being "very happy for Randy." But? "We had tried, unsuccessfully, to get a piece of material for him—or from him—that might be a hit single or turn into one." Glenn just could not goddamn understand it how the guy who came up with "Take It to the Limit" couldn't or wouldn't come up another one like it. Glenn could not get past how "Take It to the Limit" was the first Eagles single to sell a million. Their first gold single. "Maybe our only gold single." It burnt him up.

Flying around the world, beady eyes gleaming. It's not love-love-love anymore. It's me-me-me. It seems to most people that it has always been about me-me-me. Only it's cool now in 1975 to finally admit it.

Less than a year later, Tom Wolfe's essay, "The 'Me' Decade and the Third Great Awakening," was published on the cover of *New York* magazine, so inspiring the great seventies catch-all— the Me Decade. It was the new get-out clause for everything. Like if we all agree not to help each other and just concentrate on ourselves that will ultimately lead to a much fairer playing field for everyone—especially me. Now here's another beautiful crazy song about it.

The Eagles, with their detached, knowing songs and silver-tongued pop wit had become the embodiment of this new ideal. Critics disdained them for it, still clinging to forlorn hopes of a Beatles reunion, or finding Jimi Hendrix alive and well and living a secret life as an African missionary. They grew accustomed to dismissing Eagles records as cynically formulaic, as counterfeit somehow.

Radio stations loved them for it, though. No one tuned out when an Eagles hit was playing, their reach broad enough you could charge a little more for ad breaks. Concert promoters worshipped them for the same reason. By the time Tom Wolfe was coming up with his "revolutionary" ideas about the true meaning of the seventies, Eagles ticket sales were such that demand outstripped supply by five to one.

For the fans, and there were now millions of them, it was win-win. They didn't care what the Eagles supposedly stood for; no one stood for anything in America in the post-Watergate era. Nobody even cared what they looked like; they already sounded so damn good-looking in their songs. The gorgeous café-crème voice on "Best of My Love" was so moreish it could have been a woman's. Don't tell me it's that *Furry Freak Brothers*–looking fuzz-bear on the drums, I already know what the real singer of that song looks like—he/she sleeps beside me every night in my dreams.

When the Eagles sang, whichever one it was, you put your own face in there. Let hurts-so-good songs like "Lyin' Eyes" and "Take It Easy" tell *your* story. About the ones that cried while others lied. Waking up on a corner in Winslow, Arizona . . .

All the while, the shows and the hits pull *One of These Nights* and each of its three predecessors along with it, selling millions and millions of records—four million copies of *One of These Nights* alone—plus all of those radio plays that bring more and bigger royalties—"mailbox money," as they call it—which in turn make more and more fans for the Eagles, who go and buy tickets, and more records . . . on and on through 1975 and deep into '76, Glenn and Don's "satanic country rock" catching the open hearts and darker minds of millions now around the world, making a mountain of cashish, high on demand, nothing now beyond reach, an ever-widening circle that now curls itself around everything the Eagles do.

As if to demonstrate, symbolically, how far the world they have left behind has now fallen, on June 12, two days after *One of These Nights* is released, Doug Weston calls time on the Troubadour, closed officially for refurbishment. Unofficially, because, "I'd lost the basic lines of communication to the industry."

On September 30, as if to underline the point still further, the Eagles put on a vast "homecoming show" to 55,000 people at the

Anaheim speedway, where they headline a bill born of the Troubadour, featuring special guests Jackson Browne and Linda Ronstadt.

It's a special night all right. As the warm, weed-scented night falls, the five Eagles—plus J.D. Souther, of course—take the stage and are anointed as the new kings of LA—young, rich, coked-up, and free. They are more than just a talented group of young guys who hit on a winning formula. They are the first American rock stars created entirely in and of the seventies, a sound free of sixties idealism but still drawing on the roots of American music, then adding a sparkle of space dust, a new type of thing that will redefine what rock bands can be now. Coming more sincerely and purposefully from that place where artistry and commerce intersect, without prejudice. A band that will also be a corporation, a cultural landmark with the financial appeal of an investment bank, a behemoth that will exist for the next half a century, almost certainly longer; revered and reviled, remote and distant rock stars made up of everyman worker bees in jeans and sneakers.

This is the trick, ladeez-that-pleeze and gentlemen factotums. This is how it's done the right way. By the end of the year it's official: the Eagles are one of the top-grossing bands in the world, playing to almost a million people in America alone that year for ticket sales in excess of $6 million. Add on record sales and official tour merchandise, and the Eagles are looking at an annual turnover in the tens of millions.

As Linda Ronstadt observed: "The music business had a whole anti-glamour thing for a while. Now glamour is back in full style. It's starting to get like Hollywood stars again . . . it's suddenly very groovy to look like you're winning, to look like you're very rich."

The Eagles are both those things and more. They are about to find out just how much more.

22.

Hey Buddy, You're Showing

"We're trying not to go over the hill," said Don Henley, never one to fan the flames when a bucket of cold water is to hand. "As Glenn puts it, we're trying to stay lean and hungry. We started hungry for fame, fortune, whatever and we're still hungry for something. I always thought we'd make it. I always wanted to make it really bad. I was driven, a man possessed."

Being on the road for most of the year was not the fun it was supposed to be though, the ultimate indulgence of the free 'n' easy rock 'n' roll lifestyle quickly paling as the Eagles, strung out and wall-eyed after month after month after month of it, were discovering the misery behind the myth. The price of all that nice. Their survival tactics entirely predictable.

"Cocaine abuse continued to be rife," Don Felder would write, decades later. "People would wander around asking, 'Hey, you holding? You got any?' They'd disappear off to the men's room and come back with white powder rings around their nostrils, a sure indication of what they'd been up to. 'Hey buddy, you're showing,' one of us would say. A quick wipe on the back of the hand would solve the problem."

Everybody smoked primo pot and drank long-necked iced Buds. You didn't need to be in a band in 1975 to do that, it was the norm.

Rarely would anyone refuse some blow. Not in LA, baby, are you for real?

According to Felder, the band were "generally well coked up" before they even hit the stage. Roadies would "leave lines of blow on our amps, so that between songs we could go back and bend over as if we were adjusting the knobs, when actually we were snorting in front of an entire live audience."

This wasn't party-hearty time, though. This was survival, working through it. You never know if you'll get this shot again. Your next record stinks, you're gone. Like that. You gotta make the most of it. Make bank while you can. Do whatever it takes. Take whatever it takes.

"Cocaine," said Felder, "offered us the chance to keep pushing ourselves to the absolute limits when all we wanted to do was stop for a while and catch our breath . . ."

The Eagles may, as Glenn boasted, "throw the greatest traveling party of the '70s," but as the *One of These Nights* cycle finally begins to wind down, they will come to realize they haven't even got started yet. This journey is going to get longer and stranger; it is going to get much, much darker. And it is going to exact a heavy toll, details sure to be confirmed down the line.

At the center, feeding off the encroaching dusk like vampires sniffing blood, are Glenn and Don. This is no longer just about the music, although the music is a part of it. "Glenn and I would go through a series of moving in together and then moving out," Don recalled. "We'd have girlfriends and live with them for a while, and then we'd get ready to do an album and we'd move back in together. Dudes on a rampage. I was sort of the housekeeper, the tidy one. He was the lovable slob. We would get up every Sunday, watch football together, scream and yell and spill things . . ."

It sounds like fun, and it kind of is. All the parties and the girls, here at Glenn's pad in Coldwater Canyon, the place he rents from James Cagney. Glenn's towers of cigarette butts and squashed beer cans tipping over in the living areas. Don with his yellow legal pad and Glenn at the piano, talking, jabbering, bullshitting about which parts of their lives they can turn into another song dripping in toxins or melting like a chocolate heart.

At the end of 1974, Don had begun a relationship with a twenty-five-year-old would-be designer from Chicago named Loree Rodkin, then working as a party planner. Loree was no rock chick. "I was so square: no drugs, no alcohol. I don't like the taste. I've probably still only had four drinks in my life. I lived through the madness completely straight."

Don was so into Loree he rented them a love pad out in Malibu, the coastal enclave for movie mavericks and music millionaires, where mucho moolah buys you the romance of rugged, sandy cliffs, naturally blond beaches, sweeping sea vistas—and security-guarded privacy.

In mid '75, Glenn met twenty-three-year-old Janie Beggs, a Texas debutant from a successful, high-profile family, big shots in the cattle business. Soon they're living together at a big Pueblo-style house in Santa Fe.

After a while, Loree gets sick of Don's fastidiousness in the home, his womanizing when he's hanging and touring with J.D. and Glenn, and his spiraling coke habit, and leaves, a move that shakes Don to the core, especially when he discovers Loree has a new relationship with Elton John lyricist Bernie Taupin, one of the few songwriters in America doing better than Don.

Glenn, meanwhile, is doing so much blow he's destroying the lining of his nose, which requires two rounds of surgery, which still doesn't quite fix the problem—not while Glenn is still snorting his way through ounces at a time. He and Don are also both suffering from persistent stomach pain, which seems partly due to the coke, but also due to the psychic haze that is enveloping them and their rapidly disintegrating personal lives.

It's sex and drugs and rock 'n' roll. It's newfound money and newfound power. It's the shifting sands of band relationships. It's the unspoken battle *between* Glenn and Don, their relationship an unassailable fortress to the other Eagles, but on the inside, it's Don pushing for equal billing with Glenn, Don moving up from the drum stool to the lip of stage, Don standing alongside Glenn as writer, as arranger, as artist, as singer, as ladies' man, as rock star, as little brother squaring up to big brother, as dick-measuring contest, as competing visionaries for the future of the band.

But while Glenn and Don seem built for this life of Learjets and movie-star mansions, of famous rich girlfriends and armed-guard paranoia, Bernie is not, he's decided. Bernie's plan was a simple band with a country sound, a little bluegrass, a little blues, a little rock, modern but folksy. No flashy clothes or flashy cars, just the wandering minstrel life, and Bernie's plan has not fundamentally changed.

He looks around him at the decadence that surrounds the band now: the drugs, the women, the money. It eats away at him. He looks at *One of These Nights*—at his one lead vocal and three co-writing credits, none of them released as a single. He looks at Patti being cold-shouldered, at the lack of support for "I Wish You Peace" . . . He looks at all of that and hates what he sees.

In the toxic tour bubble, it festers. They get to Cincinnati at the tail end of '75. Another hotel, another room. Another soundcheck, another production meeting. The same faces, the same voices, day after day after night after day. Glenn and Don, Don and Glenn, making it all so fucking OBVIOUS what they want.

And then Don Felder . . . a great guy, but the sound has changed. New and louder frequencies altering the vibe, twisting it in Bernie's ear.

Bernie will happily admit: "I personally preferred the original four-piece group over the five-piece group with Felder, not so much to do with any criticism of Felder per se, but just the fact that another player takes up extra room and everyone has to economize."

So they're in Cincinnati, another hotel room, another production meeting, Glenn and Don arguing over some damn thing, another battle in the endless war, and Don Felder is sitting there, waiting for it all to pass.

He turns to Bernie and says: "If Don and Glenn want to control the situation, then let them . . . it's gotta be easier than fighting all the time." But Bernie looks like he wants to fight. Like he's ready.

Felder doesn't even know what they're fighting about: "Maybe Bernie was going on again about us having sold out and become too commercial. Maybe everyone was pissed because Patti was on the road again, which meant federal agents everywhere to protect her because she was the governor's daughter."

It could be anything, but the last is a constant irritation and concern. The feds are a most unwelcome addition to the tour, cramping everyone's style, especially when it comes to drugs.

In any event, Glenn, sitting in the middle of the room in an aluminum chair, started in on Bernie, who was standing in the corner with a Budweiser in his hand, about how he screwed things up every time.

Bernie gave him that fixed look. "You need to cool down, you fuckin' asshole," he said and emptied his entire beer over Glenn's head. According to Felder, "All the while, staring Glenn down, daring him to stop him. Bernie was into karate and was super-fit. Few would have taken him on. Then he stormed out onto the open balcony . . ."

Don follows Bernie outside while Glenn is too shocked and embarrassed to say anything, sitting there with Bernie's beer running down his face. Outside, Don says to Bernie: "This isn't good, man . . ." Bernie says he doesn't give a shit; tells Don he's ready to quit.

Inside, Glenn looks over at Don Henley. Shakes his head. "That guy's a fucking liability . . ."

Don nods his agreement.

And Bernie Leadon's fate is sealed.

The tour is cut short. Everyone is sick and tired. Everyone's got ulcers, diverticulitis, aching-ass disease. Everyone is sick of the sight of each other.

Bernie packs up and takes off for Hawaii.

Later, after his "amicable departure" has been made public, Bernie tells the press, "I kept asking, 'Are we going to rest next month?' I wanted to get in shape before the age of thirty. So I would have a chance at the rest of my life. I was afraid that something inside me was dying. Leaving was an act of survival."

Leaving. Being fired. What did it matter now anyway?

While Don and Glenn wrestle with the yellow legal pad and the piano in the corner, Irving has an idea. "We decided it was time to put out the first greatest hits, because we had enough hits . . ."

The first half of that sentence was certainly true, but the decision, which seemed counterintuitive at best, career-limiting at worst—major artists did not release greatest hits compilations until their careers had already peaked—was not made because the Eagles now "had enough hits" to do so. It was part of a much larger strategy on Azoff's part to wrestle away control of the band's publishing and effect a major renegotiation of their Asylum contract which would, if Irving turned the right screws, be applied retrospectively to their entire catalog.

The ball had begun to roll with the news in January 1976 that thirty-two-year-old David Geffen had been diagnosed with cancer: a tumor on his bladder that would require major surgery. In the end, the cancer was misdiagnosed, but before that became clear months later, Geffen was on his way out the door.

He had, ironically, just been promoted to vice president of Warner Brothers Pictures. David had long dreamed of graduating from music tycoon to movie producer. Now, as his moment of Hollywood glory appeared to have arrived, Geffen was knocked to his knees.

Irving Azoff saw this as just the right moment to make a move he'd been waiting to make since "Best of My Love" first hit Number 1 a year before. Citing the allegedly illegal conflict of interest that resulted from Geffen's days acting conjointly as Eagles manager, label owner, song publisher, and talent agent, Azoff launched a $10 million lawsuit against Warner Communications for the return of all outstanding Eagles royalties.

As far as Geffen was concerned, this was "bullshit." He added: "The whole issue was really created by Irving Azoff to get a settlement out of Warners."

However, it was a problem Geffen no longer had a say in. That onerous task fell to his successor, Joe Smith. Smith was a forty-seven-year-old, Massachusetts-born Yale grad who'd served in the military with the US occupation forces in post-war Okinawa.

He'd been a radio sportscaster and later music DJ in Boston, before landing a sweet ride in the promotions department of Warner Bros. back in 1961. Soon after, he became general manager. Then in 1972 he became president. Now, in 1976, Smith was expected to step into Geffen's shoes at Elektra/Asylum and make things right again. Which he was eminently more capable of doing than the flibbertigibbet Geffen.

Joe Smith was not intimidated even a little bit by the likes of Irving Azoff.

But Joe Smith knew he had to tread carefully. At the time Smith took over from Geffen, Eagles albums were selling more than a million a month. Eagles record sales now accounted for 57 percent of the label's gross.

Azoff was far from oblivious to this. "Whenever I'd call Smith," he said, "I'd tell the receptionist it was '57 percent' calling."

"There's no question," Smith recalled, "the engine that was powering the Warner music machine was the Eagles, because they sold in such incredible numbers. Jackson [Browne] broke loose too in that period, and Linda Ronstadt had her greatest success, but the Eagles were by far the biggest act we had."

One of the first calls Azoff made to Smith was to inform him he not only wanted the Eagles copyrights back, he also now demanded a significant increase in record royalties, retroactively, all the way back to the first Eagles album. Or else.

What? Smith didn't want to get to the point where he'd have to ask that question.

He found encouragement when he went through their contracts and discovered they were being paid far below the scale an act with their sales heft would normally command. The Eagles were still on a royalty rate of around 12 percent. Contemporaries like the Stones and Zeppelin were on more than double that.

A deal was done. Irving still did not rest.

Said Smith: "Whenever the Eagles had an album coming out, he would send every bill to us to be paid, whether it was the electric bill, Don Henley's car lease, anything, assuming most of it would get through." If anybody at the label dared question Azoff's accounting, he would scream down the phone, "I'll kill that Smith!"

The idea of putting out a greatest hits compilation while all this was going on, however, was not Irving's, but David Geffen's. In his last significant decision for Asylum before butterflying into a block-buster movie exec (he wished!), Geffen had come up with the idea of releasing an Eagles greatest hits.

As longtime Universal Records label exec Dante Bonutto explains: "The market for greatest hits compilations was lucrative but still fairly marginal in the mid-seventies, especially when it came to the really big artists. Unless they'd been around forever like the Beatles or the Stones, releasing a greatest hits compilation from an artist arguably still to reach the peak of their career, just didn't make sense."

But that was exactly Geffen's point. No major-league artist still on the way up released greatest hits albums; it would look arrogant. Superior. Bad for street cred.

So what? The whole world already saw the Eagles as inherently arrogant. Arrogance, though, cloaking brilliance and vulnerability, thick layers of cynicism protecting unbearably fragile personal sensitivities. As for street cred, the Eagles didn't have any. Didn't need any.

Nevertheless, Glenn and Don—Don and Glenn—were dead against it. It smelled of money-raking. But then they liked raking in money.

What they liked almost as much was that it gave them extra time to try and figure out new material for their next album. What clinched it for Irving is that it gave him one more lever to pull in his broadside relationship with Joe Smith. A zero-cost compilation likely to bring in millions was win-win for both men, however high the new royalty was.

On Tuesday, February 17, 1976, Asylum release *Their Greatest Hits (1971–1975)*. Ten tracks: two Number 1s; two Top 5s; five Top 40s. One that wasn't actually released as a single but should have been ("Desperado"). Sewn together in perfect-ten moreish-ness. To the point of being considered a stand-alone Eagles album, the focus and frame of reference cosmetically altered and gleefully enhanced to an impossible-to-resist degree to become that most elusive object of music biz desire.

All killer, no filler.

Their Greatest Hits (1971–1975) goes straight into the American albums chart at Number 4, then ascends to Number 1 the week after, where it remains for another five weeks, becoming the first album in history to receive the Recording Industry Association of America's (RIAA) new platinum certification for shipping more than one million copies, a feat achieved in its first week of release.

In Britain it also becomes the band's biggest hit, climbing to Number 2 with no commercial headwind at all. It's just a good one to play at parties, play at breakfast, play in bed or driving in a car. As the whole world is going to discover.

The vinyl is clad in another Boyd Elder sleeve with another *El Chingadero* skull, this one destined to become the best-known of all, an eagle skull set against a light blue sky, as if everything inside was already dead, already gone.

Are Glenn and Don happy about this landmark achievement, this validation of the first four Eagles records, this proof of their emergent greatness, this cash-spewing juggernaut that could support their families for the next five generations?

Don't be ridiculous. Of course they are not.

"All the record company was worried about were their quarterly reports," Don snapped. "They didn't give a shit whether the greatest hits album was good or not, they just wanted product."

Glenn and Don are the last men standing, locked in psychic and artistic struggle for the soul of the Eagles. Randy has disconnected. Felder will always be the new kid in class; you could always count on his red-hot riffs, and he could always count on his money. Bernie is gone but not forgotten.

Henley was also bent out of shape, he said, by the lack of proper context offered to the songs from *Desperado*—the title track and "Tequila Sunrise"—once removed from their conceptual surroundings.

"Typical corporate thinking," he sneered. "It's what was so frustrating, the forced marriage of art and commerce. They didn't make good bedfellows as far as we were concerned . . . Quarterly projections and stockholders and board members were their problem, not ours. I refused then and still do to have my music dictated by that."

Strong words. Defiant. Right on, man.

Meanwhile, the mushrooming success of *Their Greatest Hits (1971–75)* means Don Henley has never been so rich—or so sure of himself.

23.

Hey Joe

ernie Leadon's exit from the Eagles is announced in December 1975. He doesn't even get his own press release. For most fans news of the departure of the least interesting guy in a band not exactly known for its charisma is of little interest.

What catches the eye is the additional news that the Eagles are still a five-piece with the addition of hot-shit guitarist, singer, and songwriter, Joe Walsh.

Joe joining the Eagles was Irving Azoff's brainwave, of course. Irving had managed Joe as long as he'd managed the Eagles. Irving had put Joe on some of the band's most high-profile bills, not least the Elton John show at Wembley the previous summer. And Irving had introduced the Eagles to Joe's longtime producer, the brilliantly phlegmatic Bill Szymczyk.

What was never publicly admitted to was the fact that Irving had been sweet-talking Joe into joining the Eagles for several months. Irving was a great one for "planting seeds." Everyone saw the way the wind was blowing for Bernie. Irving was the only one prepared to act on it, though.

Walsh himself had almost given the game away when being interviewed in London that summer following the Elton show at Wembley.

"I wanna get away from the spotlight," he told *Melody Maker*'s Colin Irwin, "but that's not permanent." He'd just like to go on somebody else's tour and "play guitar with some sunglasses on without having to sing." It fit the profile of the party-hearty guy who'd rather party than do anything else ever. Yet Joe insisted there was a tear in this clown's eye: "It's kinda lonely to be the leader and the lead singer and the songwriter and make all the decisions. Every once in a while, you get down or depressed."

Behind the good housekeeping, however, Joe Walsh's arrival into the Eagles as Bernie Leadon's replacement made sense on so many levels it felt preordained, in a similar way to Faces guitarist Ronnie Wood joining the Rolling Stones did the same year. Wood's predecessor, Mick Taylor, was a blues purist, in thrall to rock but not ruled by it. A lone gunman, supremely unimpressed by the haughty Jagger and strung-out Richards, needled by them taking credit for his many exquisite contributions to the Stones catalog—not a single co-writing credit on even one album. Taylor was the best musician in the Rolling Stones and the most miserable.

Ronnie Wood replacing Taylor made being in the Stones a happier, hornier place to hang. The finesse, the out-of-the-box flourishes, the impeccable taste, all gone. Replaced by rock-star energy to the max. Fuck art, let's dance.

Same with Joe Walsh replacing Bernie Leadon in the Eagles, trying to change this water to wine. The folksy banjos and diddly fiddles, the wisps of bluegrass and vanilla vocals—all left the Eagles when Joe Walsh joined the band. Bernie Leadon took them with him. Nobody in the band was sad.

In return, the Eagles acquired the final piece of the jigsaw in what was Glenn's and Don's ultimate dream. That the Eagles be not dismissed as country rock, or soft rock, or pop rock. But acclaimed alongside the other rock titans of the era, their work taken equally seriously. And of course to continue to be evermore successful.

Joe Walsh helped turn the Eagles into the real thing. There would still be country flavors, but that would only be a small strand in the bigger, more widescreen picture. Glenn and Don were all about the big pictures. The endless possibilities. Joe brought far-out rock and get-down funk and *personality* to the Eagles. Joe Walsh made them appear *likable*, even *cool*. This was new ground.

Everybody digs Joe. So boo to Bernie. Let's rock!

The truth is, Joe Walsh joining the Eagles isn't as maybe-there's-someone-already-in-the-organization convenient as it seems. Joe is wild. Joe plays heavy and hard. Joe is not *posing*. Joe *is* it.

His big hit, "Rocky Mountain Way," had already become recognized as a cathedral-like rock classic dedicated to *the life*, joyous in its unapologetic, orgiastic revelry. His last two albums had both gone gold, both ridden the US Top 10. Yet Joe was professionally permissive and would pop up guesting on dozens of different albums over the years, with artists like B.B. King, Rick Derringer, America, Billy Preston, and his special friend Keith Moon.

Joe was an honorary member of the original Hollywood Vampires, the go-all-night, every-damn-night gang of drunken, coke-addled LA-based celebs that orbited Moon and included Ringo Starr, John Lennon, Micky Dolenz, and Alice Cooper.

Because he is an even better guitarist than he is a hang—and Joe is a great hang, getcha ass over here!—Joe is coveted by Humble Pie *and* the Who. His name is still said to be in the hat for the Stones should Ronnie Wood fuck up or the Faces get back together. And if Keef thinks Ronnie is a cool cat to keep around . . .

Joe plays slide that sounds like a bear who hasn't slept for three nights and doesn't intend to start now. But Joe's in no hurry to make a move; Joe just loves to hang and bang on his guitar and on that weathered old bong and shiny silver spoon when he's not banging the guitar.

Joe is not a gun-for-hire. He writes big, dirty riffs. With big, hooky melodies and fun stuff like the guitar talk box, a new invention from the future that lends Joe an extra, ice-cut kinda cool. He was awesome, he was wasted, but he sure knew his shit.

Irving argues that Joe joining the Eagles is the perfect move. The smart call. It certainly works for him, already being manager of both.

Don Henley is not convinced. Yes, Joe would bring rock cred and some real edge to the music. But this guy's crazy, right? Bernie was boring, but he didn't trash hotel rooms. He wasn't always lit up.

But then Bernie was uptight. Joe Walsh—not so much.

They discuss it for weeks before Henley agrees to accept Walsh into the Eagles. Irving is the man smoothing the way, calming Don's nerves, assuring him that Joe is just what they need, absolutely the right guy to replace Bernie and keep the band cooking on the road.

The clincher is when Irving assures Don, hand to God: Joe will play exactly what he's told to play. Sing whatever they want him to sing. Joe is the perfect choice to take on the gig, no stranger on the shore, a fun-loving rock 'n' roll guy, not a stick-up-the-ass health freak like Bernie, followed everywhere by his girlfriend and the feds.

Don is coke-sweat intense and sees all sides. Reluctantly he agrees. With certain reservations. Joe is summoned to Don's palatial spread in the Hollywood heavens, where Don lays down the law. Line by line.

Freaked out, Joe goes to Don's oldest friend, Richard Bowden—better known to the band as Balloon Dick—and asks him to tell

Don to lighten the fuck up and stop worrying all the time. Richard tells Joe that Don *needs* to worry, needs to fret, because that's his natural state and if Joe actually leaves well alone and allows Don to be Don, all will be fine. Joe shrugs his shoulders and lets Don be.

"I told him: 'Just let Don be tense. He's always been that way. When he solves one problem, he just moves on to something else to worry about.'"

Bonus bump. The band agree to also bring in Joe's old road buddy, Joe Vitale, as a second drummer in the touring band for when Don is up front singing. The Two Joes are inseparably high. And at night, full of thoughts.

One predawn hotel hootenanny found them hatching a plan for Vitale to formally join the Eagles, as Walsh had. Don and Glenn shut that shit down fast, show Joe the bad face, and things start to settle.

The good news: the crowds love Joe, even the toned-down version of himself that he presents to avoid breaking Henley's law about the music being the only reason for being onstage. Glenn tells a newspaper: "The guitar playing in the band and the musical platforms are much more to my liking now . . ."

Don Felder, who had himself been brought in to toughen up the Eagles sound, observed, "Joe's voice was a lot more nasal than Bernie's and the sound of the vocal harmonies changed dramatically. [But] personally I liked Joe a lot. He's such an easy to love character, like a favorite drunken uncle . . ."

There was nothing put on about Joe. The life of the party, even on those days when they were "hungover, out of drugs, or feeling sick with sinus infections from bad blow out of Cuba."

Glenn and Don are surprised though not entirely shocked to learn that Joe carries a chainsaw in his luggage to carve up hotel room furniture and take off the doors so that he can turn their suites into one huge party room. Joe likes doing what he calls "hog rails": long, thick white lines of cocaine. Smoothing it out with man-size screwdrivers—quadruple vodka and fresh-squeezed orange juice, or just the mixer from the bottle, the vodka being the only real essential.

Joe likes water fights, pranks with glue guns. Joe likes what one girlfriend calls his "kink scenes"—soft-core bondage and S&M, all very consenting and safe, just more fun when you've been up for five days straight and are still trying to stay high.

"Monstering," Joe calls it.

Joe likes abandoning rental cars in the most unlikely spots, leaving vapor trails of fun and destruction in his wake, all of the energy he can no longer burn by going crazy onstage finding an outlet away from it. An exit wound.

Joe discovers that he likes being in a band, especially this band, where Irving indulges his wild side and he doesn't have to worry about anything other than playing his ass off every night. There's none of the hassle and responsibility of his solo career, and Joe views responsibility in the same way that a vampire views the rising sun. He keeps his head down, his nose full, and his guitar turned the fuck up, and by the time he comes off the road, he's the fifth Eagle.

"This was a different age," Walsh would later say. "We could do anything we wanted, so we did. And Irving's role was to keep us out of prison, basically." Like the time the Eagles hit Chicago and Joe invited his good buddies John Belushi and Dan Aykroyd over to his suite at the Astor Towers hotel, where the three amigos set about destroying the place—which turned out to be the owner's private apartment. "We had to check out with a lawyer and a construction foreman," Joe recalled. "But Irving took care of it. Without Irving, I'd *still* be in Chicago."

Once the dust has settled, Don offers the blandest of takes on Joe's rocky induction: "Well, Joe was and is his own man; he's always been an independent entity, even as a member of the group.

He had a fine solo career going before our manager suggested bringing him into the Eagles."

He admitted there had been a measure of trepidation in the band. Joe was a brilliant player with his own sound and groove, and great, great company. But that kind of energy can also be disruptive, a pain in the ass. Certainly, if you're Don Henley, you totally don't need the hassle. Yet somehow it worked. As Don astutely put it to David Browne in 2016, "Joe has always been able to live in both worlds."

Now all they needed to do was make the next album. No pressure, but it better be good. The best. Why? Look around you. In the summer of 1976, Rod Stewart is enjoying his biggest American chart success for five years with Number 1 hits "Tonight's the Night" and "The Killing of Georgie (Part I and II)."

The former, taken ironically, though you never really knew with Rod, could be any Laurel Canyon croon from the good times, though lavishly gussied up in the studio, along with his then girlfriend Britt Ekland heavy breathing in French over the—um—crescendo. It could be the Eagles—if the Eagles were ever fun.

But with "The Killing of Georgie," Rod threw down the songwriting gauntlet, while utilizing exactly the same country-lite, smooth-rock, metropolitan soul that Glenn and Don had been aiming for their whole lives and still hadn't quite got to yet. Rod made it seem effortless. For Rod, it was.

Though far from a prolific songwriter, Stewart had the magic touch on the radio and still enjoyed mainstream critical favor. He was having a hot summer. Next year might be different. Last year it was Elton. This year it's new dick on the block Bruce Springsteen.

Glenn and Don see all of this, and with the fervor of the newly crowned, believe themselves to be above all of them. In the groggy summer of 1976, the only real rivals to the Eagles are, improbably,

a recently revived for the nth time raggle-taggle band of old blooz-
ers from London called Fleetwood Mac.

Huh?

Strange but true, but only strange if you were old enough to
remember the original, long-suffering Fleetwood Mac fronted by
their messiah-like guitarist and angelic singer: sweet, doomed Peter
Green. But none of the incandescent hits that shot them into the sun
in the UK in the late sixties made more than a ripple in America,
where the closest they got to a hit was Santana's other-level version
of Green's "Black Magic Woman."

Years later, stranded in California, scraping by on occasional
low-charting albums and a steady diet of bread-and-butter gigs
around the country where long hair still mattered, Fleetwood Mac
had been through so many line-up changes—so many alarming
tales of acid casualties, cult worshippers, alcoholics, and rip-offs—
it seemed there could be no way back.

Then Mick Fleetwood was introduced by chance to the previously unknown singer Stevie Nicks and her singing and guitar-
playing boyfriend, Lindsey Buckingham. Their first album together,
simply titled *Fleetwood Mac*—emphasizing the launch of a fresh
new look and sound, a whole new band in fact—was released a
month after *One of These Nights* and would eventually follow it to
Number 1 in September 1976—fifty-eight weeks after it first
entered the chart.

Suddenly, the Eagles faced strong competition for the crown of
California's Coolest. More chicks liked Fleetwood Mac too. West
Hollywood was jammed that summer with boutiques selling the
kind of witch-queen wardrobe that Stevie Nicks favored onstage—
the elaborate silks and scarves, the bippity-boppity hats and floaty
Snow-White dresses, the shaking tambourines and wild, gypsy-
woman trinkets.

Stevie has become America's beautiful sprite goddess, a smoky-voiced siren with more than a hint of Garbo beneath the Shirley Temple facade of golden ringlets and brown doe eyes. As 1976 rolls along, Stevie's major contribution to the *Fleetwood Mac* album, the compelling "Rhiannon," becomes one of the biggest-selling singles of the year. Its ethereal opening chords building to a spiritual tornado coming from every car radio on every freeway across the country that summer.

When they start work on the follow-up—a record that will become, two years later, *Rumours*, now one of the biggest-sellers of all time—John and Christine McVie (the "Mac" of the band name) were divorcing and Lindsey and Stevie were on–off, mostly off. A situation aided, in no small part, by the fact that Stevie had begun an affair with another singer in a huge American band then working on a new album: Don Henley.

"He was *really* cute," Nicks gushed, "and he was elegant. Don taught me how to spend money . . . He didn't visibly set out to do that. I just watched him. He was okay with buying a house like *that*—or sending a Learjet to pick you up."

Sending Learjets to pick up chicks had become such a habit for the Eagles by then that Henley would coin the phrase: "Love 'em and Lear 'em." A trite, locker-room joke that took on a more literal meaning once the band got into sending their Learjet back to LA to ferry the most beautiful girls to and from whichever Midwest outpost they happened to currently be in.

This was a practice that became known as "the third encore," a debauched gathering that would follow every gig, featuring the band, their entourage, hangers-on, bizheads, "and as many beautiful girls as we'd meet from the airport to the hotel."

Stevie didn't care. She had begun 1975 as a waitress. She ended the year as a millionairess with an even richer boyfriend. "He is sexy," she added, needlessly. What began as a casual hook-up, however, would quickly deepen into a more serious relationship that would have unforeseen long-term consequences.

When the Eagles' summer '76 tour commenced on July 2 at the 23,000-capacity Greensboro Coliseum in North Carolina, special guests on the bill were America's other SoCal sensations, Fleetwood Mac.

Long before they met, Don Henley had begun wooing Stevie Nicks in a series of phone calls. Just like millions of other twenty-something American men, Don had fallen hard for Stevie based solely on her TV appearances and the pictures he saw of her in newspapers and music magazines.

Moving in the same Hollyweird circles, he'd heard whispers of the troubles Stevie and Lindsey were going through. Stevie, for her part, had cooed about the Eagles in *Rolling Stone*, describing Don and Glenn as: "the Errol Flynns and the Tyrone Powers" of seventies rock.

The afternoon of their first show together, with the bands in adjacent dressing rooms, Stevie freaked out when she arrived to find a huge bouquet of dozens of red roses waiting at her dressing table. Along with a handwritten card: "To Stevie, Best of My Love—Tonight? Love, Don."

Beside herself with embarrassment, Stevie hurriedly looked around the room to see if Lindsey had seen the flowers. Only to spy Mick Fleetwood and John McVie doubled over with laughter. The flowers had not come from Henley but from her joshing bandmates. Stevie was so furious she refused to speak to either of them for the rest of the night.

But while Don had not sent the flowers, he had already invited Stevie out on a date. Followed by another and another. When the bands performed a special US Bicentennial Fourth of July show together at Tampa Stadium, Florida, as the 74,000 blissfully high fans singing and swaying inside the venue they nicknamed the Big Sombrero can attest, the "marriage" between LA's newest, hippest, coolest, most successful bands is consummated.

Fleetwood Mac on first, unrecognizable from the beer-bellied old blues bruisers they had been before the arrival of LA natives Buckingham and Nicks.

Then the Eagles, unrecognizable from the genteel, pedal-steel picking house hippies of five years before.

Both bands now transformed into big time, guitar-wailing, coke-gobbling, cock-strutting, in Stevie's case, full-body contact, Lear-jetted Rock Stars—emphasis on capitals "R" and "S."

The Eagles and Fleetwood Mac. They are perfect for each other.

A week later, during a short break from the tour, the two bands found themselves back in Florida. The Eagles were renting a house on the water with a mobile recording truck, putting the finishing touches on some of the tracks that would be on their next album. Fleetwood Mac were staying in a five-star hotel in Miami.

The band were all in the large breakfast room late one morning when a long black limo pulled up outside and a uniformed chauffeur got out carrying an armful of expensive, gift-wrapped presents—for Stevie. From Don.

"There's a stereo, a bunch of cool records," she recalled. "There's incredible flowers and fruits, a beautiful display. The limousine driver is putting all this out on the table and I'm going, 'Oh please . . . *please* . . . this is not going to go down well.' And they want to know who this is from. And Lindsey is *not* happy."

Later, back home in LA, Stevie becomes a regular guest at the mountaintop retreat in Coldwater Canyon that Don shares with Glenn. She never invites Don over to the more modest house she is renting in West Hollywood. Really, this is Don's trip and Stevie gets that. Until she finds out she is pregnant. Now the true test of their relationship is revealed when Stevie gives in to pressure—from others, from herself—to have an abortion. Stevie, at twenty-eight, has only just become a rock star; she decides the others are right and that she isn't about to give that up to have a baby. A decision she will one day soon regret.

Don certainly didn't force her into it. Though she saw his easy consent as a sign he didn't want a serious relationship.

After the procedure is complete, she finds out the unborn fetus was that of a girl. Stevie names the unborn baby Sara. Three years later, her song about the aborted child, "Sara," becomes another Top 10 hit for Fleetwood Mac. Stevie never, ever forgives herself—or the father.

It's around this time Stevie also begins seeing J.D. Souther, usually while Don is away on tour. A little later, she will also have an affair with Joe Walsh. "We had an incredible time together," she would recall, her face lighting up. "Those Eagles were an interesting bunch of guys . . ."

Lindsey Buckingham, meanwhile, seems determined to push her away even further. Shutting her ideas down in the studio, talking over her, disparaging everything she tries to do. Some of that animus would find itself into the songs both Lindsey and Stevie were writing for *Rumours*: the guitarist's bitter pill, "Go Your Own Way," with its nasty accusatory lines, "Packing up, shacking up, is all you want to do," which so upset Stevie she insisted Lindsey remove them from the final mix. He flat-out refused. And Nicks's heavy-lidded response, "Dreams," with its arch refrain: "Oh, thunder only happens when it's raining / Players only love you when they're playing . . ."

Don Henley doesn't care, tucked up safe and sound on the beef-colored leather couch of his Learjet, his drink freshened every thirty minutes by a goddess in an airplane stewardess uniform, silver platter of crème-de-la-crème Charlie at hand, his focus entirely on the songs he and Glenn Frey are writing for the next Eagles album, the one they already have the title for, after one of the songs they haven't actually finished yet but already know is *the one*—"Hotel California."

24.

The Gods

Looking back many years and lifetimes later, Don Henley put it like this: "Most people who make it in the music industry are not prepared. Success can be just as scary as failure, if not scarier. And some people don't actually live through it."

The truth is, with two Number 1 albums in a row, the Eagles now have so much fame, so much money, so much self-validation they have no idea what to do with it all. The sold-out summer tour with Joe, the *Greatest Hits* beginning to outsell all their other albums combined, the resultant back catalog sales, the resultant millions in merchandise . . . it's insane. It's buckets and truckloads and planeloads of insane.

"We take Learjets the way other people take taxis," Don Felder boasts to one journalist. They'd hire them, Elvis-style, to fly in food and cases of Château Lafite Rothschild when Henley celebrated his birthday. "We drink champagne like water and snort almost enough cocaine to finance a Third World country . . ."

They buy fast-ass cars and big-blouse houses, they lavish crazy, over-the-top gifts upon their crazy, over-the-top women. Glenn now takes his tennis coach on the road. Don takes a masseur for his bad back. They employ their friends as glorified gofers and give them phony job titles like "transportation manager" and "ground transportation manager."

They keep them on the payroll to stay awake and keep smiling. And still they can't spend it all, can't make a dent in it, because it comes in so quickly and in such large amounts that it's like being swamped by a giant wave of delicious green shit.

IT'S HARD TO KNOW *who to trust, who to cling to outside of the immediate circle of the band and the organization and the people going through exactly the same thing.*

"People came out from under every rock," said Don.

Old high school friends. Distant relatives. Former work buddies. Guys you met once when you were ten years old who just want to look you up and tell you how well you're doing. Maybe offer you a once-in-a-lifetime "investment opportunity," or an early stake in some other can't-miss idea, maybe just some expensive-ass guitars, maybe half of Bolivia delivered to your door by naked serving wenches from the other side of the rainbow—the one Geffen named his part-owned club after on the Strip, the Rainbow Bar & Grill.

Everywhere they go, they are being told so many compelling things by so many amazingly interesting people they can't even hear what they're saying anymore. They can't even hear themselves.

Glenn and Don—Don and Glenn.

It's relentless, endless; it makes you fucking paranoid because everywhere you look—on your pillow, outside your window, knocking on your back door—there is a manically smiling face. Everywhere you go there are bag carriers and drivers and ground transportation managers and tennis coaches and masseurs, and drug dealers and groupies and moneymen snaking around cos they're great and you're great and the whole fucking world is great, man!

All smiling at you, all there for you, all telling you exactly what they think you want to hear because you're the guy, baby, you're the man, the one standing in the spotlight, putting on a show, on and offstage, drowning in a tsunami of cash, a hard rain of love, that might never end.

By the time they'd done their third, sold-out "homecoming show" in a row at the 18,000-capacity LA Forum in October, Glenn and Don have a new collective nickname that starts out as a joke among the Eagles' road crew then catches on with everyone, even Irving.

The Gods.

Neither of them has the crackling charisma of Crazy Joe. But they have cultivated their own kind of hip: the ice-cool Marlboro Man that is Glenn Frey; the smooth and chiseled rock God that Don Henley has willed himself to be.

Even Randy Meisner and Don Felder feel it. Soon they are calling Glenn and Don "the Gods," too.

Even though Don Felder has the studly looks and leisurely presence to be a rock star, he leaves it all behind when he exits the stage each night. Don lives a life away from the rest. He and Susan have two kids now and a family to look out for. Once preparations for a new album begin, once Henley and Frey move back into another secluded Hollywood mansion to start pulling it together, Don Felder leases a beach house in Malibu for the summer. He's sitting around one day, watching his daughter play in the paddling pool, cradling his old acoustic twelve-string guitar as he takes in the view, inhales the vibe, wondering how life could possibly get any better.

He absentmindedly starts to strum. Sitting there in the 'Bu, looking out over the deep cerulean sea, basking in the rays, Don breathes in the good feeling and lets it out again on the tinkling guitar.

"I remember sitting in the living room, with the doors all wide open, on a spectacular July day," Felder recalled. "I had a bathing suit on, and I was sitting on this couch, soaking wet, thinking the world is a wonderful place to be."

He's not there to write a song, specifically, he's just tickling out some chords that sound like something might happen to them if he starts to push them far enough. An idea slips into his mind for a verse, then a chorus. It sounds a little bit Latin but with a little reggae rhythm maybe, Don's not sure.

The only reggae he's really been exposed to is the stuff other white rock stars have begun dabbling in, the big breakthrough coming the previous summer when Eric Clapton scored his only US Number 1 single with his white-bread version of Bob Marley's "I Shot the Sheriff." Now everyone is jumping on the bandwagon, including the Stones with their boogie-reggae track, "Luxury" from the It's Only Rock 'n' Roll album. Elton John has also tried his hand with "Jamaica Jerk-Off" from Goodbye Yellow Brick Road. Even Led Zeppelin had come up with their own bulldozer reggae in their punningly titled "D'Yer Mak'er" (the title a play on the word "Jamaica" when said with a cockney accent), which had been a Top 20 hit in the US in 1973.

All of these were either heavily stylized, tongue-in-cheek attempts at insinuating reggae into their music, or, as with Clapton, sincere but heavily sugared attempts at commercializing the form.

Don Felder wasn't aiming for any of those elements while he was noodling on his guitar. If there was a lilt—whether it be Latin or reggae—it was not pre-planned. "It was about thirty-two bars long," he said, "a sparkling little gem that fell out of the spectacular view before me. The hairs on the back of my neck were standing up . . ."

He rushes to the little four-track recorder he keeps in the spare bedroom to get the idea down before it vanishes. He adds a bass *line, finds some kind of cha-cha-cha beat, and, when he's done, lays it down, leaves it for a while, plays with the kids, waits to see if it's half as good as he thinks it is when he returns to it.*

Comes back a few hours later, listens delightedly, and wonders how it would sound with Joe Walsh playing on it too, so he writes a couple of descending guitar lines and mixes it all down. He puts it on a cassette with a bunch of other ideas and sends it to "the Gods," wondering whether any of it will get their attention.

"I knew it was unique but didn't know if it was appropriate for the Eagles," he admitted. "It was kind of reggae, almost an abstract guitar part for what was on the radio back then. When I gave Henley the cassette it had eight or ten different song ideas on it. He came back and said: 'I really love this one track on your tape, the one that sounds like a matador or something . . . like you're in Mexico.'"

Don Henley is driving late at night the first time he listens to the tape, sweeping down through Benedict Canyon along the narrow roads that bear him south toward Beverly Hills. This is haunted LA, a place full of the ghosts of old movie stars whose restless spirits lurk in the hillside mansions that hide in the creases of the hills, the weird sounds that bounce through the nighttime air, the screams that came from Cielo Drive mistaken for the howls of coyotes that run wild and scavenge here, the cool night winds a welcome respite from the choking heat and smog down below, the all-enveloping dark of the more deserted stretches of road, where the hairpins need a deft touch on the brakes.

Don is driving here when he slips Felder's demo into the cassette player, mentally discarding most of what he hears, thinking none of these ideas move him in the way he wants to be moved, in a way that cuts through to the currently inchoate, unexpressed idea that he wants to capture for the next Eagles album, something that gets at the alienation and the impermanence, the unreality of the life he is living now, here in this vast thrumming city that nonetheless feels utterly deserted, without a single human soul to connect to on nights like this, nights when he guns his dream machine through the haunted canyons and searches for what Glenn calls "the perfect ambiguity" that will sum up all that this really means.

Don said of the Felder demo, "I remember thinking, 'This has potential; I think we can make something interesting out of this.'"

For months now he has been living the life he needs to lead in order to write. He makes up and breaks up, breaks up and makes up—with Loree, with Stevie, with the host of other beautiful, smart, willing women who pass through his shiny-new rock-star life, far removed from the country-boy life he almost led—using it all as fuel for his creative drive, the spermic grit that makes the pearl necklace, and he starts to wonder more and more where life ends and art begins, whether somehow subconsciously he is finding the teeth that fit his wounds, breaking up and living in romantic chaos simply because it makes for better art, gets him going in just the right wrong direction, gets the creative fluids simmering.

Because he can feel it, almost taste it as he drives through the dark canyon on that night, feel it as he starts to write with Glenn, as they discuss the big ideas that will become the next Eagles album, both of them experiencing this strange new euphoria that is starting to overtake them, the feeling that everything is about to come to some kind of crazy, finish-line peak, that a cosmic and distant summit is about to be scaled, that their lives and careers are going to get to a point where they can never forget, never repeat, never escape.

Singing in sweet, bitter harmony: "Welcome to the . . ."

Don puts the melody to Felder's guitar demo while he is driving. "I write a lot of songs in my car," he explains. "It's the only place I can get any privacy . . ."

He gives the track a working title: "Mexican Reggae."

The God drives down from his Olympus, a heavenly new song in his head, a song he already suspects will say what he has been trying all of this time to say . . .

GLENN AND DON write in the usual way: alone together, at night, the yellow legal pad and the grand piano, the big, empty mansion with its perfumed ghosts, where they can talk and think and watch ball games, and toot and smoke and chug-a-lug while they try to distil everything that has happened and everything they feel. Only they are not coming up with the usual results.

They encounter the same problem every band eventually faces after they've sold their first ten million records: having succeeded on the premise that they are about the common man and his true-life experiences, their songs telling stories of small-town life in everyday America, suddenly they find they just can't relate. No more "All alone at the end of an evening" for Glenn and Don, who now reside so far over the rainbow they shit diamonds into pots of gold.

They talk about it, trying to remember exactly when it happened. The day they found out for sure they were no longer living on that street corner in Winslow, Arizona, that it is no longer a part of who they are. When you're as rich and famous as Glenn and Don are in America in 1976, standing around on corners unnoticed and hitching a ride is a simple pleasure no longer within your reach.

To try and repeat those sentiments in a song is not only impossible, it is dishonest. Worse: fake. Leave all that blue-collar, working man shtick to new saints in the city like Bruce Springsteen (the irony, as years later Broooce concedes, is that he "never worked a day in my life"). Glenn and Don have bigger fish to fry now. Their heads full of the "crystal visions" Stevie Nicks is singing about else-where in night-owl LA, they tell each other they are going to take the Eagles' own brand of "California music" in an unexpected new direction, no longer the shirt-and-jeans simplicity of the days when they still looked like they had just come offstage at the Troubadour, but something else entirely.

A perfect ambiguity. A grand decadence. A Southern California gothic that meets with the post-Watergate, post-Manson, post-anything-you-can-think-of times. The words of the Gods.

Once they have it nailed, Don can't wait to talk you through it. The new material focused on the same themes that ran through all of their work, says Don. They knew they were on to something the moment they entered the studio again with Bill, exploring dark themes "constructed in an atmosphere of excitement and produc-tivity. And okay, a little debauchery, here and there."

Recording takes place, as before, at Criteria in Miami, and back "home" at the Record Plant in LA. The summer tour with Fleetwood Mac keeps growing, so some of the album is made on the fly. But Glenn and Don have never been so serious before, never been surer—or more under pressure.

"We were under the microscope for sure," said Glenn. "Everybody was going to look at the next record we made and pass judgment. Don and I were going, 'Man, this better be good.'" Don complained that it was impossible for the band to take the time off they needed "in order to get our heads together, to regain a sense of perspective that we had lost."

Instead they choose to simply go with it, to double down and not look back. They want their millions of fans to be amazed, but they are no longer trying hard to please them. It's time for the Gods to turn their cards face up, show you what they've got. Warm smell of colitas rising up through the air.

One of the first things Don and Glenn write together is a majestic soul ballad replete with pure B.B. guitar aches, called "Wasted Time," a song that tapped directly into Henley's time with Loree Rodkin. "Failed relationships," Don sighed. "Nothing inspires or catalyzes a great ballad like a failed relationship. Still, it's a very empathetic song, I think."

Maybe. But there is an icy chill to much of "Wasted Time," in which he uses the second person to address his subject:

> You don't care much for a stranger's touch
> But you can't hold your man . . .

The orchestration starts big and grows from there, becomes overwhelming, Henley so obviously lost in his self-absorption the music is allowed to carry on as a "Reprise" that opens side two. Don's fix on Loree becomes a way into the real meat of the record for him, as he begins to finalize the words to fit Don Felder's "Mexican Reggae" tune.

He becomes more explicit. "There's something of every girl I've ever been with in all of my songs. They're combinations of characters, like fiction. Some of the more derogatory parts of 'Hotel California' however are definitely about Loree Rodkin . . ."

To wit: "Her mind is Tiffany twisted / She got the Mercedes-Benz . . ."

"That's about her," Don was happy to share, "and I wouldn't be crowing if I were Ms. Rodkin. As far as I'm concerned, she's the Norma Desmond of her generation."

Wow.

But Don and Glenn need something bigger than the simple rancor of wasted love to say what they really want to say. Henley's real breakthrough is using the hotel as both rock parable and occult symbol. Everyone knows how a hotel feels—the generic luxury, the transience, the fleeting nature of the experience—but for a band, and for anyone that travels a lot, it becomes something more, a kind of soul prison that provides the same experience day after day, month after month, fade-in, fade-out, that homogenizes every city, blurs every show, that depersonalizes and diminishes, that traps you in a maze of mirrors.

According to Don, "Beverly Hills was still a mythical place to us." The mythical hotel that went with it "a symbol . . . the locus of all that LA had come to mean for us," which he characterized as "the end of the innocence." The recurring theme of all his best songs.

As the years sped by like the lights of a speeding train, "Hotel California" took on far more perverse symbolism for those that sought it out. The song was about heroin addiction, it was about cannibalism, it was about devil worship. Most of this was conjecture built around the fifth verse, which speaks explicitly of a diabolical feast in which an attempt is made to "kill the beast."

Mention of "the beast" certainly tweaked speculation, for who else could that be but the fallen angel, Lucifer himself? As did reference to "the master's chambers'—a magus, perchance? The feast—ritual ceremony. Steely knives—blood sacrifice. Just hadda be, right?

Another popular theory was that Anton LaVey, a dark-world character who drove a coroner's van and walked his pet black leopard, Zoltan, through the streets of San Francisco, had lured the Eagles into the temple of his self-styled Church of Satan (whose mangled doctrine built on the conceits of Ayn Rand and Friedrich Nietzsche) and that the lyrics were about their subsequent deal with the devil. Hence the references to heaven and hell.

There was also the suggestion that cryptic messages that could only be detected by playing the song backward revealed disturbing couplets such as: "Yeah, Satan hears this / He had me believe in him." And: "Yeah, Satan / He organized his own religion."

This was hardly the first time, of course, that rock artists had been accused of devil worship or satanism. Elvis Presley stood accused early on of doing the devil's work with his dangerously rhythmic gyrations and head-turning beats. While other stars of Presley's generation like Little Richard and Jerry Lee Lewis were so convinced of the intrinsic ungodliness of their music, they would eventually give up years of their respective careers to wrestling painfully with the idea that what they'd been doing was not just seditious but fundamentally perverted. It was a notion compounded by the commonly held belief that the blues—the forefather of rock 'n' roll—was propagated by itinerant black men who had been taught to play while sitting atop gravestones at midnight, or, in the case of Robert Johnson, passed on by the Devil himself, encountered after dark at a certain crossroads.

However, compared to the more intentionally subversive ideas being espoused just a decade later, what the original fifties generation of rock 'n' rollers was up to is now seen as woefully innocent, quaint almost. The image of Aleister Crowley—after Merlin, the most famous English wizard in literature—had been added at the personal request of John Lennon to the cover of *Sgt. Pepper* three years before a stoned Jimmy Page instructed engineer Terry Manning to scratch Crowley-isms into the run-out grooves of the third Led Zeppelin album. One album later, and Zeppelin would also be accused of applying backward masking to their signature opus, "Stairway to Heaven." The claim: that if you spun the track backward it would reveal a satanic message—"There's no escaping it / It's my sweet Satan!"

The Rolling Stones—whose founding guitarist Brian was into paganism, Zen, Moroccan tapestries, and very heavy drugs, famously held séances at the London flat he shared with his witchy-woman girlfriend Anita Pallenberg, before driving off to the countryside in the dead of night to hunt for UFOs—had released *Their Satanic Majesties Request* album while Frey and Henley were still small-town boys dreaming of something bigger and weirder.

By the early seventies, there were dozens of musical artists and filmmakers all flirting with the "secret knowledge." From the comparatively innocent output of Hammer House of Horror movies to the clearly more serious *The Exorcist*. From the relatively infantile musical stylings of Black Sabbath and Alice Cooper to the far more dedicatedly authentic exposition of occult lore by artists like Graham Bond and, most infamously, David Bowie.

Also living in LA at the time the Eagles were working on *Hotel California*, Bowie's 1976 album, *Station to Station*, was riven with Orphic imagery. Bowie made no secret of having dabbled in occult rituals, fueled by mountainous supplies of cocaine, a practice that reached its terrifying apotheosis when he called in a white witch to successfully effect an exorcism of his Hollywood mansion.

"There was something horrible permeating the air in LA in those days," Bowie would later claim. "The stench of Manson and the Sharon Tate murders." Hallucinating twenty-four hours a day, Bowie lived in a perpetual state of paranoia, convinced a cabal of female occultists were attempting to steal his sperm to make "a devil baby," culminating in a megalomaniacal rant: "I believe that rock 'n' roll is dangerous. It could well bring about a very evil feeling in the West. I do want to rule the world."

Also involved in a solemn mission to climb vertiginous mountains of cocaine at the same time as endeavoring to make the best music of their lives, neither Frey nor Henley were hanging quite as far over the side of the ledge as Bowie, but they were working in similar prohibited spheres of influence. Said Glenn, "We decided to create something strange, just to see if we could do it." For him, though, it was less about Aleister Crowley and more about John Fowles, the British author whose mystical 1965 novel *The Magus* he had recently finished reading—and rereading.

"We take this guy and make him like a character in *The Magus*, where every time he walks through a door, there's a new version of reality." He said he and Don "wanted to write a song that was sort of like an episode of *The Twilight Zone*. All of our songs were cinematic, but we wanted to open up with [a montage]. It was just one shot to the next—a picture of a guy on the highway, a picture of the hotel, the guy walks in, the door opens, strange people [appear]."

The kiss-off, the line about being able to "check out any time you like" but never actually being able to leave, was whispered to be based on Jackson Browne's beautiful but troubled wife, Phyllis Major, who had tragically committed suicide. But the line meant something different to everybody who heard it. Everyone knew what it really meant—to them.

Phyllis was just thirty. Jackson was in the studio recording his fourth album, *The Pretender*, the night it happened. Some say he never came back. He wrote a song about his wife's death, "Sleep's Dark and Silent Gate." Two and half minutes of elegiac gloss disguised as self-examination.

Better was Don's line. In other words, you can check out, die, but you're still woven into the fibers of the cosmos, like it or not. No one escapes fate.

"Glenn was great at conceptualizing," observed Felder. "He'll say: 'I can see this guy driving in the desert at night, and you can see the lights of LA, way off on the horizon . . .' Henley gets the picture and goes from there. He was an English literature major. He writes really great prose. He can take those snapshots and put them into just two or three lines."

The song "Hotel California" was perfect from every angle, even the most diffuse and unflattering. Just like California itself, it was a canvas on which to frame whatever it was you wanted its meaning to be.

"I've learned over the years that one word, 'California,' carries with it all kinds of connotations, powerful imagery, mystique, etc., that fires the imaginations of people in all corners of the globe," said Don. "There's a built-in mythology that comes with that word, an American cultural mythology that has been created by both the film and the music industry."

(Hey, man, Don's been up all night again *reading*.)

It's that cultural mythology that fires the rest of the songs. Don drags another masterpiece from deep inside for the track that will conclude the album, "The Last Resort." If "Hotel California" is almost painfully personal, then "The Last Resort" is about the universal, in this case the planet itself.

"This is a concept album, there's no way to hide it," said Don. "But it's not set in the Old West, the cowboy thing, you know. It's more urban this time. It's our bicentennial year, you know, the country is 200 years old, so we figured since we are the Eagles and the eagle is our national symbol, that we were obliged to make some kind of a little bicentennial statement using California as a microcosm of the whole United States, or the whole world, if you will, and to try to wake people up and say, 'We've been okay so far, for 200 years, but we're gonna have to change if we're gonna continue to be around.'"

Glenn stands back in frank awe, calls "The Last Resort," "Henley's opus." Explaining that it was the first time that Don, on his own, took it upon himself to write such an epic story.

They were concerned about the environment and interested in anti-nuclear benefit concerts, said Glenn. Don had gone to the next level as a lyricist on that song. The message: "We're constantly

screwing up paradise." Soon there will be "no more new frontiers."
He added: "There's enough crap floating around the planet that we
can't even use . . . It's unfortunate but that is sort of what happens."

J.D. brings them "New Kid in Town," a song with a sure-fire-hit
chorus that they finish up together. J.D. sees it as a straight-up
Western metaphor in the style of "Desperado." "At some point
some kid would come riding into town that was much faster than
you and he'd say so, and then he'd prove it," he explained. "We
were just writing about our replacements . . ."

Don, meantime, still had Loree on his mind—or maybe this time
it's Stevie he's thinking of, or maybe someone no one is supposed to
know about—when he declared: "It's about the fleeting, fickle
nature of love and romance. It's also about the fleeting nature of
fame, especially in the music business. We were basically saying,
'Look, we know we're red-hot right now, but we also know that
somebody's going to come along and replace us—both in music and
in love.'"

In rehearsal, Joe Walsh comes up with a roasting guitar lick that
roars into a fire. Don recalled: "One day, Joe just busted out that
crazy riff and I said, 'What in the hell is that? We've got to figure
out some way to make a song out of that!' But we really couldn't
sing over that riff, so Glenn came up with the idea of what is a tra-
ditional blues or R & B staple—the 'one chord' song, although
there are obviously other chords in there, too."

There were also some classic Eagles lines about "the right people," "the right pills," "outrageous parties," and "heavenly bills."

Don claimed not to recall exactly who came up with which lyrics. He and Glenn had reached a point of creative symbiosis where,
"[they] were always finishing each other's sentences." They had, he
said, "a kind of telepathy going on . . ."

Glenn recalled the moment he got the title, though. He was in a
car with one of the band's favorite drug dealers known as the

Count. As they merged onto the overflowing freeway, the Count hit the gas, much to Glenn's alarm. "What do you mean slow down?" the Count yelled, aghast at the very idea. "This is life in the fast lane . . ." That one sticks.

Later, Don would lament the fact "Life in the Fast Lane" turned "into a celebration of exactly what we were trying to warn them about. Everybody's got cocaine now, no matter how shitty it is. I could hardly listen to that song when we were recording it, because I was getting high a lot at the time and the song made me ill." He added: "We were trying to paint a picture that cocaine wasn't that great. It turns on you." The fans heard it differently.

Joe brings them "Pretty Maids All in a Row" all on his own-some. Everyone is shocked. Not an ounce of bravado, no showboating guitar, this is a poignant, musically lush pop ballad that might have come from the pen of Todd Rundgren, all swooning-harmony vocals and a silk-smooth melody guaranteed to bring glass tears to your cocaine eyes.

Randy Meisner comes in with "Try and Love Again," his own almost unbearably autobiographical ballad: Randy is going through a divorce and feeling more uncertain than ever about his place in the band. It all comes out in one of his most expressive musical moments. Only Randy, man.

They take a riff of Felder's that he calls "Iron Lung" and turn it into a tune they rename "Victim of Love" after J.D.'s throwaway comment that "being in love is like being the victim of a car wreck . . ."

They rehearse them, work them up, wonder what it is they've got. Go again—and again. By March 1976, they are ready to record.

Bill Szymczyk is in the producer's chair again. They want Bill, need that tougher edge, want him even more now they've got Joe Walsh, but Bill still wants to record in Miami, at Criteria, and you know, *Hotel California* is what it says on the sleeve—a California

album—in fact *the* California album. Starting it in Miami seems . . .
off. Don moans but sucks it up, and they rent a house near the
beach. Big place, barefoot servants, the best coke in America. They
want everything to be *just right* for this one.

"At this stage in their career, the Eagles were pursuing perfection," said Szymczyk, looking back, "and in the process of editing
I'd hear, 'Well, see if you can do that, Coach'—which was my nickname back then. This might refer to replacing one drum fill with
another fill that was a little better, so there'd be an edit at the front
and an edit at the end. That's the kind of perfection we were dealing with."

Once the basic tracks for "Hotel California" had been assembled, it took nearly three days to record the closing guitar solos,
Felder and Walsh trading ouch-hot licks side by side in the control
room in a hypnotic slow dance of aching arpeggio and raw, bleeding emotion.

Felder had gone in thinking he and Joe would simply improvise,
go for the burn, see what shakes from the tree. Henley and Frey had
other ideas. "Joe and I started jamming," Felder recalled, when
Don leapt up. "No, no, stop. It's not right!"

Felder stopped. "I said, 'What do you mean it's not right?' And
he said, 'You've got to play it just like the demo.' Only problem was,
I did that demo a year earlier. I couldn't even remember what was
on it." Felder was forced to call his housekeeper in Malibu and get
her to play the original cassette recording down the phone. "We
recorded it," Felder shook his head, "and I had to sit in Miami and
play exactly what was on the demo."

Don Henley is OTT tetchy, crawling with creative tension and
pent-up feeling. He and Glenn get into a fight before they leave for
Miami and Don says fuck this and goes to stay with Irving.

Glenn now gets closer to Joe and that fuels Don's paranoia. Does
he really like Joe? Does he really want him in the band? Then

there's the situation with Randy. The dude seems to have checked out, spinning in a vicious circle in which his only relief is to withdraw, causing Don and Glenn to sideline him even more.

"Success changed everything," Randy would later reflect. "We were real close up until the year of *Hotel California*. I just didn't feel like I was part of the group at that point." Randy with his long, straight girl's hair and soft, warm eyes. "When we first started, we were really close, like brothers. We'd sit around, smoke a doob together, drink a beer, and have a good time. By 1976, we couldn't sit down like guys anymore. It was all business. The friendships were kind of gone at that point . . ."

SOMEONE SHOULD HAVE *thrown an arm around Randy, told him straight. This is what bands are, man. This is what they become when they start making the multi-zeros. You can't be squeamish about it, not while you're still cashing the checks. Don't forget, this ain't just any band, Randy. This is the biggest band in America, with the highest-selling record of the year, about to make an album that will take everyone to places very few people ever get to visit. So, you know, maybe don't worry so much about the bullshit; quit whining and start fucking feeling it, you know?*

Because this is history, brother. This is art.

You are playing with the Gods.

25.

Eagles Poker

The house they rent in Miami is not just any house. It is 461 Ocean Boulevard, where Eric Clapton stayed while he made his '74 "comeback" record, an album he named after the place. It's in Golden Beach, which is actually a tiny island between the intracoastal waterway and the Atlantic Ocean, a luxury-first millionaires' habitat just like the California enclaves that Glenn and Don have grown accustomed to.

The big house at 461 is right on the beach, a white stucco mansion with glittering ocean views and towering palms in its manicured gardens. There they can kick back, drink beer, snort coke, play touch football out on the sand—and when they're not doing that, get on with the serious business at Criteria.

From the start, Glenn and Don set impossibly high standards, like they're trying to surpass the *Greatest Hits* record at a single stroke. Applying the laser-like focus only high-grade cocaine can bring. "Whether it was engineering, writing, singing, playing, tracking, or editing, it was all done under the most intense scrutiny," Felder revealed. "We often wound up erasing performances that were fiery, motivated, and inspired. If a take had a tiny human glitch, one note out of tune, even if all the rest sounded fine, we'd junk it and do it again."

The pressure cranks. Sessions start between 2 and 3 p.m. every day and extend on through the night into the next morning. "One by one the others would arrive, bleary-eyed, disheveled, sniffing, or coughing, suffering from the excesses of the previous night."

Downtime gets filled with games of "Eagles poker"—played with a sixty-five-card deck containing a fifth suit of cards, allowing for five of a kind, which becomes dangerous as thousands of dollars change hands and grievances begin to blister and burst.

The five members of the band also have to reconfigure the odds. For it is now that a clear power shift in the relationship between Glenn and Don begins to take place. Now, suddenly, it's more Don than Glenn.

It causes friction, but even Glenn is beginning to realize that Don is the man with the plan, the voice of the hits, and that he is winning their psychic struggle for control of the band. He is tetchy, moody, tense—typical Don. He is driving them onward toward his vision for *Hotel California*, a lucid, waking dream of the kind of audio perfection achieved by very few artists.

Don wants to capitalize on this moment where everything he has worked for is now happening, where long-held fantasies are suddenly, tantalizingly, within reach. He drives them on, seemingly oblivious to the collateral damage. Don sings lead on five of the eight songs that have vocals. Then bans everyone from the control room while he does it. Glenn sings lead on just one.

"It became an agonizingly slow process," shuddered Felder. "Taking five times as long to make the record as it should have with tempers being lost along the way."

They monster the drugs, float in the booze, do their best to ride it out in the studio. Someone invents a game called "cut out man," where they buy piles of girlie magazines and wrestling publications and cut out various pictures to make a story that they put up on a pinboard.

Black Sabbath hire an adjoining studio to make a record called *Technical Ecstasy*. They're even bigger coke fiends and booze hounds than the Eagles and they make a fuck of a lot more noise. Several times Don and Bill have to abandon versions of "The Last Resort" because the tapes pick up the dark, sonic boom of Sabbath issuing from next door.

When the Eagles finally vacate and Sabbath move into the main room, Sabbath bassist Geezer Butler says: "Before we could start recording, we had to scrape all the cocaine out of the mixing board. I think they'd left about a pound of cocaine in the board."

They record "Victim of Love" live in the studio as a five-piece, except for the vocals (they're so pleased with this that the run-out grooves of the album's first pressing are engraved "V.O.L. is a five-piece live"). Felder, who came up with the initial idea, is supposed to get his first lead vocal on the song, but Henley gives that idea the thumbs down. "He sang it dozens of times over the space of a week, over and over. It simply did not come up to band standards." Glenn agreed: "Don Felder, for all of his talents as a guitar player, was not a singer."

It's Irving who has to take Felder to dinner and break the news: Felder tells Irving it's not fair. That he feels that Henley has just taken the song from him. Irving gives it some there-there, a little coke and sympathy. Then points Felder back to what Henley had actually done with "his" song. "There was no way to argue with my vocal versus Don Henley's vocal."

No shit, Sherlock.

Glenn had said he wanted the record to be filmic. Well, it was certainly taking as long as a Hollywood blockbuster to make. For Don, it was *The Godfather Part II*, everything about it made for the big screen, as epic in its creation as in its realization. Despite the endless night hours in the studio and the relationships stretched taut by his determination to make something immortal, Don Henley is in his element.

Reflecting on the months of toil, Don tells *Rolling Stone* they got saddled "with that perfectionist label" because they were always looking "to up our game." If the Eagles were perceived as seekers of some sort of musical perfection there were "no apologies to be made for that." He had always seen the simple brutalism of punk rock as "a cover-up for lack of ability."

He did concede, however, that "obsessive perfectionism can be oppressive, stifling, paralyzing. Never let the great be the enemy of the good. We understood that. There should always be—and will be—a wart or a little clutter here and there. Life is messy, and rock 'n' roll is part of life."

Now that school was out, even the others, still hurting from the months of doing exactly what they were told by Don, could only stand back and marvel. In its ten songs, beginning with "Hotel California" and ending with "The Last Resort," it was clear this was the Eagles' masterpiece, a shimmering mirage in which you could actually see the ghosts gliding ominously through the neon ooze of small-hours LA.

A far more convincing concept album than the overly contrived *Desperado*, nearly half a century later *Hotel California* is now rightly regarded as the quintessential late-seventies American musical text, a true document of a time when the ultimate Hollywood highs and subterranean LA lows were blurred beyond recognition, blinded by white-powdered double visions, and buried beneath greenback mountains. A truly gothic American fable.

The recording finally completed to his satisfaction, Henley turns his attention to the album sleeve, which would create its own art, its own enduring mysteries. John Kosh, a Brit from London known professionally just by his surname, had designed the cover of *Abbey Road*, worked for the Beatles' Apple label, and handled John and Yoko's "War Is Over" campaign before moving out to LA in '73, where he art-directed sleeves for Jimmy Buffett and Bob Dylan.

Don briefs him on exactly what he wants from the *Hotel California* shoot. Specifically, a hotel with "a slightly sinister edge." Kosh knows exactly where to go to find one of those. He shoots an exterior of the Beverly Hills Hotel at dusk, using a cherry picker to elevate the photographer David Armstrong sixty feet above Sunset Boulevard to get the shot.

For the interior, Kosh scouts sleazier places that he can mock up. He settles on the lobby of a fleapit named the Lido Apartments on the corner of Yucca and Wilcox. He fills its cavernous space, all-white arches and black chandeliers, with friends and acquaintances: "I want a collection of people from all walks of life," Henley has told him. "It's people on the edge, on the fringes of society . . ."

For the inner gatefold, the band stand surrounded by this cast of characters, the most mysterious of whom is a figure, hidden in shadow and standing on the balcony looking down on the scene below. It doesn't take long after the album is released for rumors to start that the figure is Anton LaVey—furthering the sold-their-souls-to-Satan line of inquiry. But as Koch pointed out, "Nobody knows what the sinister figure lurking in the balcony window is doing—or who he is. I assume he must have been a benign spirit, as *Hotel California* went platinum immediately—and then some!"

Hotel California is released on December 8, 1976. It becomes the second consecutive Eagles record to ship platinum, reaching Number 4 on the *Billboard* Top 200 in the week of release and hitting Number 1 for the first time a month later. It will spend eight weeks there on its way to selling almost six million copies in its first year alone.

The first single is "New Kid in Town," the only track on the album with lead vocals by Glenn, which also goes to Number 1, at the end of February, its sumptuous harmonies and killer chorus belying a tale every bit as bitter as it sounds sweet. Like a John Lennon song sung by Paul McCartney.

Then the full-length version of "Hotel California" is released as a single in February while "New Kid" is still at Number 1; Don and Glenn flat-out refuse to let it be edited down into a more radio-friendly format. It is vital that all six minutes thirty seconds of it be kept fully intact, they insist. If American radio didn't want to play it because of that, that was their loss. And they were proved right. It hit Number 1 for one week in April and for the rest of all eternity on radio.

Only this time no one is fooled about the real intention behind the song. Where "New Kid" is positively drowsy in its exposition, "Hotel California" immediately assumes the status of a "Stairway to Heaven" or a "Bohemian Rhapsody," minus the virtuoso grandstanding, closer in spirit and execution to the cinematic musical vistas of Ennio Morricone, perhaps, or John Barry. This is musical statement writ large, a new connection to a place at once more real and more mystical. It goes on to win the Grammy Award for Record of the Year, but everybody already acknowledges its attainment long before that plastic accolade.

According to Henley, the fifth Eagles album of original material was the result of the momentum steadily been building since the very start. He acknowledged their worldwide sales had also been boosted by "the enormous and somewhat unexpected success" of *Their Greatest Hits (1971–1975)*. By *Hotel California* "the circumstances couldn't have been better; the world was ready and waiting." It certainly was.

You can say that again—and Don will. People loved it. People bought it. But did the world truly understand it? That was the question Don really wanted answered. It was an album filled with mystery and imagination; it had Glenn's "perfect ambiguity." Yet while it was a giant commercial hit, *Hotel California* was not the resounding critical success Don had imagined it would be.

As if to prove a point, *Rolling Stone* give their January '77 cover to Jackson Browne, not the Eagles. Their album review, by Charley Walters, does not run until the February issue, and begins: "*Hotel California* showcases both the best and worst tendencies of Los Angeles situated rock, but more strikingly, its lyrics present a convincing and unflattering portrait of the milieu itself."

Well, uh, thanks, I guess.

Meanwhile, longtime Eagles skeptic Robert Christgau writes grudgingly in the *Village Voice*: "Speaking strictly as a nonfan, I'd grant that this is their most substantial if not their most enjoyable LP—they couldn't have written any of the songs on side one, or even the pretentious and condescending 'The Last Resort,' without caring about their California theme down deep."

Frey hits back when he speaks to Barbara Charone in an exclusive interview he and Henley give, deliberately and provocatively, to *Crawdaddy!* one of *Rolling Stone*'s competitors.

They rail against the music press who had considered the Eagles "those West Coast assholes." Frey says, "What they want to do is be on that hipper-than-hip trip. So they have this negative attitude. What they hate is the individual, not the music."

Still, the accusations hit home. Reviewers who pour scorn on the band are added to a "punch on sight" list. A list that grows very long very quickly.

Don also uses the *Crawdaddy* article to shoot back at the critics. "People talk about Jackson's lyrics, but they don't seem to talk about ours. It's not that they don't look at us as good songwriters, but they just seem to emphasize the ones that were hits rather than the ones that weren't." He added: "I think our songs have more to do with the streets than Bruce Springsteen's."

It's easy to feel for Don. He has just released an album that, even now, in 1977, he intuits will outlive the band and its members, that will take its place in the pantheon of twentieth-century American art. And he has done it by playing a complex game with ideas of time and place. The Eagles are an American band, a Californian band, but by being overt about the place, by using it as a metaphor for their wider situation and the condition of contemporary fame—haunted by strangers and familiar ghosts—he has transmuted "California music" from nebulous label to a symbol for what life has become in the latter half of the American century.

Peered at through that lens, it is easy to see why snarking critics and blithe dismissals of the band's inestimable ability to write chart-topping melodies made Don and Glenn so pissed. They are already major-league rock stars. Now they are bona fide artists, too. They are rich beyond counting, famous beyond measure, at the peak of everything. All by their own hands.

One thing they know for sure. It's all downhill from here.

26.

The Nest among the Stars

Exactly one week before the release of *Hotel California*, a new band from England—a frightening-looking bunch of gobby, cigarette-chewing youths called the Sex Pistols—made their first TV appearance, promoting their debut single, "Anarchy in the UK."

It was on Thames TV's flagship early-evening magazine show, *Today*, broadcast live in the Greater London area every weeknight since 1968. In an age when the UK had just three TV channels, none of which broadcast anything during the day and very rarely anything past midnight, the *Today* show was a biggie. Scheduled for broadcast each evening when most family households were sitting down together to have their "tea" in front of the telly, *Today* entertained a near-captive nightly audience of over ten million.

Last-minute replacements for Queen, who'd bailed after Freddie Mercury needed emergency dental surgery, the Sex Pistols had brought with them an entourage, including then-unknown future punk-goth spider-queen Siouxsie Sioux. As was the norm in live TV back then, to keep everyone happy while they waited their turn, the production crew kept them all fed with booze.

The show's host, fifty-three-year-old Bill Grundy, also sauntered over with a full glass in his hand. Grundy was a heavyweight figure in British television. He had fronted coverage of elections and the main political party conferences. On the night of President

Kennedy's assassination, he had been handpicked to anchor the late-night news special. Grundy was also a producer, working on the award-winning history series *All Our Yesterdays* and the fearless current affairs strand *World in Action*.

Conducting a live, three-minute spot with a bunch of penniless pop hopefuls that had never been on TV before was meat and drink for a man of Grundy's depthless talents and looong experience. Wriggling with earthwormy self-assurance, Bill was more than happy to join in with a free drink. He'd already had a few anyway, as was Bill's wont. This was the last item of the show—what the heck!

"They're as drunk as I am," Bill woozily declared, eleven seconds into the piece. It was all jolly convivial. Bill guzzled his drink and ogled the girls in their skin-tight punk attire, swastika armband to the fore, and the Pistols' singer, a strangely childlike weirdo with orange hair and the farcical name Johnny Rotten, sat there staring marble-eyed into space.

When the band's guitarist Steve Jones responded to being asked what they had done with their reported £30,000 record company advance by saying: "We fucking spent it, 'int we?" and Johnny Rotten muttered the word "shit" under his breath, a disgruntled Grundy turned his attention back to the girls.

Teased by a dyed-blonde Siouxsie Sioux who told him coyly, "I always wanted to meet you," Grundy responded, "Did you really? We'll meet afterward, shall we?"

Cue: music history in the making.

Jones to Grundy: "You dirty sod. You dirty old man."

Grundy to Jones: "Well, keep going, chief. Keep going. Go on. You've got another five seconds. Say something outrageous!"

Jones: "You dirty bastard."

Grundy: "Go on, again."

Jones: "You dirty fucker."

Grundy: "What a clever boy!"

Jones: "What a fucking rotter."

The front page of the following morning's *Daily Mirror*—then the UK's biggest-selling daily tabloid—led with the story under the now famous headline: THE FILTH AND THE FURY! In the story they demanded to know: "Who are these punks?"

The front page of the *Daily Express* (God, Queen, country) ran with: FURY AT FILTHY TV CHAT. While the august *Daily Telegraph* finessed the message into: 4-LETTER WORDS ROCK TV.

There were two seismic outcomes from this media feeding frenzy. The first was that Thames Television suspended Grundy and, though he was later reinstated, the interview effectively ended his career.

The second: the birth of punk rock.

As Jones astutely described it in his memoir, *Lonely Boy*, "Grundy was the big dividing line in the Sex Pistols' story. Before it, we were all about the music, but from then on it was all about the media. In some ways it was our finest moment, but in others it was the beginning of the end."

There was one other major consequence: a new ground zero in the history of pop music where stadium-surfing "dinosaurs" (as Rotten scornfully branded them) like the Eagles—and the Stones, Led Zep, Rod Stewart, Elton, Queen, and anyone else who'd had the temerity to come before the Sex Pistols—would first be discredited then hastily discarded, like waving a bad smell out of a hotel suite the morning after another morning after.

There was nothing peaceful or easy about the Sex Pistols and the dozens of ultra-attitudinal punk groups that sprang up overnight in the wake of the Grundy TV massacre. When London Conservative councilor Bernard Brook Partridge declared the Pistols to be "unbelievably nauseating," it only burnished their rebel-rocker image still further. "They are the antithesis of humankind," Brook Partridge thundered. "I would like to see somebody dig a very, very large, exceedingly deep hole and drop the whole bloody lot down it."

You couldn't buy publicity like that. The Eagles couldn't, that's for sure.

Meanwhile, back in LA, Fleetwood Mac also released a fiery new single that month: "Go Your Own Way," a song as brimming over with vitriol as the Pistols' song, but with a spoonful-of-sugar melody and soaring harmony vocals that belied the very real emotion behind the lyrics. It was also wildly popular, quickly climbing the US singles charts until it peaked at Number 10 in March—the first Fleetwood Mac single ever to reach the US Top 10. By then, "New Kid in Town" had already gone to Number 1, while *Hotel California* still nestled atop the albums chart. But only for another week, before being transplanted by the new Fleetwood Mac album, *Rumours*.

That was on April 2. For the next two weeks *Rumours* sat prettily at Number 1. On April 16, *Hotel California* went back to Number 1—its fourth time to do so—and stayed there for another five weeks. Then on May 21, *Rumours* replaced it at the top again. And stayed there for the next twenty-eight weeks—bar one week in July when *Barry Manilow Live* hit the top. *Rumours* would continue on at Number 1 right into January 1978, when it was finally dislodged from the top by the disco, hit-laden *Saturday Night Fever* soundtrack, which didn't move again until July.

Just as the Eagles had finally left Earth's orbit and found their own cosmology to preside over, they suddenly felt under siege. On one hand, denounced by a next-generation breed of artists—punk in the UK, new wave in the US—that saw them as the enemy: super rich, super cokey, super out of touch with reality, as evoked by the anti-hippy stance of the new street kidz with their short, spiky hair and no-flare jeans.

On the other hand, being beaten at their own game by their closest musical rivals, Fleetwood Mac. The disco bullshit Glenn and Don didn't get too bent out of shape about. Everyone knew that stuff was garbage, fish food for the water-breathers. But the disdain being heaped on the Eagles by the new punk rockers—and most especially, their new-wave supporting music critic acolytes preaching the punk gospel—rubbed them both raw. They had been battling for credibility since the very first Eagles record. Now, just as they reached the apotheosis of a monumentally successful career, it was being denied them again—and again for all the wrong reasons.

Glenn hated punk on principle, the same way he'd hated the New York Dolls and all that other "fake crap," glam-rock shizzola. Ironically, Glenn was the most punk of anybody in the Eagles; he didn't favor the leather jacket, but he certainly had the scowl and the razor-sharp put-downs.

Don was more sensitive. "We were beginning to see press articles about how we were passé," he grumbled. "Those kinds of jabs were part of the inspiration" for a new song he was working on called "The Long Run," its acid chorus: "Who is gonna make it / We'll find out in the long run . . ."

What really rankled though was the success of Fleetwood Mac.

Fleetwood Fucking Mac, man!

Are you fucking kidding me, dude?

Even as the band are out on the longest, most lucrative tour of their lives, the Fleetwood Mac thing shadows them: the easy comparisons, the critical Venn-diagramming, the subliminal suggestion that all the really heavy rumors could be tracked back to a certain occult hotel in California.

The Fleetwood Mac thing haunts Don, especially. He pores over the numbers with Irving: *Hotel California* is certified platinum in its first week of release, sells almost ten million copies in its first year of existence, and goes to Number 1 in six countries; *Rumours* sells over ten million worldwide in its first *month* and also goes to Number 1 in six countries. There are three singles from *Hotel*

California, two of which go to number 1 in America, the third of which gets to Number 11. There are four singles released from *Rumours*, one of which goes to Number 1 but all four of which hit the Top 10.

At the 20th Annual Grammy Awards, in February 1978, hosted by John Denver and broadcast live on network TV from the Shrine Auditorium in LA, the single, "Hotel California" won Record of the Year, but *Rumours* won Album of the Year. But that was okay, actually, because "New Kid in Town" also scored a Grammy—for Best Arrangement for Voices.

Sports nut Glenn Frey sees it like this. Final score: two for the Eagles, one for the Mac. Only Glenn's not there to enjoy the victory. None of the Eagles are there. They have *refused* to go. Never mind that maybe thirty-five million people will watch the show. Fuck that shit.

Irving had showed them the way, refusing requests for the band to attend or perform at the ceremony unless a win was guaranteed. Today, with viewing figures for the Grammys not even half that 1978 number, they could probably make that kind of deal. Back then it was unthinkable. There were no Eagles there that night at the Shrine to collect their trophies. Confirming the growing impression of the Eagles as an overentitled, overindulged group of rich assholes.

TV balladeer and most recent Grammy host Andy Williams collects the award for them, while Glenn and Don and the others sit at home watching. Irving calls it "one of the great moments of rock 'n' roll." As the media pick up on the Eagles' no-show and the reason for it, Don tells the *LA Times*, "The whole idea of a contest to see who is best doesn't appeal to us."

Don already knows who is best, thanks all the same.

27.

The Party Plane

"It's very romantic," Don says of the record that spends all of 1977 drilling into the hearts and minds of American youth, taking them to that dreamlike, haunted place that is the real-life Hotel California. "It gets a hold on you. You love it and you hate it. It's a whore, but it's a fertile mother. LA to me is what America is all about."

The tour, man. Don't forget the tour. They started out again in March with two sold-out shows at the 15,000-capacity Nassau Coliseum on Long Island. Went straight from there to Madison Square Garden, the big one, 20k crazy. Hey, man, get a picture of the band's name in lights above those big fuckin' Madison Square doors!

The rest is all Lears and presidential suites, armed security, and fawning music bizzy himbos. Girls that get it and dealers that give it. They can't move without it any more. They don't want to.

Back in the UK they do four sold-out nights at Wembley Arena, London's biggest indoor venue. They do multiple nights everywhere now, including two sell-outs at Bingley Hall in Stafford, the biggest indoor venue in the country, able to hold 15,000 if everyone breathes in and keeps their hands to themselves.

In America that summer it's all stadiums all the time. Helicopters. Luxury backstage quarters, tent town for rock aristos, everyone in their own plush, one-night-only dungeon.

Millions of fans buy tickets and T-shirts and beers and a rapidly expanding line of official merchandise that makes so much money each night the roadies have to stamp the bundles of cash into plastic trash bins with their feet. Like crushing grapes, only no mess. Credit cards were still ancillary. Nice warm cash was still the norm.

Henley struggled with the guilt of it all, poor guy: "You know that you don't deserve it. You get too much money and too much of everything when you're too young, and it comes really quickly. And it messed me up for a while. I grew up in a town of 2,400 people. My dad didn't believe in credit cards, he paid cash for everything. And suddenly I had a gold American Express card, which I was embarrassed to take out of my wallet because I'd never done that before."

The new stage set had been designed by Ken Graham and featured a giant projection of the David Alexander photograph of the Beverly Hills Hotel before which the band would emerge in silhouette, as in a crazy half-dream. The show no longer opened with the a cappella "Seven Bridges Road" that had long begun every Eagles gig. Now, Don Felder stepped forward to play the opening starlit guitar chords to "Hotel California" . . .

Cue: pandemonium. Every single time.

"Every night there would be thunderous applause and this incredible noise rising out of the darkness," Felder recalled. "Don's voice would float out from behind the drum kit, strangely disembodied, leading the fans along that dark desert highway . . ."

For two hours each night, those who hold a ticket are transported to that place, the one Don Henley conjured from thin air, the one that they yearn for through the long California haze of 1977. Don's voice, Felder's guitar, Walsh's solo, Glenn and Randy joined on the eternal, ethereal harmonies . . . it's all there right in front of them, and beyond it, the hotel itself, gleaming in Ken Graham's head-swimming lighting design, a permanent, moody

Los Angeles twilight where the palms stand skeletal against the sky and the strange, empty towers of the building wink seductively, drawing them inward toward the magic that is all around and now within them.

Don Felder gets as close as anyone to defining exactly what this magic is. "Whenever anyone asks me what the Hotel California is about," he says, "I tell them it's whatever you want it to be . . ."

It's magic up there on that stage each and every night, but the other twenty-two hours of the day . . . The Learjet, aka "the Party Plane," is forever in the sky and has battle lines drawn within it. Don has his quarters, Glenn has his. Each has their "friendly" section of the road crew, employees, and hangers on.

Between them stands Irving. This three-legged stool is now the established power base of the Eagles. It's Irving's job to make sure those three legs stay the same length, keep the whole thing in balance.

Nobody is taking it easy anymore. As Marc Eliot later testifies: "To many veterans of the road crew, the extent of the band's self-indulgence seemed worse than ever." Henley and Frey were no longer brother artists perched in the Eagles' Nest polishing up gold. They were now "constantly in each other's faces, their conflicts over the band's leadership fueled by ever increasing amounts of cocaine."

Things don't so much boil over as never stop hubble-bubbling. Especially when the road crew are hanging with the band all the time, playing cards, playing softball, sharing the drugs, getting high on the bosses' supply. The head electrician Joe Berry tells Eliot: "Nobody could miss the 'Glenn and Don show.' By now what went on between them was more entertaining than the actual performance. They'd shout at each other, argue over the slightest thing, threaten to kick each other's ass, and sooner or later one of them would storm off the stage."

The crew nicknamed Henley "Massa Don" he was such a pain in the ass. It's Don's way or the highway, baby.

He now traveled with his own special king-size bed and mattress. "The tour seamstress made a special cover for it, with handles, to make it easier to pack it in the truck every night," said Berry. "It went everywhere and never once got used, because no hotel would allow us to bring it in."

Don loses it with road manager Richie Fernandez when the Party Plane touches down in Montreal one night and the special-floor hotel suites are double booked. Don complains bitterly to Irving. Irving fires Richie. Tells him he was going to do it anyway because he was so fucking stoned, he almost got them busted as they passed through Canadian customs.

Massa Don and Massa Irving.

With long-serving and always loyal Richie out, guilty of crossing the increasingly blurred white lines between band and crew, between the rest of the band and Don and Glenn, between the nest of stars and the earthly realm, the crew give the tour a new nickname—"The Prison California."

The good times end with Richie. No more "third encore" parties every night, no more handing out 3D button badges and passes to the hot girls in the audience, no more getting stoned with the band, no more love 'em and Lear 'em. No more F.U.N.

"All of the decisions concerning the operation of the tour were now being made by the triumvirate of Irving, Don, and Glenn," complained Randy Meisner, now occupying a space one above the crew and, as the most detached and conflicted member of the Eagles, the hyena at the rear of the pack.

"The only problem was, Don and Glenn were no longer speaking directly to one another. If you needed to get something resolved, even other members of the band, you had to go through their individual road captains. Glenn had Jimmy Collins; Don had Tony Taibi."

This was a power struggle that Glenn knew he could no longer win, however. As Felder observed, "We suddenly had two presidents vying for the same position. Don would usually back down in the end, knowing that to push Glenn too far would be unwise, but when they had one of their cocaine-induced arguments, the clouds descended . . . Don would sit silently in his part of the Learjet and Glenn in his."

When you think about it—and Don does, because Don can think about almost nothing else—the human brain is not wired to get everything it wants, when it wants, all the time. It is not wired to handle extreme and overwhelming amounts of money and fame and adulation, and sex and drugs and no pain whatsoever.

Don knows this because all he has to do is look around. Every band that this has ever happened to—from the Stones to the Doors on down—has suffered its casualties from all of this excess. He just has to talk to Stevie to hear about the same madness in Fleetwood Mac. At least the Eagles aren't all fucking one another. That's one complication he doesn't have to worry about.

But it is madness. Madness and war . . . War with Glenn . . . He remembers when this band started. Four equal parts, best buds swearing on their lives that if any of them left, that would be the end for all of them.

But that's not real life, not how things play out. Right now, in 1977, it is Don's crystal vision, Don's after-midnight bias, Don's post-everything aesthetic that out of all of the artists working today is the one that chimes best with the times, is the one that fires the collective imagination of young America.

Don is the chosen one among the chosen ones, and he knows this now, so no fucking wonder he gets tetchy, no wonder he likes things his own way, because when he awakes late in the p.m. each day, he realizes how tenuous and unlikely this whole enterprise is, how glancingly rare and how fleeting. That you have to hold on to it while you can, but holding on comes at a price, a price both physical and psychological.

It's why one of his shoulders hangs an inch and a half lower than the other. The drumming does that. The drumming and the coke and the constant stress and tension, contracting his muscles, forcing them to snap his neck and shoulders in a vice, giving him endless headaches.

It's why he employs a masseur and has the road crew carry that damn bed everywhere. Because if Don doesn't make the show, there is no fucking show, geddit? And nobody gets paid.

Everyone is suffering. Glenn's still struggling with the chronic gut ache and the nasal nightmares. Randy's nursing a nasty ulcer. Felder is doing too much blow for a health freak with a yoga-loving wife and two young kids waiting for him back home. Fuck it, they're *all* doing too much blow, they're *all* drinking too goddamn much, they're *all* trying to make the endless party last just one more night. One more night when they don't have to think about this *stuff* all of the time.

There is not a single day of this godforsaken tour that runs on and on for an entire year, not a single fucking night when Don Henley is not thinking about himself and the Eagles, about how they can sound better, write better, look better, live better, make even more money, get even bigger, become even more famous.

High up in that nest of stars, where the nightmares still find him. So yeah, you will have to forgive Don if he is bad-tempered and irascible and strung extra tight tonight. Like you will have to forgive the others for acting like assholes, taking out their resentments in childish, passive-aggressive ways. This is just how they get through.

Glenn with his cruel nicknames—not for Don, of course, not to his face, but for the crew, even for Felder, who he calls "Spot" once he catches sight of a small bald patch on the back of his head. Glenn

is a good mimic, and he puts it to evil effect, ripping into his chosen
target with a deadly, scornful wit.

Only kidding, man! (Fuck you, asshole.)

Then there's Randy Meisner and Joe Walsh, both big fans of
Chuck Berry. Joe thinks it's cute and Randy always smiles when
Joe duckwalks across the stage à la Chuck during his guitar solos,
which pisses Don off big time, because there isn't any duckwalking
in the Hotel California, did he have to spell it out?

Joe laughs it off. Joe finds everything funny, man. But Randy,
who no longer kids himself the band is as much his as it is Don's,
burns up inside. He does not appreciate "the star trip that Don is
on . . ."

It all comes to a head when the tour gets to the steaming South.
Memphis time, my brother, Tennessee. They all get excited because
they are scheduled to visit Graceland for an audience with the King.
The new princelings of American rock, hoping to be anointed by
Elvis himself.

But at the last minute one of the Memphis Mafia calls and
cancels—the King is too unwell to receive visitors.

The band are bummed out. Was he really ill or just couldn't be
bothered?

They suspect the latter. Until the shock news comes in just weeks
later that Elvis has died. Fat and fucked at forty-two, found face
down on the floor of his gold and leather private bathroom. The
one with its own waiting area for guests.

They are in Cincinnati when they hear the sad news. They have
just sold out the 50,000-plus Riverfront Stadium. Randy, Joe, and
Don Felder drown their sorrows, get high, and Randy finally cracks,
tells Don and Joe that he is sick of Glenn's and Don's bullshit, sick
of feeling like an also-ran in his own band, has had it up to here.

His stomach ulcer is giving him hell, he says, he is so goddamned
tired after months and years on the road while his wife and

children are still a million miles away back home in Nebraska. This is it for me, man.

Joe and Don try to talk Randy down off the ledge, try and stop him from doing something stoopid. They even joke that the three of them should form a band of their own, and Randy wonders if that isn't exactly what they should do. Don and Joe laugh and say, no, that is exactly what they shouldn't do.

Two nights later Randy has the flu as well as the stomach ulcer.

He is drinking and his throat is sore. For months on end he's been singing night after night, and each night he's expected to close out the encores with "Take It to the Limit," climaxing in that final, endlessly warbling high note, one that only Randy in the band can sing, the note that sends the crowds delirious, lone spotlight at the ready.

They are in the wings and about to go out for the final encores when Randy tells Glenn and Don that he won't be singing it tonight; in fact he wouldn't be going back out onstage at all. Glenn listens to all this and is beside himself. What the fuck is Randy whining about now, man?

"You pussy," Glenn hisses. Randy takes a swing at him, Glenn fights back, then they're going at it and have to be separated by some of the crew.

The backstage cops go to break it up. Don gives them the face and tells them: "Stay out of this. This is personal and it's private. *Real* fucking private." The cops back off.

Henley would later claim that Randy had simply been too wasted to sing the damn song. That Randy had "been up all-night doing drugs with two chicks in a hotel room." That in itself was no capital offense on a rock tour in the seventies, but Randy always seemed to be sick, or threatening to leave the band, complaining it was destroying his marriage. "There was always something . . ."

The irony is that Glenn has far more patience with Randy than Don does. He tries and tries with the guy, but Randy has become his own worst enemy. Don sees elements of self-sabotage in the way Randy carries himself, knowing that if he acts out for long enough, the decision he cannot bring himself to make will eventually be made for him.

Taking a swing at Glenn makes that decision easy for all concerned. Although Randy apologizes a few days later and the tour limps on for a few more weeks, it is *over*. A day after the final show, Irving issues the briefest of statements to the press that says Randy Meisner has left the Eagles due to "exhaustion."

Yeah, right. Exhaustion with Glenn and Don. Exhaustion with fucking Irving.

Exhausted by the Gods and their nest in the stars . . .

28.

Interlude:
Irving and Randy

Irving tells Randy, don't worry, baby, he'll manage his solo career. Randy says, sure. Asylum has a leaving member clause that it exercises for Randy's debut solo album, called simply Randy Meisner and released in June 1978. The record features no new material from Randy; instead there's a dull reworking of "Take It to the Limit," one so-so song by J.D. and Glenn called "Bad Man," and a bunch of makeweights.

Randy plays bass on just one tune, a cover of the Drifters' "Save the Last Dance for Me." Irving manages to get "Bad Man" onto the soundtrack of a film called FM, but the album doesn't sell, and Irving doesn't book a lot of dates for his first solo tour because they're not selling tickets, and Randy becomes paranoid and convinces himself that Glenn and Don are secretly working with Irving to blackball him.

Randy confronts Irving, who, according to Randy, takes him into a corridor and yells at him to get the fuck out and never come back.

Irving, unsurprisingly, has a different take: "He couldn't get a deal or a play date because he couldn't put asses in seats," he shrugged. "He was unbookable. I may not be the most diplomatic guy in the world, but I did try to help Randy at first, until his self-destructiveness became too much."

Now it's over for Randy. The things he never really wanted but that came to him anyway are now gone again.

He will release six more solo albums between 1980 and 2005 and only two of them will chart, and then only in the country charts, and then only modestly. He will fall back into that comforting kind of half-world fame that he always craved, while the work he did with the Eagles will mean that money should never be a problem again.

It's easy to look at Randy Meisner and wonder what he lost, especially when some of the bad things in life head his way. But really, as the next few years unwind, the question is best turned on its head.

What have the Eagles lost now that Randy has gone?

"He was a wonderful Midwestern guy with a great heart and a loving soul," Don Felder recalled. "Randy Meisner was a very gentle soul," agreed Henry Diltz. "Pisces. A quiet and friendly guy. No aggressive vibe at all. Very sweet. He was so there and open."

The all-American band has lost another measure of its original bloodline, its direct connection to the heart of the Midwest, the man who put the "easy" into "Take It Easy."

In the non-pejorative sense, Randy represents the simple life—a beer, a joint, some music on a Saturday night, the kind of life that the Eagles set out to write about and sell. And then somewhere down the line, left behind, shed like the skin of an old rattlesnake, transitioning into something new and darker, something that Don took and turned into the Hotel California, a place that became the antithesis of what Randy Meisner was about.

So Randy got sad and self-destructive, and that gorgeous pure voice was gone and then so was he . . .

"I thought, my God it's taking its toll," Randy says years later. "I don't want to end up hating anybody . . . I wish I could have left in a different way, but how are you gonna be nice when you leave?"

It was a good question.

29.

Can't Tell You Why

Irving, Don, and Glenn replace Randy with his shadow.

This long thin shadow has a name: Timothy B. Schmit. Tim is a true Eagle in that he was born in Oakland, California, and grew up down the track in Sacramento.

Tim does the usual young muso stuff, a folk band (Tim, Tom, and Ron—adorable) and a no-hits surf band (the old-sounding New Breed), and then he auditions for Poco, but loses out to . . . Randy Meisner.

But when Randy then quit to join the Eagles, Tim got the Poco gig, which he held until '77, writing and singing the closest thing Poco ever got to a hit, "Keep on Tryin'," which peaked at Number 50 in 1975. When Randy quit the Eagles, they knew exactly where to go to find his replacement.

As Glenn recalled, when Tim replaced Randy in Poco, "He just plugged in and played the same parts." He even sang in a similar high register. Glenn saw no reason why Tim couldn't do the same thing for the Eagles.

But when he ran his brilliant idea by Irving, he was immediately shot down. Irving related the story of how he'd actually been in a hotel bar recently where Poco were staying and, according to Irving, "Timothy was smashed out of his mind, and he was gacked up. Now, you sure about this?"

"Gack" was new LA code for coke. The inference, that Schmit might just be Randy by another name in more ways than the merely musical.

Glenn shot right back. "Irving, if you'd been in a band for eleven years and you were still making $250 a week, working forty weeks a year, maybe you'd be a little smashed and gacked up yourself."

So sure was Glenn that Don didn't even bother to argue, it was a no-brainer, and the gig was offered to Tim before he'd even played a note with the band.

Glenn was right. Tim was perfect. He looked good, sang high, played great bass. He was the right age, same as Don, a year older than Glenn. He knew the ropes, had seen the underside, and most of all knew that joining the Eagles was the once-in-a-lifetime golden ticket you do not fuck up. You hold your hands up to heaven, stare up toward that nest in the stars, and give thanks to the Gods. Both of them.

One other thing Glenn and Don bet on: Tim will never make waves. He won't get unhappy because the band isn't going in the direction he wants, or because he doesn't get enough songs on albums.

Tim's married with kids. He lives right across the street from J.D. He's a vegetarian, yoga-loving health freak, one of nature's born sidemen. Sure, on the road there is often gack. And booze and whatever comes your way. But he is good people. He will not get in Don's face or crawl too far up Glenn's ass. Tim is perfect.

J.D. is the one who tips him off—Randy's gone, bro, it's a done deal, and you better be ready because the call is coming. Tim is just about to head out on tour again with Poco when Glenn phones. Tim's a straight-up guy, but he's ready to drop everything. He tells Glenn: "Where do you want me and when? I'm definitely in."

But Glenn says, actually, no hurry, it's cool. Do your tour. Tim is grateful for the courtesy but tells Irving he can't head out on the road without letting his bandmates know he's quitting, so Irving allows him that privilege.

"The important thing to me was not to have management do it," Schmit explained. "That happened to me once before. Where somebody left the group and they didn't talk to me personally, I didn't like that. I thought it was odd, actually. So I told management that I was going to go tell [the other Poco members], and I went to everybody's house and told them."

That's who the Eagles are getting now. A real straight shooter, just like Bernie and Randy used to be, minus the baggage of him thinking he has any real say in the band or anything at all to do with it. Tim's cool with all of that. Come on, who wouldn't be, in his position?

Sure enough he slots right in. You can't even see the join. Tim slides right in next to Don Felder, another dude who still can't quite believe his luck, even though he's just co-written the band's biggest hit.

Only snag: the band Timothy B. Schmit joins is a burnt-out wreck. It will still make him famous; it just won't stick around long enough for him to enjoy it as much. It will make him a millionaire, while keeping him a relative pauper musically (only three co-writing credits).

But Tim has beamed up to the Starship just as it's about to reenter Earth's atmosphere at a terrifying, life-altering velocity. Sure beats the shit out of growing old in Poco though, am I right? My *man*.

30.
Tough Little Sons of Bitches

Looking back years later, Glenn Frey would quip to Lloyd Bradley: "I was one of the richest men in the rock business, but I didn't live anywhere." Thinking back to 1971, he recalled: "When Geffen first signed the Eagles, he sent us up there to play a bar for a month to sharpen up, and I said then that's where I'll buy my first house."

"Up there" is Aspen, Colorado. What had been a nineteenth-century boom town gone to seed had been reborn with the advent of the Aspen Mountain ski resort, which drew the rich, including movie stars and celebrities and, by the late seventies, rock stars and their people. It was where art and commerce met drugs and politics and it was cool to carry and shoot your guns. Hell, this was the place where Hunter S. Thompson ran for sheriff on a Freak Power ticket—and only narrowly lost.

In the wake of the license to print money that *Hotel California* has become, Glenn Frey buys a vast estate on the side of one of the most spectacular of Aspen's mountains, as a retreat from the world, as a place where only money can take you—and put some distance between you and everyone that wants you. Somewhere to regroup and think. Glenn's new eyrie among the stars.

From here, he can survey the scorched earth that *Hotel California* has left in its wake. Eagles may make "California music," but the elements that brought it about no longer exist. Bernie and Randy are gone. The early sound has gone. They are no longer the young post-hippies that drove out to Joshua Tree, got stoned, and stared into the clouds. Now they are up there in the skies looking down and things are very different.

The era of empire may be underway for the Eagles. But way down below, among the record buyers, the people who really decide how long this dream lasts, the older certainties are being challenged.

The album that everyone buys after *Hotel California* and *Rumours* finally fall away is *Saturday Night Fever*, the Bee Gees soundtrack to the movie that ignites the disco craze.

England has its summer of punk rock, the media landscape shape-shifting, the musical culture overhauled. In America it becomes new wave, and suddenly the kids aren't dressed in denim anymore. They no longer dream the old dreams that the Eagles and Fleetwood Mac are selling. They dream the new dreams that the Bee Gees and Blondie sell. Something spikier, more urban, more modern, more *now*. Something that Glenn, frozen up there in the stars, does not really feel. Or even see as much of a threat. Not yet.

Irving Azoff, meanwhile, his antennae more finely attuned to which way the wind is blowing, chooses this moment to do a David Geffen and decide that managing the biggest band in the world is not quite enough for him. Just as Geffen had before him, he covets the world of movie production, of Hollywood highs.

He dips a toe in the water as an executive producer on the 1978 film *FM*, a comedy-drama about a radio DJ who thinks his station has "become too commercial" and tries to take it back—some irony right there. But the reviews are uniformly bad and the movie tanks. However, the soundtrack—complete with "Bad Man" from Randy's solo record and also "Life in the Fast Lane"—does a million copies.

Now Irving's got the bug.

He comes up with another great idea: a movie based around the song "Hotel California," a kind of darker, deep-dive version of *A Hard Day's Night*.

As chance would have it, Julia Phillips, red hot as the co-producer of *Close Encounters of the Third Kind*, the biggest movie of the year with a worldwide gross of $288 million, has the same idea. She gets in touch with Irving. They agree to huddle, a meeting she later writes about in her bestselling memoir *You'll Never Eat Lunch in This Town Again*.

She says Irving tells her he "hates music." Yeah, and?

Irving sets a meeting for Julia with Glenn and Don.

Don's view on the movie business? "Movie pukes, we called 'em. Ray Stark had tried to get us to let him make a movie out of 'Desperado,' which went badly. They always thought we should be excited or flattered because they wanted to make movies out of our songs. In fact we didn't want anything to do with it."

Something they make all too apparent at the meeting with Julia, which descends into a "he said, she said" charade, Julia later claiming that Glenn and Don were aloof and arrogant, hoovered up the cocaine she offered then split.

Don responded in kind. "She's a liar," he told Marc Eliot angrily, going on to claim that Phillips had brought out a "huge ashtray filled with a mound of coke." He added: "I don't remember if she went ahead and did some, but I know for certain we didn't."

To this day, there is still no movie of "Hotel California."

It's the feeling of co-piloting the great rocket ship that really keeps Don and Glenn on the hook, whatever coke-enflamed argument they might be having that day.

"There was a certain intensity," Glenn acknowledges later. "Perhaps a lot of it was bluff because we were skinny little guys with long hair and patched denim pants . . ."

But it's hard to tell how much is bluff when they wake up back in LA in 1978 with nothing to worry about, except the monumental hangovers—and how in hell they are going to follow up all of . . . that.

"We're a bunch of tough little sons of bitches," said Don. "But we were in a dark place. We were doing way too many drugs, just fucked up all the time because we felt this tremendous pressure— the Big Machine demanded to be fed. Momentum had to be maintained. The corporate stockholders had expectations; jobs were on the line. We should have taken a year off or hired a band psychiatrist. Or both."

They don't do either.

31

Some Dance to Remember

The follow-up to *Hotel California* begins with grand plans.

They know it has to be at least as good as *Hotel California*. They know it has to be at least as *big*.

Don and Glenn, in conference over the mirror with the snowy peaks, decide therefore it has to be a *double* album, always the mark of a band at the end of its peak-of-empire phase. It will not just equal *Hotel California*, they decide, as another ounce of primo-primo vanishes up their noses, it will total-eclipse it.

Fuck, yeah!

It will take all the disco beats and new wave know-it-alls and shove them back in their shitboxes where they belong, fuck you all very, very much!

They already have a title they think says everything about where they are now: *The Long Run*, from Don's new song. The only problem is, they have no other songs as good, and they are so sick of the sight of one another it makes it almost impossible for them all to be in the same room at the same time. Glenn and Don most of all.

"It had stopped being fun," said Glenn. "We no longer trusted each other's instincts."

"We were having fights all the time about the songs," said Don, "enormous fights about one word—for days on end."

"It made us very paranoid," Joe Walsh said. "People started asking us, 'What are you going to do now?' and we didn't know. We ended up on the next album in Miami with the tapes running, but nobody knowing what was going on. We lost perspective. We just kinda sat around in a daze—for months."

For all his candor, Joe is being disingenuous. In May '78, just as the Eagles are turning on each other in the studio, immersed in white flake and bad takes, Joe Walsh releases a solo single, his first since joining the Eagles. It's called "Life's Been Good to Me" and it is instantly hailed as one of the greatest rock songs of all time.

If "Rocky Mountain Way" was all anyone real ever knew about Joe Walsh, it would be enough. It's a stone-cold classic, whatever you cut your coke with. Now, though, Joe had gifted the world an even greater rock classic to admire, Joe crooning the chorus, "Life's been good to me so faaarrr," like a genie riding his magic carpet.

It's the most bitingly funny, scarily accurate satire on the excesses of the era and its most outrageous stars, Joe explaining with a shrug: "I live in hotels, tear out the walls / I have accountants pay for it all . . ."

Musically, "Life's Been Good" was also a revelation—an unlikely it-shouldn't-work-but-does amalgam of reggae, prog rock, badass boogie, acoustic, electric, eclectic, and cool. Indeed, it sounds exactly like the kind of genius idea, expertly executed, that the Eagles were fruitlessly searching to find for their own album. It was next-level. Self-aware enough for punk, musically sophisticated enough to have Eagles fans purring. Indeed, the rest of the band all appear on the track, its album version clocking in at over eight epic minutes (edited down to a fighting-fit four minutes for the single).

Walsh had also recorded the album it came from, *But Seriously, Folks* . . . in Miami, during the many lulls in the band's stop-start, mostly-stop sessions for their next album. Did Joe think to offer it to the guys? Did Joe maybe decide this was too good not to keep for himself? Hmmm. It was certainly a question Don Henley must have asked himself when "Life's Been Good" got to Number 12 that summer. It even hit the Top 20 in Britain. Followed by the album, also Top 20 in the UK and Number 8 in the US, where it would quickly go platinum. Meanwhile, the best the band had come up with so far was the one song Timothy B. Schmit had brought with him.

As Glenn ruefully described it, it was hard to cope with anything rationally once you got used to "this lifestyle of limos, private jets, first-class hotels, and people doing what you told them to." Plus, he confessed, "both Henley and I had developed drug habits, which didn't help matters."

To borrow a phrase from their friend Jackson, they were running on empty.

"When we began the process of recording, we were completely burned out," Don told *Rolling Stone*. "We were physically, emotionally, spiritually, and creatively exhausted. Our collective tank was empty." The tortuous making of *The Long Run* was his "least favorite time" making an album.

The first of what would become five studios was booked for March 1978 and Bill Szymczyk got ready for what he already suspected would be the longest, most tortuous production gig of his career. "If it *had* been a double LP," said Bill, acidly, "we might still be working on it today."

But then he wasn't the one trying to write the immortal songs. As Glenn put it: "If you were to ask a struggling, twenty-five-year-old musician: 'How would you like to sell eighteen million albums?' he'd say: 'Yeah! Damn right I would.' The next question is: 'But how would you like to try to make one as good as the one that sold millions and millions of records?'"

The idea that Don eventually comes up with, the concept behind *The Long Run*, is to do with time. How time moves, leaves you for dead just when you feel you've got all the time in the world. Just as the hotel in "Hotel California" was a multichambered mansion, each room a luxurious prison cell purchased with the price of a soul, *The Long Run* pits the Eagles not against their contemporaries or their successors, but against the true judge of artistic achievement, time itself.

The bitter irony: "The group was breaking apart, imploding under the pressure, and yet we were writing about longevity, posterity. Turns out we were right . . ."

Time was their new enemy. "The record company expectations were unreasonably high," complained Felder. "Irving would call or come down in person and tell us what they wanted. We'd sit and listen to what they had to say, and Don would say quietly, 'Don't rush us, Irving. They'll get it when it's done.' He was often the one who stood up to the executives and put them in their place. I think maybe because it took the greatest toll on him."

Don Henley was now thirty. He wore his years like a badge of pride. You need a decision on something Eagles, Don is the man to see. Now, for the first time he is feeling the heat of the situation he created for himself, that he strong-willed into existence.

"Everybody wanted to be a lead singer, to write the songs, and it just can't work that way. Somebody's got to take charge and somehow it had shifted to me, and I felt enormous pressure to come up with all the lyrics since Glenn had sort of backed off. In essence, we were all just too strung out. Everything was a drama. All kinds of little wars were going on within the group, little mutinies and games being played."

Henley was reaping all that he had sown. He had staged the soft-power coup that put him at the forefront of the band. It was his artistry that had shaped the Eagles' biggest hits. Now the record company and the rest of the band wanted more of it and the well had run dry, at least temporarily. He didn't know what to do. Glenn didn't either. Or said he didn't.

Having made Asylum what some estimated to be around $250 million with the *Greatest Hits* and *Hotel California*, it's no wonder label chief Joe Smith falls down on his knees in thanks when Irving gives him the good news, in March 1978, that the band are back in the studio with Bill. Joe can already hear the cash registers singing.

He offers the band a million-dollar bonus if they deliver in time for a Christmas release. That's when Irving gives Joe the bad news. They haven't finished writing. More accurately, they haven't even started writing. Joe reels at the news. But this is supposed to be a double album, grander in scope even than *Hotel California*. Relax, Irving assures Joe, the boys will figure it out.

In the studio in Miami, the only one who has anything usable is the new guy. Tim has the melody and some words of an almost-completed tune he'd already been kicking around called "I Can't Tell You Why."

Glenn tells him: "Let's not do a Richie Furay, Poco-sounding song. Let's do an R & B song. You could sing [it] like Smokey Robinson." As he and Don help Tim finish up "I Can't Tell You Why," Don calls it "straight-up Al Green"—a pretty accurate description of its lush, blue-eyed-soul sound, like the Bee Gees but with something to actually say.

Tim can't believe his luck. The first song finished for the new record, and it's one of *his*. "I just kept pinching myself," he told Joe Bosso. Don and Glenn had helped him hugely, "but it was one of those songs that was just there . . . I was like, 'Yes! This is an amazing debut for me.'" During the final mix, Don had looked at him and said, "There's your first hit."

The rest of the session passes without progress, however, and before they pack up and leave Miami the usual backbiting and arguments quickly turn into something more serious. A new fissure opens between Glenn Frey and Don Felder. Felder complains he is missing his family during the long stretches away.

"Don and Glenn seemed burned out," Felder recalled. "They spent hours in stony silence facing each other, neither one able to suggest any new lyrics, each one staring at Don's trademark cigarette butts, which he left standing around on every available work surface."

Tim, who is where Felder was at the start of *One of These Nights*, says of the impending apocalypse: "I knew that there was some squabbling—I mean, it was obvious; it couldn't be hidden—but I had no idea how truly serious it was . . . I didn't know how heavy the issues were."

Irving, in full crisis-management mode, pulled them out of the studio and put them back on the road, hoping it might unblock the drains, get the mood jumping again. It didn't. Once it became clear things were shaky, Irving extended the tour. Consequently, there is no new Eagles album ready for release that Christmas. Instead, Don pushes for the band to record a single, a cover of Charles Brown's cheesy "Please Come Home for Christmas," one of Don's favorite Christmas songs. It gets to Number 18 in the charts then vanishes again.

Out on the road, new resentments gnaw at them. It's as if the lack of new songs is a stomach ulcer, burning a hole in their guts. Don gets more introverted and crankier. Glenn keeps himself amused by picking on what Felder calls his "random victims," ripe for humiliation. "He'd amplify something in your voice or your character and act it out for an admiring, laughing audience."

In rehearsal one day, Glenn announces, "And now let's hear it, gents, for Fingers Felder, singing his Number 1 hit, 'Hotel California' . . ." Glenn does an uncannily accurate if unnecessarily cruel impression of the way Felder sidles up to the microphone to sing, like a man approaching a sheer drop from a cliff. Everyone from the band and crew joins in the laughter.

Glenn's impressions are lethally good. This one twists Felder up even more than usual, because he knows there is a grain of truth in it. Don Felder doesn't like singing much, especially because he can always feel Glenn's eyes burning into his back, waiting for any kind of bum note. Today it's just too goddamn much. Felder follows Glenn into the men's room. He takes Glenn's shirt in one hand and makes a fist with the other.

"You humiliate me in public like that again, Roach, and I'm gonna break your fucking nose." "Roach" is Glenn's new nickname, after his habit of always having a lit joint in hand. He tells Felder to cool it, it's just a joke, man, lighten up! But Felder sees the look of shock on Glenn's face. And something else: doubt.

Don Felder doesn't know it yet, but he has just crossed the line.

32.

Some Dance to Forget

After an entire fucking year, they finally get something, an inkling, a wisp of a vibe.

They are back in the studio. It's the summer of 1979. The new record still has just one finished track, but this time . . . at last . . . something happens. They have a song, really just a riff, called "Heartache Tonight." Glenn's old buddy Bob Seger gave him the title. Glenn and J.D. were jamming on it at his place and sort of hit on the riff while they were listening to Sam Cooke. They kept chugging and turned it into a verse. Bob was in town and happened to come over. They played him the chorus.

Bob Seger remembers it this way in a 2007 interview he gave to author-songwriter Ken Sharp: "[Glenn] had this little thing: 'Somebody's gonna hurt somebody.' He wanted to write a shuffle. So we're playing that groove, and Glenn's singing the verses, and suddenly, out of the blue, the chorus came into my head. 'There's gonna be a heartache tonight, heartache tonight, I know . . .' I started singing that and Glenn goes: 'Yeah!'"

Next thing, Glenn was on the phone to Joe Walsh. It was the early hours of the morning, but Joe came straight over and plugged in his guitar "and comes up with the bridge. Then J.D. came in right after Walsh that same night. He'd help Glenn with lyrics."

When Don showed up the next day he also sat down and started writing lyrics.

In Miami, Glenn lays down a vocal track for "Heartache Tonight," and Joe Walsh feels it happening at last. "The creative stalemate was broken that night," he tells the *LA Times*. "Glenn went out and sung his ass off. We knew then we were off the hook a little. We had a single.

"The next break came when we recorded 'The Long Run.' When Henley sang those words, we knew we had the beginning of a concept. The next step was 'The Sad Café.' Again it was the words. That's when we were finally able to say to ourselves, 'This is going to be okay . . .'"

"The Long Run" is almost therapy, its jolly lilt contradicting the emotional pain. It is Don talking to Don about the hurrying, the worrying.

It is Don opening up more directly than ever before:

"I did some damage / I know it's true . . ."

Although he is writing about love and loss and the still-crazy life so different to the small-town one he originally seemed destined for, he finds a way in his artistry to pull the lens wider and turn the song from one that ponders the length and strength of love to another that makes it clear what "The Long Run" really is.

"Who is gonna make it? / We'll find out in the long run . . ."

Yes, it's about love, but also creativity, ambition, longevity . . . all of the questions that an artist asks themselves about their work and its place in the world. Will the Eagles outlive new wave and disco? Will the mystical Hotel California hold any meaning once the seventies are done and everyone's lives have moved on?

He will find out, we all will, in the long run.

Then comes "The Sad Café." Another emotionally windswept ballad that works on several levels: on the surface, a straight love-lost song. Beneath it, a desperately sad memento of times past, a eulogy for the band and the time and place that birthed them.

It's a fitting close to what will become the last Eagles record for decades—men looking back on their youth, with all of the melancholy that entails. Just like the Hotel California, the Sad Café is both real and metaphor. It is the Troubadour and Dan Tana's, it is all of the nights they spent there, laughing, dreaming, trying to make it out of their ordinary lives and upward into the stars.

"The song is about the demise of the club, the passing of the glory years," Don said, waxing lyrical. "The crowd that hung out in the Troubadour and the bands that were performing there were changing. The train tracks that had run down the middle of Santa Monica Boulevard had been ripped out. The train no longer came through—the same train that Steve Martin had once led an entire Troubadour audience to hop aboard and ride up to La Cienega Boulevard, then walk back to the club. Those remarkable freewheeling times were receding into the distance."

"The Sad Café" was perfect Henley, perfect Eagles.

"In the City" was primetime Joe Walsh, awash with knowing, slash-and-burn guitars and wry lyrics, high aboard the same victim-of-success train as Don and Glenn, testifying about city streets that "don't have much pity . . . When you're down that's where you'll stay . . ." Joe had originally co-written the song with veteran film composer Barry De Vorzon for the 1979 cult movie classic The Warriors, which appeared on the official soundtrack album released six months before The Long Run.

The other standout track on the album was the monumental "King of Hollywood," with Glenn and Don vying for who can sound the more sinister on a sordid tale of the casting-couch consciousness that now existed everywhere in 1970s America, not just Hollywood—and an eerie glimpse into the behind-closed-doors proclivities of a singer whose chickens would soon come home to roost. Or as Don sings it: "His Jacuzzi runneth over."

This was their sign-off from the stars. Their most revealing glimpse inside the minds of the rock elite. The rest of the album, though, reflected their least sympathetic side. Their creatively burnt-out, leave-me-the-fuck-alone side. Their nothing-left-to-say side. Lightweight ditties like "The Disco Strangler," a bitter tirade against the vacuity of disco culture in the late seventies, "the melody without a cure." Or the just plain nasty "Those Shoes," another chauffeur-driven excursion into the after-hours of late-night LA and hard-fixing on the attendant "Desperation in the singles bars / All those jerkoffs in their fancy cars . . ."

There were also two tracks that were just embarrassing: "Teenage Jail" and "The Greeks Don't Want No Freaks," songs that Henley will later admit make him laugh when he hears them. Not because they are funny. Because they are sad. The former is clearly the Eagles' response to punk and new wave. Dirge rhythm, strutting guitars: a fifteen-line song with no chorus and no need to ever listen to it again. Ick. The latter, another nod—or pogo—to Elvis Costello–style punk put-downs, replete with retro guitars and cringe-inducing "humor." Dads all dancing in their dad sunglasses.

When it was finally over, they couldn't wait to get away from each other. "That record took three years and cost $800,000, and we burned out," said Don.

They staggered away from the creation of The Long Run and fled in the night to their dark corners. By September 1979, however, the Eagles were back on tour, beginning in Japan with four sold-out nights at the 14,000-capacity Nippon Budokan in Tokyo. But they all know it's over, even if they are not yet ready to admit it. Henley talks about one more record to go out on—maybe even a double (sound familiar?)—but when he truly starts to think about what that might be like he goes back to his hotel suite and hangs up the "Do Not Disturb" sign.

Irving feels it too. He notes that the early Eagles records were made in weeks. Now they are costing them years. Irving has helped make them and himself richer than they ever knew possible. All that they dreamed of they now have. What was left, really? "The thing that holds them is the music," Irving sums up, "and if the music doesn't hold them, they could disintegrate in a second . . ."

For a little while longer, at least, the music holds. *The Long Run*, released in September 1979, debuts at Number 2 on the *Billboard* chart, goes to Number 1 the following week, and stays there for two months. It goes to Number 1 in Australia, Canada, and Japan, and Number 4 in the UK. "Heartache Tonight," the lead-off single, goes to Number 1 in America in November. Two more singles, "The Long Run," in January, and "I Can't Tell You Why," in April, both reach the Top 10 and keep the whole thing rolling. "Heartache Tonight" wins a Grammy. *The Long Run* shifts seven million units.

America is still hungry, it seems, for America's biggest band. The critics are not. They sense the weakness, the fading grandeur, the hubris behind "The Disco Strangler" and "The Greeks Don't Want No Freaks." Reviewing *The Long Run* for *Rolling Stone*, Dave Marsh writes, "The fact that this pack of cliché-mongers is one of the biggest 'rock' bands today is perhaps the most pathetic commentary I know about the current state of the musical world." For Marsh, *The Long Run* is "a bitter, writhing, difficult record, full of piss and vinegar and poisoned expectations."

Don Felder recalls in his memoir how "Don's perfectionism and Bill's professionalism" meant they were continuously "raising the bar for us to leap over." To the point where "we took that bar and hit each other over the head with it." For Felder, that resulted in some of their "gutsiest, most spontaneous performances" being left behind in the relentless search for musical El Dorado.

The tour continues their long, slow descent. The shows seem strangely muted. There is no fanfare as they open with "Hotel California," just the silhouetted figures cradling their guitars at the front, and the voice, tentative sounding, coming like a whisper from the back where Don is sheltered behind his drums.

With six of the first ten songs each night coming from the just-released *The Long Run*, it makes for an unexpectedly low-key first half of the show. It's not until what becomes known as the Joe Walsh part of the show—toward the end, after Glenn introduces Joe's candidacy for the presidency with the words: "We need a good guitar player in the White House"—that the evening finally takes off.

Beginning, inexplicably, with a rousing version of "Turn to Stone," a track from Joe's *Barnstorm* album, before segueing into "Life's Been Good," Joe's biggest solo hit, then straight into "Life in the Fast Lane," which Don Henley sings but which Joe Walsh had left his mark all over, and which closes the show.

First encore: Joe's bludgeoning "Rocky Mountain Way," a rock classic as totemic in its way as anything the Eagles had done (second only to "Hotel California"). It felt symbolic each night when Joe finished off playing "Take It Easy" by pretending to smash his acoustic guitar. A self-mocking moment largely lost on encore-fevered audiences.

Apart from the odd interview that Joe Walsh gives to guitar magazines that want to know all about his playing style and equipment, Irving limits interaction with the press to just Glenn and Don, who give nothing away. The *Rolling Stone* interview, for which the writer tagged along with the band on and off for almost two years, claims Don has compared himself to God on tour. Reading this, Don spits out his soup and starts writing angry letters to *Rolling Stone*.

They play Japan, Hawaii, the East Coast of America, and then swing through the Deep South. Tickets get sold in bundles. Venues sell out. Don't they always?

They play three sold-out shows at the LA Forum. They play a series of benefit shows for the band's pet causes, and also for Governor Jerry Brown—now Linda Ronstadt's boyfriend—and Senator Alan Cranston, the last show of another endless tour, in Long Beach on the last night of July 1980.

At the Cranston Benefit, Glenn thinks that Felder disrespects the senator when he comes backstage before the show to thank the band for their efforts, and Don responds with a sullen, "You're welcome, Senator . . . I guess." It leads to another backstage row, with beer bottles smashed against the wall. "I felt Don Felder insulted Senator Cranston under his breath, and I confronted him with it," said Frey matter-of-factly.

True to the word Felder gave him when things last got physical, he waits until they are about to step out on the stage and says, "What you did back there, you're an asshole for doing that . . ."

HO-LEE FUCKKK, Glenn is stewing now. He's up on that stage for the final show on this godforsaken tour and Don fucking Felder is living rent-free inside his head. That fucker has overstepped the line . . . Again.

Roach keeps glaring across at Fingers's skinny ass, the anger rising and rising until he can't hold on to it anymore, until he thinks he might fuckin' explode if he doesn't do something about it.

They're playing "Best of My Love." Glenn gets up close to Felder, makes the crowd think they're singing in sweet harmony and says in his ear: "Fuck you. When we get off this stage, I'm kicking your ass . . ."

Felder, who has been drinking Jack Daniel's and has had about as much of this shit as he can stand, starts hissing back. "Only three more songs till I kick *your* ass, pal," he tells Glenn. "Get ready . . ."

The final number of the night before the encores is "Life in the Fast Lane." They play it and run off. Glenn waits in the wings for the first encore. He's screaming, "That FUCKING FELDER!!!"

The crew try to keep them apart. Somehow they manage to churn through the encores without attacking each other. The gig ends. Most of the band split for the limos waiting at the backstage door. Glenn doesn't. He stands around with the Cranstons, watching as Don Felder grabs an old guitar and smashes it against a wall.

The Cranstons split in a hurry. This is decidedly not their scene.

Glenn glares at Felder. "Typical of you to smash your cheapest guitar . . ."

Typical of Glenn to go for the cheapest shot.

Felder strides out to his limo before anything else can happen.

It really is all over now.

33.

His Jacuzzi Runneth Over

The Eagles finally get around to making a double album with their first live collection, *Eagles Live*, released in November 1980. A melding of tapes recorded during some shows at the LA Forum in 1976, plus the July 1980 shows in Santa Monica and Long Beach. All of the pickups and overdubs are done individually in the studio with Bill Szymczyk. Don and Glenn mix the record on separate coasts. Bill jokes that *Eagles Live* "is brought to you by Federal Express." *Rolling Stone*'s Record Guide calls it "probably the most heavily overdubbed live album in history."

So fucking what, asshole? The record does its job, which is to deliver the final album of the band's contract with Asylum. Once it's released, they are free as birds. There is no more music left to hold them together. No more tours to toil through. The album sleeve reads, "Thank you and goodnight."

Glenn can't wait to get the fuck out of Dodge. Don calls it "a horrible relief." There are no public announcements about the band's future for another two years, by which time everyone has already figured out what the deal is. The Eagles have landed. Crash-landed. Here comes the new decade and they're not in it.

Glenn tells Lloyd Bradley, "Toward the end, we just wanted to get the record finished and released. It is a very polished album—but none of us wanted to go through that again." Once the decision was made to fold the band, "I experienced an overwhelming sense of relief."

The new decade would not be kind to the Eagles. One thing the 1980s reviled more than any other was the 1970s. The music, the fashion, the food, the TV—and, especially, bands like the Eagles. They were now seen as misanthropes, cynics, zillionaire mountain-top dwellers gazing down with contempt on the rest of us.

"I suppose a lot of good art down through the ages has come out of turmoil and stress, but this was just too much," Henley shook. "This misanthrope business has always been a complete mystery to me. We were critical, but for fair reasons. We cared about our fellow man; we cared about the ecology; we cared about the Indians; we cared about nuclear energy. And so we would point out what was wrong. I don't consider that to be misanthropic. We were arrogant, sure," he added. "You have to be arrogant if you're going to be in a rock 'n' roll band. But, you know, I thought we were pretty nice people all in all."

"I'm through my *Playmate* period," Frey declared. "I constantly ask myself what I think of women. Lately I've been feeling much less physical, you know, where you meet a real pretty girl and immediately attach all these great qualities to her. But women are objects for men, whether or not sex objects. They're a goal. That's the way we're brought up."

THEN SOMETHING HAPPENS at Don Henley's place that appears to confirm people's worst suspicions about the Eagles.

A week before Thanksgiving, Don made a call to a Madam X— Alex Adams, then LA's go-to celebrity brothel queen, and requested "the usual": young girl escorts. Even though he was now in a relationship with *Battlestar Galactica* star Maren Jensen, who's away on a trip, this was a party, dude! The end of the tour! The end of the band, for fuck's sake! Gimme a break!!

Roadies were invited, other musicians and trusted friends, a mansion full of party-hearty guys looking to let off a little steam. Rivers of booze, primo coke, plastic sacks full of top-line weed, and a shit ton of "disco biscuits": Quaaludes. Madam X reportedly sent over two underage girls—one sixteen, the other just turned fifteen, both homeless runaways, an endless "talent pool" Madam X routinely "fished in." One of the girls was allegedly from a violently abusive home and was still a virgin.

As soon as the girls arrived the fun began, starting with the coke to get them jumping, followed by the 'ludes to stop them freaking out, along with as much pot smoke and anything-on-the-rocks as they could get down them. Followed by a visit to the Jacuzzi where, it was later claimed, "candid" Polaroid pictures were taken.

What happened next depends on who you believe, or what the lawyers will allow writers like this one to say in print. But an emergency phone call was made to the cops in the early hours. When they arrived at the house, they discovered that a sixteen-year-old girl had overdosed. A hastily assembled team of anonymous fixers was already on the scene. Don was arrested and charged with possession of marijuana, cocaine, and Quaaludes, and contributing to the delinquency of a minor. He was fined $2,500, put on two years' probation, and ordered to attend drug counseling.

"I had no idea how old she was, and I had no idea she was doing that many drugs," Don pleaded. "I didn't have sex with her. Yes, she was a hooker. Yes, there were roadies and guys at my house. We were having a farewell to the Eagles."

The story being told behind the scenes, however, was far from simple. When the fire department and paramedics arrived, they walked in on a scene they described as "Sodom and Gomorrah" with drugs, vomit, and booze everywhere. Both teenage girls were totally naked, although the younger of the two had begun to dress.

The paramedics did CPR on the unconscious girl, as she was unresponsive, then she went into seizures. They got her into the ambulance and sped off. Someone had allegedly told the younger runaway they would "take care" of her and to stay close and keep her pretty mouth shut. She left with her friend in the ambulance.

Later at the hospital she is said to have been given a bus ticket and a fat envelope stuffed with cash. She is said to have left town as per her instructions, later that same day.

In the end, though, there were just too many people waiting with their hands out and the secret did not stay secret for long.

The elder of the two girls recovered from her ordeal. A year later she was found dead near the 101 Freeway, the unfortunate victim, apparently, of a drug overdose. She had been staying at a local shelter where friends and co-workers said she'd cleaned up and was trying to turn her life around.

Don began to see himself as the victim here. It was a party, dude! He didn't know the chick was underage! Coulda happened to anybody . . .

As Don tells *GQ* magazine a decade later: "[The fire department] just flat-out lied to me. They said, 'Well, by law, we're supposed to take this little girl to the hospital, but if you'll take care of her, we'll leave her here . . . We're not here to get anyone busted.'"

"She was fine by the time they got there." He added: "I got all of them out of the house; I took complete blame for everything. I was stupid; I could have flushed everything down the toilet. I didn't want this girl dying in my house; I wanted to get her medical attention. I did what I thought was best, and I paid the price."

The price is reputational damage that takes decades to disperse. It feels like a queasy end to an era of unfettered excess.

Untouchable no more.

When Maren Jansen returns from her trip, she doesn't know what to make of Don's story. But her troubles have only just begun. She falls ill soon after with Epstein-Barr syndrome. Don nurses her. It takes almost three years to get her properly diagnosed. In the meantime, Don makes a solo record with his new writing partner Danny Kortchmar, *I Can't Stand Still*, and dedicates it to Maren.

"We hibernated," he claimed, while their world continued to grow ever crazier. Shortly before the LA bust, they had survived a terrifying emergency landing in a Learjet, Don having to throw Maren clear of the cabin, fearing the plane was about to catch fire. Shortly after the bust, Don's mother was diagnosed with breast cancer. He began to believe that the party bust has a political element—a drive to "clean up" the entertainment business, with many of Hollywood's dealers, madams, and party people giving information to politicians and the police.

To top it off, Maren now has two stalkers to go along with all of the Eagles crazies trying to get closer to Don. The shooting of John Lennon by Mark Chapman in December 1980 brings those fears too close to home.

"IT WAS A TERRIBLE YEAR," Don acknowledged in a strange postscript to the end of a once-great American band. One nobody talks about publicly for fear of retribution—and because by 1980 the Eagles are already presumed dead, if not forgotten. Some sleazy, over-zonked, has-been rock star exploited a couple of willing groupies? Tell me something I don't know, dude.

34.

You Just Can't Kill the Beast

Hyde Park, London, the last Sunday of June 2022.

On a bright, warm evening in front of around 65,000 fans—an undulating blancmange of lifelong stoners, late-middle-aged day-trippers, rich tourists, and the merely curious, sons and daughters dragged along against their will to something they are promised will be very special—the Eagles meander unannounced onto the stage and turn the clock back to 1972, gliding into an a cappella version of "Seven Bridges Road" before lifting their twinkling acoustic guitars and seeing out the rest of the song with the kind of spirit that hasn't been seen here since Laurel Canyon in 1969.

The whole scene is too baby-boomer beautiful for words.

The second number is "One of These Nights" and from where I'm standing about 300 feet from the front, it sounds sluggish, takes a moment for us to recognize, but chugs along pleasingly once it gets going, and when Don sings you know it must be real or as close to real as you and they can get at this late stage of the game.

"New Kid in Town," sung by Vince Gill, keeps the mellow, sunny-afternoon-at-the-fair vibe going. There are thousands of people here, but it doesn't feel overcrowded. If you want to, you can gently work your way to the front. But you don't want to because you are fine right where you are on the grass, sun beaming down, glass of Pimm's and organic lemonade in hand.

The figures onstage are too tiny and nondescript to be enjoyed in the old-fashioned way. The screens either side of the stage help a little, but your eyes soon wander off again. To the still-bright blue sky, the tall and ancient trees, the people milling around dreamily as though they haven't noticed there is a band playing some songs they might recall. Hyde Park on a balmy June evening is delightful.

So are the band obviously, but wait, what are they playing now? I don't recognize it. Spooky guitar, tribal beat—yes, of course, "Witchy Woman." Even better than the record, check out that coiling, snakebite solo from Joe Walsh. That's unexpected and not really necessary, actually, but thanks, that was very nice.

What next? Oh, Don Henley is coming to the front of the stage to speak. A month shy of his seventy-fifth birthday, Don starts by explaining to the crowd that he "can't see you but I can hear you" then apologizes for the two consecutive years' worth of cancellations, due to the fact "Mother Nature had different plans." There are still some people in their COVID-era masks, but no one wants to be reminded of all that. Tonight we dance to remember only the good times.

Then Don relays his mission statement, and this is key: "Our mission this evening is to give you about a two-hour vacation from all the horrible headlines and all the chaos that's happening out in the world. It's not that we don't care about those things, just that we need a little break. So sit back, relax, and enjoy the music. It'll all be there in the morning when you get up . . ."

This is what the Eagles are all about a half-century down the road. Taking it easy. Those fifty years since the first Eagles album have left the world almost unrecognizable. It's the same for the band.

There is now only one founding member left in the Eagles: Don Henley.

Bernie Leadon left when he did.

Randy Meisner left when he did.

Don Felder left when he did—following a long period of fuming discontent, after being forced to "sign papers" reducing his financial stake in the band. That had been for their first reformation, the Hell Freezes Over tour in 1994.

As Felder scathingly put it in his memoir, *Heaven and Hell: My Life in the Eagles, 1974–2001*: "It felt to me like we'd all been on the same farm eating from the same trough, but two pigs had gotten so fat they were crowding everyone else out. If I were to try to force myself into the trough, I'd be run off the farm. I didn't want that to happen. The farm was all I knew. Reluctantly and with bile in my throat, I signed their damn papers. The so-called equal partnership was over."

Felder goes on to describe the legal dissolution of the band in 2000 in favor of a company called NEA, owned by Don Henley and Glenn Frey, which then—purely coincidentally—resulted in his firing. That was over twenty years ago now. The band kept on trucking, touring as a four-piece again for the next eleven years, selling even more of everything as their legend just grew.

Since Don Felder fell to earth there have been various line-ups of the Eagles—even one that included Bernie Leadon between 2013 and 2016—cleaning up on the classic rock live circuit. Stadium mayhem, whatever the names of the guys in the band. Nobody batting an eye.

Then Glenn Frey died, and all bets were off. Glenn died on January 18, 2016, at Columbia University Irving Medical Center, in New York City. He was sixty-seven. Official cause of death: complications of rheumatoid arthritis, acute ulcerative colitis, and pneumonia. Not a very rock 'n' roll death for a guy whose idols all went down in flames in car crashes and gunfights. Nor was the news greeted with much ceremony—shocking to Eagles fans, meh to the rest.

Eight days earlier, David Bowie had died, and the world came to a standstill. Front-page news from London to LA. Deep-dive TV and radio tributes globe-wide. A river of internet tears.

Two weeks before that, Lemmy of the legendary heavy metal band Motörhead died. The Eagles had sold more copies of their worst-selling record than Motörhead did in their entire forty-year career. But in the UK and other parts of Europe it was Lemmy's grizzly visage that got all the attention. Nobody really even knew what Glenn Frey looked like anymore. It wasn't like he'd done much lately. Had he?

Merle Haggard, who was the kind of genuine no-fucks-given country outlaw Glenn wished he could have been, but had only one modest hit, "Okie from Muskogee," that anyone other than his fans could actually name, let alone hum—even Merle Haggard got better press than Glenn Frey did when he, too, died in April 2016.

Ten days later Prince would be found dead of an accidental drug overdose and the international pop world went back into mourning. Later the same year Leonard Cohen would die, as would George Michael. All given a carousel of media send-offs, critical revaluations, fond adieus.

Glenn Frey picked up kindly worded obits in old familiar haunts like *Rolling Stone* and the *LA Times*, but mainstream ripples were few. The day after his death, the headline on the front page of the New York *Daily News* sneered: FREY'S DEATH IS SAD, BUT I STILL LOATHE THE EAGLES. The article declared, "Hating the Eagles defines whether a music fan is a fan of music or a bandwagon jumper." It said the music of the Eagles could be best described as "pop pap . . . a warm glass of milk to get you to bed." It cited Steely Dan lyrics and *Big Lebowski* scenes and albums by other seventies artists (Bowie, Lou Reed, the Stones, Neil Young) as proof that "The Eagles were, quite simply, the worst rock 'n' roll band." There was a more formal tribute to Frey run alongside, but really, thanks for nothing.

It was the blessing and curse of the Eagles that apart from Joe Walsh no one ever really knew what they looked like, only what they sounded like. That was something no one could forget. But it was hard to put faces to it.

Was Glenn Frey missed that summer evening in Hyde Park? Of course. But not enough to prevent thousands buying tickets to see the Eagles, even if the band on that stage now included only one original Eagle.

Bernie had bailed after Glenn checked out. Few had really noticed he'd been back. Seventy-four-year-old Joe was still there to bring a bit of life to it. But only just. At one point at Hyde Park he leans into the mic and croaks: "I had a lot more fun being twenty in the seventies than being seventy in the twenties." It's a good line, it gets a hearty, appreciative laugh, and he says it at every show now. But even Still-Crazy Joe only came into the picture on the fifth multimillion-selling Eagles album. Tim is still here, and still a great, ready-made stand-in for Randy, but he only came in for the final two stadium-gods years of the late seventies.

And there was Vince Gill, who sang both "New Kid in Town" and "Take It to the Limit" better than Glenn and Randy ever did, though minus the fraught, snow-blinded edge. Vince handles most of Glenn's songs, only suffering by comparison slightly on "Lyin' Eyes," which lacks Frey's sneering candor, but which the crowd helps cover for by singing the chorus for him.

Vince, a mainstream country star in his own right in America, is authentic, dependable—but he is not Glenn. Even when Glenn's son Deacon Frey joins the band onstage halfway through to sing "Peaceful Easy Feeling" and "Take It Easy"—at a glance, looking just like his father at the same age; at first hearing, sounding a little like his father at the same age—he is still not actually his father. None of it seems to matter. Everyone seems happy enough to see him walk on and play. No one seems to much mind when he departs again.

The Eagles is now a family affair. On recent tours Don had also brought in his son, Will, to play guitar. Kids and grandkids congregate freely at any show they want to go to. Backstage, although Irving still rules the roost—whether in person or via a military-op-style combo of sophisticated online dominion and besuited on-site henchmen—Glenn's daughter, Taylor Frey, has now effectively become the band's road manager. There are no drugs, outside the prescription medicines all men in their mid-seventies are familiar with.

None of it matters to the people in the crowd, very few of whom appear to be dancing or doing much moving in time to the music at all. Maybe one or two—Americans, mostly. Women, not girls. Everybody else—just watching the screens, taking it in, soaking up the late-afternoon sun. Musically, there are no surprises. The Eagles haven't released any new songs for over fifteen years. They don't need to.

The show long ago evolved to meet the low-maintenance needs of its avid audience. Mostly it's repeat business, the tours getting bigger and more lucrative every year. The twenty-three-song set list, including encores, is a live best-of, a jukebox show, which now includes two of Joe's biggest hits in "Life's Been Good" and "Rocky Mountain Way" *and* his ancient James Gang near-hit, "Funk #49."

It also includes Don stepping up to do "The Boys of Summer," which he dedicates to recently deceased Foo Fighters drummer Taylor Hawkins. That's as exciting as it gets, though, the song performed faithfully enough but hardly crackling with energy. Even the side-stage screens are only showing stock footage of sea waves crashing into a shore.

There are other people on that stage who you don't even notice because they never get their image on the screens. People like guitarist Steuart Smith, who quietly took over Don Felder's spot and has kept it warm ever since, while never officially becoming an Eagle. Steuart celebrated his seventieth birthday two days ago, has been touring with the Eagles for two decades—and no one in this crowd really knows who he is, or really cares. Not even when he trades those vicious guitar lines on "Hotel California" with Joe.

There also appears to be a keyboardist up there . . . is that John Corey, the guy Don Henley brought into his solo band in the eighties? Don brought him into the extended Eagles touring band for the Hell Freezes Over tour and . . . Wait, no, it's Will Hollis, right? Came in right around the time Felder got the boot.

Then some old guy in a suit playing accordion. Hey, that's Michael Thompson, right? Michael has also been around since the big reinvention in the nineties, and he can play almost anything. At least it looks like him . . . probably. And is that Joe Vitale still stepping up to handle the drums whenever Don strolls to the front to sing and play guitar? Or maybe Scott Crago, who also came into the touring band back in '94. It's hard to tell from a distance and the screens are so monochromatic and focused only on the person singing, they are little or no help.

In the end, though, none of those pesky details get in the way. Or the fact that they have only released one album in the forty-three years since *The Long Run*. Or not had a hit single since 1980. People still buy Eagles tix and merch and back-cat shit by the ton. Just like they snapped up the *History of the Eagles* DVD, added the *Eagles Greatest Hits Volume 2* to *Their Greatest Hits (1971–1975)*. The latter has now sold over forty million copies worldwide; the former a mere fifteen million. And in case you missed it, *The Best of the Eagles*, in 1985, which sold over a million in the UK alone. Or *The Legend of Eagles* ('88), *The Very Best of the Eagles* ('94), *Selected Works 1972–1999* (2000), *The Very Best of the Eagles* ('01), *The Very Best of / The Complete Greatest Hits* ('03), *Eagles* ('05), *The Studio Albums 1972–1979* ('13), and last but only until the next go round, *Legacy* ('18). Combined sales worldwide: millions and millions and millions.

Then the live albums—three multi-squillion sellers so far. The DVDs, which scored them another ninety platinum awards until the bottom fell out of that market with the advent of Netflix and streaming. The Wikipedia entry for all this stuff alone runs to several pages.

Here at Hyde Park in the summer of 2022, however, it's all a blur. None of it matters to the huge crowd gathered, thousands of whom have opted to pay £185 each for the Primary Entry Ticket & Hotel Experience and/or £309 each for the Gold Circle Ticket & Hotel Experience. Conservative estimates suggest the Eagles will take away over £10 million in ticket sales alone just for this one show. Add on the millions from merch, refreshments, VIP packages, and rejuvenated back-cat sales, and some say the band will double that figure. Maybe more.

The days of cheap jug wine and a couple of hand-rolled reefers being the only desired accouterments at an Eagles show are so long ago only the fans whose memories are now longer than their hair can remember them.

Ladies and gentlemen, this is not the Eagles. This is a wrong-end-of-the-spyglass, highly manicured, decoratively curated remembrance of rock past. It's a beautiful eighth wonder of the music world, a spectacle to behold, a pyramid for the Old Gods. But don't fool yourself. You're actually back in Egypt with the desert sun on your back and a sword in your hand, feeding on slave girls and slaying Christians.

This is a time machine—the effect all-encompassing. Thanks to the can't-see-the-join miracle of cutting-edge, twenty-first-century "production values," even if Don and Joe are the only ones left to look at, they actually sound better now than they did back in their heyday. It's the same, of course, for all the old monster bands still roaming the earth. The Stones (just Mick and Keith left from the originals), the Who (just Pete and Roger), Queen (just Brian and Roger).

The Eagles' great advantage: all those bands still have to dress up and act the part when they fake-swagger onto the stage. The Eagles never did that so don't have to pretend to do it now. Everyone knows the Eagles were never badass. They were born looking nondescript. At Hyde Park they just stand there on the stage, same as they always did. Until Joe wakes up toward the end. It feels charming and harmless, like watching a classic old movie on TV with snacks.

As long as Don is still there to supply that sugar-fire honey voice and there are others to do passable impersonations of Glenn and Randy singing their songs, and the tech ensures the rest stays perfectly in sync, everyone goes home happy. Even the band.

This is not the Eagles that walked away from it all in 1980, half in desperate relief, half in hog heaven at having Proven Everyone Wrong, now in a hurry to vamoose. That band died forty years ago. That gang of storm riders ain't never coming back to town.

Don Henley confirmed it at the time when asked in an interview when the band would play together again, to which he famously responded, "When hell freezes over." Glenn Frey was even more blunt: "I just rule out the possibility of putting the Eagles back together for a Lost Youth and Greed tour."

Irving stood over the stricken beast and willed it to hoist itself back up, however painful that was, but he knew he was shit-out-of-luck when both Don and Glenn came to him separately in 1982 to play him the solo albums they had recorded.

Glenn's record, *No Fun Aloud*, was deemed "an agreeable, well-crafted little record," by the *New York Times*—which said it all. It was fine, fun, perfectly forgettable. One minor hit, the corny "The One You Love," about a girl "left blue" by a recalcitrant ex-lover. It reached Number 15 and was never heard of again.

The album hardly fared better, creeping to Number 32. Glenn co-wrote five of its ten songs with good ole Jack Tempchin. Aimed at Billy Joel territory, it very nearly made it but fell down with thrift store "crowd pleasers" like the abject "Partytown." The other half of the album comprised underheated covers like the soporific "Sea Cruise." Curtis Stigers with better hair.

Don's album, *I Can't Stand Still*, was only marginally better. Replacing Frey's hollow, good-timey vibe with a more po-faced, issue-driven agenda. The only standout, "Dirty Laundry," Don's angry riposte to the years of bad press, not least the raking-over his name got following his conviction for the fallout from that "farewell party" at his house. As usual, not everybody got the reference. But Don wasn't letting it go, determined to show how *he* was actually the wounded party.

The single did surprisingly well, reaching the Top 5 in America. The album, however, stalled at Number 24. Neither solo album made platinum; both struggled to go gold. Irving's attitude was: whatever. Irving, who now presided over a sprawling empire of movies, recording artists, tours, deals, and secret handshakes, decided sure, he'd handle this solo malarkey. Be it on their own messed-up heads. It might even hasten the return of the Eagles if they both crap out. And if they don't—win-win.

Things rarely got better than that for Glenn Frey. Only one of the five solo albums he released over the next decade squeezed into the American Top 30. Only two of his solo singles made the Top 20—the buttery, decidedly unsexy "Sexy Girl" and the formulaic pop-lite "True Love," both co-written with Jack.

If it hadn't been for his invitation to sing "The Heat Is On," the undeniable theme tune to the 1984 Eddie Murphy blockbuster *Beverly Hills Cop*, written by movie soundtrack vets, Harold Faltermeyer and Keith Forsey, Glenn Frey might never have revisited the Top 5 outside the Eagles. With the massive success of the movie, "The Heat Is On" became the impossible-to-escape hit of the year, reaching Number 2. A feat Frey managed to duplicate under similar circumstances the following year with "You Belong to the City," from the soundtrack of the hottest TV show of 1985, *Miami Vice*.

Even though he secured a cameo role as an airline pilot in the corresponding episode, which later led to a co-starring role in a seven-ep storyline of TV crime drama *Wiseguy*, Glenn's nascent acting career stalled after he landed the lead role in the 1993 show *South of Sunset*, playing former Hollywood security chief turned private detective Cody McMahon. A cheapo, copycat version of *Miami Vice*, the show got canceled after just one episode.

There were a handful of small parts in movies like *Let's Get Harry* (a gang of plumbers rescue a pal from a Colombian drug lord) and his old *Rolling Stone* pal Cameron Crowe's third movie as a director, *Jerry Maguire*. But nothing that caught fire for him. The name Glenn Frey simply no longer resonated with the wider public. His only major chart hits had both been artist-non-specific and his only major acting roles went by in a flash.

Things went better for Don Henley's solo career. Each of his three albums released in the eighties did better than the last, culminating in 1989 with *The End of Innocence*, which eventually sold more than six million copies in America, off the back of the five Top 30 "radio hits," and the title track making the Top 10.

By then the Don Henley of the Eagles, vaguely recalled as bearded, sitting down at the back hiding behind a helmet of curly hair and a straggly beard-mask, was history. Now came a stocky, middle-aged man in a sharkskin suit. Short hair, designer stubble, scowl on puffy-cheeked face. The sound, too, had altered dramatically. No need anymore for sweet acoustic guitars when you can find all you need on a synth or computer file.

The turning point for Don had come on his second album, *Building the Perfect Beast*, on the track that would become his best-selling and most self-defining hit, "The Boys of Summer." It had begun as an entirely "electronic" demo by Tom Petty and the Heartbreakers guitarist Mike Campbell. Experimenting with one of the very first Lin drum machines, Campbell had come up with what he hoped would be a fresh flavor for the next Petty/Heartbreakers album, *Southern Accents*.

When both Petty and producer Jimmy Iovine dismissed the track as "too jazzy," the guitarist was "completely deflated." So he rewrote the chords on the chorus and when Iovine heard it, he suggested Campbell play it for Henley, then in the process of scouting for fresh material for his next solo album. Jimmy made some calls and Mike drove straight over to Don's opulent mansion in LA.

"It was just me and him," Campbell recalled. "We sat at a big table. He sat at the other end like the judge, totally quiet and didn't bat an eye, just listened with his eyes closed. And then he said, 'Okay, maybe I can do something with that.'"

Mike had never actually met Don before and found him impossible to read. "He was so serious." Mike drove away in his car that day expecting to hear no more. Until two weeks later, when Don phoned him out of the blue and told the astonished guitarist: "I've just written my best song for ten years."

And he had. It was also his last truly great song, with or without the Eagles. Elegiac, haunted, a look back at the spirit of 1969 no longer cloaked in occult metaphor as on "Hotel California" but taken straight, no chaser. The final verse nut-shelling a life of regret, if not repentance: "Out on the road today," Don sings plaintively,

"I saw a Deadhead sticker on a Cadillac," itself the perfect meta-phor for the way the yuppie generation of the eighties had appro-priated and subsumed the hippy ideals of the long-time-gone sixties. "Don't look back, you can never look back."

Except, it becomes clear, Don has no other choice but to con-stantly look back. "Those days are gone forever," he decides finally, "I should just let them go but . . ."

He can't.

"I have no regrets," Don still insisted years later, asked yet again to look back and pass judgment. "A lot of people in the media attach more importance to bands that came out of the sixties than bands that came out of the seventies, so I don't know how the Eagles will be remembered. Someday, though, I think people may look back and say: 'Some of that stuff was pretty good after all.'"

He was right. The Eagles had written and recorded scores of brilliantly executed, impossible to ignore songs. More than that, they had come to embody a particular space and time that no lon-ger existed outside the pages of books and magazines that gloried in that "golden" era. The longer the eighties wore on, the more what the Eagles came to represent was looked back on as somehow more authentic than the increasingly micromanaged way the big-gest music artists now operated. Leaving the seventies with the appearance of being the more fun time when rock rolled without rules, without shame, without letting anything get in its way.

At the same time the advent of American classic rock radio meant the big, forever songs of the Eagles and other giants of their time were played more now than when they had first been hits. Hey man, it doesn't get much better than rolling down the highway with the top down and on the radio there's "Hotel California" followed by "Stairway to Heaven" followed by "Sweet Home Alabama" fol-lowed by . . .

By 1986 the Eagles were being offered millions to reunite.

"I don't think so," Glenn was quoted as saying in *Interview* in 1986. "We were offered two million dollars to play the [first] US Festival [in 1983] and two and a half million to play the second one ['84]. One of my managers at the time said: 'Come on, you rehearse for a couple of weeks, you play the gig, that's it.' He had just gotten a divorce from his wife, and I said: 'I'll go rehearse with the Eagles if you'll go back for a couple of weeks with your wife.'"

He took a meaningful drag on his cigarette. "I can't see myself at age forty-one, up on stage, with a beer belly, singing 'Take it Easy.' Without a reunion, the Eagles are forever young, like James Dean."

"When hell freezes over."

Don always did write great lines. For almost fifteen years it held true.

35.

Electric Eden

"So, this is British Summer Time," Don Henley jokes, coming to the front of the Hyde Park stage to sing "Best of My Love." He goes into a little ramble about how "this month this band is marking fifty years," for which he receives ripples of applause. He goes on to explain how the first Eagles album had been released in June 1972. Not only that but that it had been recorded here in London. More whooping, more ripples.

Then he says, his voice quavering, though whether through genuine emotion or just old age it is impossible to tell: "In case we don't pass this way again, I want to thank you all, on behalf of the band and crew, for letting us into your lives, for embracing these songs, taking them into your hearts and your homes—we appreciate it very much. It's been a hell of a ride."

It was something he said every night of the tour, versions of it. Here in the third decade of the twenty-first century, it's no longer about what's "real." It's about what works. For you. In your head. Your phone. Online outta sight.

And nobody cares because none of it matters. This is the era of flawless vocals and clean instrumentation, of perfect timing and a set list polished until it shines so hard it's like having silver poured into your skull. Nobody wants to hear songs from the new album, which is why the Eagles have only released one album since *The*

Long Run. That's one album in forty-three years. A double—surprise, surprise!—called *Long Road Out of Eden*, it came out in 2007, and boy was it long and boy did it sell and sell and sell. Only snag: no one could name even one song from it now, except maybe the single, a warmed-up version of an ancient J.D. ditty called "How Long," which, pointedly, was not a hit. Anywhere. Which helps explain why they don't bother playing it live anymore—and why they have never recorded another album and now never will. As Timothy Schmit explained in September 2022, when *Eden* first came out, "We put in five to seven of those songs [into the live set]. But we don't do them anymore because there wasn't a big reaction. When people come to see the Eagles, they want to hear 'Best of My Love,' 'One of These Nights,' all these things. So we give it to them."

It's the right call. The Eagles have been on a "farewell" tour now for more years than the original, living-breathing band existed. It began in 1994 with the Hell Freezes Over tour and accompanying live double album of the same name.

At the time, it seemed like a cute way of getting over the fact that Glenn and Don had gone back on their words and finally reformed the band for one of those Lost Youth and Greed tours. Nearly thirty years later nobody's holding anybody to their word about anything anymore. All those people who paid hundreds of dollars to see the Eagles on their rumored to be "final" tour, didn't feel cheated when it turned out to be just the start of a decades-long victory lap; they were thrilled they actually got a chance to see the Eagles again.

The only people complaining were those who wouldn't be seen dead at an Eagles show anyway. As for the band, they are no longer empire building, no longer in the business of winning over casual fans. It's their long-standing hard core that are keeping them going; everybody else made up their minds about the Eagles long ago. The stats are just too crazy. So that even their 1998 induction into the Rock and Roll Hall of Fame—replete with the unexpected sight of all seven original band members onstage performing "Hotel California" together—is dwarfed by the staggering fact that exactly ten years later, *Their Greatest Hits (1971–1975)* became the biggest-selling compilation album in the world. Or that *Hotel California* was officially the biggest-selling album of the twentieth century at twenty-six million.

But even those numbers don't fully convey how unfathomably deep in our consciousness the Eagles now reside. During the first Gulf War, the US-led assault on Iraqi-held Kuwait, according to the *LA Times*, US Marines placed a neat, hand-painted sign above one bombed-out barracks doorway labeled: "Hotel California: Check In. Never Leave."

Their most famous song's occult status has also metastasized into urban legends about the "real" Hotel California. It was an old church taken over by devil worshippers. It was originally a psychiatric hospital stuffed with certified lunatics. It was a secret club run by cannibals. It was actually a barely disguised depiction of Aleister Crowley's infamous loch-side monastery in Scotland, Boleskine House. It was Hugh Hefner's Playboy Mansion in Hollywood.

In Chicago, inmates renamed Cook County Jail the Hotel California, principally because it was on California Street. But really because if you read the lyrics right it perfectly described that hell on earth.

The Hotel California is now more famous than the Bates Motel. In the notorious *American Horror Story: Hotel* 2015 season, it appears as a secret torture chamber, where death meets desire in an LA full of ghosts. All the big shows have had "Hotel California" providing the atmosphere, from scary-wary in *The X-Files* and *The Sopranos*, to funny-yummy in *Absolutely Fabulous* and *Entourage*.

Testifying on Russian influence over American affairs before the Senate Judiciary Committee in July 2017, businessman William Browder observed solemnly: "There's no such thing as a former intelligence officer in Russia. It's like the Hotel California. You can check out any time you like, but never leave."

In April 2022, Nicolas Hénin, a French journalist held by the Islamic State in Syria, testified that he and other hostages were forced by their captors to sing a depraved parody of "Hotel California," retitled "Hotel Osama."

"It was terrifying for us, a joke for them," said Hénin, who said the words to "Hotel Osama" included the original lyrics from "Hotel California" about checking in but never leaving, but with a twist. "If you try, you'll die Mr. Bigley style," Hénin said the lyrics went, a reference to British engineer Kenneth Bigley, who was beheaded in 2004 by Jordanian Abu Musab al-Zarqawi, head of the al-Qaeda terror network in Iraq.

Face it: everybody has their version of "Hotel California." Everybody knows what you mean.

As this book was going to press, three men in New York had been criminally charged with possessing about 100 pages stolen from Don Henley's handwritten notes and lyrics for the album *Hotel California*. Glenn Horowitz, Craig Inciardi, and Edward Kosinski were accused of trying to sell the stolen materials, worth more than $1 million, and lying to auction houses, prospective buyers, and law enforcement.

Meanwhile, back at base camp, what Irving Azoff discovered before anyone else was that the people who pay the most for their concert tickets are always the happiest, always feel like "the lucky ones" with the overpriced platinum tickets in their hands. Like going to see Elton John, who also appeared on the Hyde Park stage that summer, just two nights before the Eagles. Or the Stones, who return for a second show at Hyde Park the following Sunday.

Everybody who's into their music and knows albums wants to be able to say they saw the Eagles at least once.

The Eagles have so many instantly recognizable hits they don't need to write any more. Everybody's happy with them being right where they are. Everybody buzzing on the knowledge that this probably really is the last time the band will pass this way again. The way they sing along to "Heartache Tonight," to "Best of My Love," to "Life in the Fast Lane," to "Desperado" and "Tequila Sunrise" and every other number in their twenty-three-song set. Simple but sincere emotions, music taken easy, life in the slow lane at last.

This is not the solipsistic seventies where you clamped on the headphones, burned a juicy lucy, and fell spellbound into the shadowy realm of "Hotel California," a song your ma and pa would never get. These days it's all about communing in public with these sacred, ancient texts, with sharing the collective high of proximity to thousands of others, the bigger the crowd, the greater the personal affirmation. Shows like this are no longer about *them*—the band—they are about *us*, the crowd. Whatever the name of the singer or bassist or guitarist or whoever is now.

The midsummer sky has darkened but is still blue when the opening, still shimmering chords of "Hotel California" finally come slinking out into the night. As always it gets the biggest cheer of the night. Like welcoming Dracula home to his castle hidden high on the mountain. The side screens no longer concern themselves with images of whichever old man it is up there singing and playing. They fill instead with the cover image from *Hotel California*. Tall, windswept palms lining the dark desert highway, so much more evocative than the sight of ordinary fellows doing once-extraordinary things.

Perhaps the best moment at Hyde Park is the final encore, when Deacon Frey returns to the stage—bringing with him John

McEnroe on guitar along with his wife, the singer Patty Smyth. With his gym-trim figure and impish leprechaun smile, wielding a left-handed acoustic guitar like an old pro, John McEnroe looks more rock 'n' roll even than Joe Walsh, who he naturally gravitates toward.

The band burst into "Already Gone" and for the first time all evening the joint is genuinely rocking. Albeit gently.

By the time the number tumbles to its conclusion, the sky has still not fully faded to black, but everyone slowly departs the stage as though ready for bed.

As he stands there drinking in the applause, Don Henley jokes to the audience: "You've got to work in the morning." It's an older man's joke and the older audience gets it.

"Thank you so much," says Don, exiting slowly stage right. "We love you. Hope to see you again. Take care of one another."

Everybody leaves in no particular hurry as over the PA Glen Campbell's "Wichita Lineman," an early country rock forebear, burbles comfortingly, Campbell's peerless tenor still "searchin' in the sun for another overload . . ."

You could say the same for Don. Or anybody.

ACKNOWLEDGMENTS

The author wishes to thank the following people, all of whom were crucial to the writing of this book: Anna Valentine, Matthew Hamilton, Linda Wall, Jon Hotten, and Damian McGee.

SOURCES

Life in the Fast Lane draws on the author's forty-five-year archive of interviews not just with members of the Eagles but with hundreds of other significant figures from the same period, including fellow rock stars, artist managers, record company executives, concert promoters, radio and TV producers and presenters, tour crew members, girlfriends, and friends of friends. Along with the insights gained from a lifetime working in the music business, variously, as journalist, record company executive, press officer, management consultant, TV and radio presenter and producer, and, latterly, podcaster and live performer. Working toward a unique distillation, told in novelistic literary form.

The most impressive archive of material for the world this book describes, outside the author's work, belongs to *Rolling Stone*. The legend says the Woodstock-gen *Stone* chin-strokers lined up to purposely shoot the Eagles down. The reality was that no American rock band of the seventies more reflected the increasingly slick transition *Rolling Stone* underwent than the Eagles. From rootsy dope-an'-denim to glittering penthouse-grade suck-$e$$.

And of course, not just for the Eagles. Digital isn't everything. Poring over ancient copies of *Rolling Stone*, *Creem*, *Crawdaddy*, *Village Voice*, and the like, it's the heady glimpses into authentic seventies culture that hold sway. The full-page ads for "state of the art" stereo speakers the size of a wall. The half-page ad-shares for coke spoons on necklaces, coke spoons hidden inside little brown medicine bottles, the tiny spoon attached to the inside of the lid, exotic-looking water-bongs, fancy roach clips and chillums, classy and discreet. Just the smell of the pages, like traveling back in time to a room full of smoke.

Rolling Stone has a magnificent archive recalling a world now vanished, you are urged to subscribe and enjoy. But also, in the flesh, a taste of the real thing. This is the world the Eagles were born in—the realm they exemplified and ruled over. There is a real contact-high just holding those yellowed pages.

Very similar to poring over geriatric original copies of seventies-era British music paper giants like *Melody Maker*, *New Musical Express*, *Sounds*, and their short-lived but infinitely hipper offshoots *Let It Rock* and *Street Life*. Then in more recent times, *Classic Rock*, *Uncut*, and *Mojo*. All invaluable for stories and vibes.

The Eagles, however, always attracted a much broader range of media interest, inspiring some great reporting over the years in cultural beauty-spots like *Vanity Fair*, *GQ*, all the *Times*—LA, *New York*, London—from the *New Yorker* to *LIFE*, from *Grazia* to the *Guardian*, *Playboy* to *Arena*, from Carson to Letterman, Howard Stern to the BBC, TMZ to vulture.com. They became one of those seventies giants you could write about and make the story say *anything*. The Eagles were rock's Great Gatsby.

Cameron Crowe, with his peerless insight from the inside, first for *Rolling Stone*, then later in his films, most prominently, *Almost Famous*, is the most welcoming guide to some of the best—and worst—of those days. Cameron Crowe really *got* the Eagles.

Also, Marc Eliot, Barney Hoskyns, Stephen Davis, Ben Fong-Torres, and all those other notable biographers who have written so well on the drama of the Eagles. All these strands—along with the full panoply of Eagles-related documentaries you can find online, from being right on stage with them at Mount Olympus stadium shows to hanging out wasted-on-the-plane, to the occasionally well-informed rants of some bad-brains YouTuber—form the basis of the crossfire picture that developed almost of its own accord.

Gazing in bored admiration at Glenn Frey doing his best to act tough in *Miami Vice*, staring at Henley struggling to look interesting, miming on TV to "Boys of Summer." It's amazing the insights that stuff gives you after years thinking about, then writing a book with the Eagles—and 1970s America—at its fulcrum. After the Beatles broke up and Manson was blamed for spoiling the fun for everyone in LA. Especially in Laurel Canyon. And down below on the boulevard. How the Eagles got blamed for all that, for the seventies, like being rich and famous and higher than God on the best shit in all of Hollywood was a *bad* thing.

For further Eagles-related reading, the author recommends these:

Babitz, Eve. *I Used to Be Charming: The Rest of Eve Babitz* (The New York Review of Books, Inc, 2019)

Browne, David. *Crosby, Stills, Nash and Young: The Wild, Definitive Saga of Rock's Greatest Supergroup* (Da Capo Press, 2019)

Brownstein, Ronald. *Rock Me on the Water: 1974. The Year Los Angeles Transformed Movies, Music, Television and Politics* (Harper, 2021)

Carvello, Dorothy. *Anything for a Hit: An A&R Woman's Story of Surviving the Music Industry* (Chicago Review Press, 2018)

Casey, Kristin. *Rock Monster: My Life with Joe Walsh* (Rare Bird Books, 2018)

Collins, Judy. *Sweet Judy Blue Eyes: My Life in Music* (Crown, 2011)

Crosby, David. *Long Time Gone* (Doubleday, 1988)

Crosby, David and Gottlieb, Carl. *Since Then: How I Survived Everything and Lived to Tell About It* (Putnam Pub Group, 2006)

Dannen, Frederic. *Hit Men: Power Brokers and Fast Money Inside the Music Business* (Times Books, 1990)

David, Clive and DeCurtis, Anthony. *The Soundtrack of My Life* (Simon & Schuster, 2013)

Davis, Stephen. *Gold Dust Woman: The Biography of Stevie Nicks* (St. Martin's Press, 2017)

Doggett, Peter. *Crosby, Stills, Nash & Young: The Biography* (Bodley Head, 2019)

Einarson, John. *Mr. Tambourine Man: The Life and Legacy of the Byrds' Gene Clark* (Backbeat, 2005)

Eliot, Marc. *To the Limit: The Untold Story of the Eagles* (Little, Brown, 1998)

Felder, Don with Holden, Wendy. *Heaven and Hell: My Life in the Eagles (1974–2001)* (Weidenfeld & Nicolson, 2007)

Fleetwood, Mick and Bozza, Anthony. *Play On: Now, Then and Fleetwood Mac* (Hodder & Stoughton, 2014)

Fleetwood, Mick and Davis, Stephen. *Fleetwood: My Life and Adventures in Fleetwood Mac* (William Morrow, 1990)

Fong-Torres, Ben. *Eagles: Take It to the Limit* (Welbeck Publishing, 2020)

Fong-Torres, Ben. *Hickory Wind: The Biography of Gram Parsons* (This Day in Music Books, 2020)

Fong-Torres, Ben. *Not Fade Away: A Backstage Pass to 20 Years of Rock & Roll* (Backbeat, 1999)

Forgo, Rik. *Eagles: Before the Band* (Time Passages LLC, 2019)

Forgo, Rik and Cafarelli, Steve. *Eagles: Up Ahead in the Distance (The Eagles Trilogy)* (Time Passages LLC, 2022)

Giguere, Russ and Wren Collins, Ashley. *Along Comes the Association: Beyond Folk Rock and Three-piece Suits* (Rare Bird Books, 2020)

Glatt, John. *Live at the Fillmore East and West* (Lyons Press, 2014)

Goodman, Fred. *The Mansion on the Hill: Dylan, Young, Geffen, Springsteen, and the Head-On Collision of Rock and Commerce* (Vintage, 1998)

Greenfield, Robert. *The Last Sultan: The Life and Times of Ahmet Ertegun* (Simon & Schuster, 2011)

Hepworth, David. *Uncommon People: The Rise and Fall of the Rock Stars* (Henry Holt and Co., 2017)

Hillman, Chris. *Time Between: My Life as a Byrd, Burrito Brother, and Beyond* (BMG Books, 2020)

Hoskyns, Barney. *Hotel California: Singer-Songwriters and Cocaine Cowboys in the LA Canyons 1967–1976* (Fourth Estate, 2005)

Hoskyns, Barney. *Waiting For the Sun: Strange Days, Weird Scenes, and the Sound of Los Angeles* (Backbeat, 2009)

Hughes, Glenn with McIver, Joel. *Glenn Hughes: The Autobiography* (Foruli Codex, 2017)

John, Elton. *Me* (Macmillan, 2019)

Johns, Glyn. *Sound Man* (Blue Rider Press, 2014)

King, Thomas R. *David Geffen: A Biography of New Hollywood* (Hutchinson, 2000)

LIFE. *Eagles: Their Story. Their Music. Their Lives* (LIFE, 2021)

LIFE. *Fleetwood Mac 40 Years Later* (LIFE, 2016)

Mayer, David N. *Twenty Thousand Roads: The Ballad of Gram Parsons and His Cosmic American Music* (Bloomsbury, 2008)

Nash, Graham. *Wild Tales* (Crown, 2013)

Norman, Philip. *Sir Elton: The Definitive Biography* (Pan, 2019)

Raynes, Dale. *The Eagles Trivia Book: Uncover the Epic History & Facts Every Fan Should Know!* (Bridge Press, 2021)

Roberts, David. *Stephen Stills: Change Partners: The Definitive Biography* (Red Planet, 2016)

Rogan, Johnny. *Byrds: Requiem for the Timeless: Volume 2: The Lives of Gene Clark, Michael Clarke, Kevin Kelley, Gram Parsons, Clarence White and Skip Battin* (Rogan House, 2017)

Ronstadt, Linda. *Simple Dreams: A Musical Memoir* (Simon & Schuster, 2013)

Shapiro, Marc. *The Story of the Eagles: The Long Run* (Omnibus Press, 1995)

Singular, Stephen. *The Rise and Rise of David Geffen* (Birch Lane Press, 1997)

Stein, Seymour with Murphy, Gareth. *Siren Song* (St. Martin's Press, 2018)

Thomas, Nick. *Joe Walsh: From the James Gang to the Eagles* (Guardian Express Media, 2022)

Uncut. *Ultimate Music Guide: The Eagles* (Uncut, 2022)

Wall, Mick. *Love Becomes a Funeral Pyre: A Biography of The Doors* (Orion, 2014)

Wall, Mick. *When Giants Walked the Earth: A Biography of Led Zeppelin* (Orion, 2008)

Yaffe, David. *Reckless Daughter: A Portrait of Joni Mitchell* (Sarah Crichton Books, 2017)

Young, Neil. *Waging Heavy Peace: A Hippie Dream* (Blue Rider Press, 2012)

QUOTED LYRICS

227   "Hotel California" by Eagles from *Hotel California* (Asylum, 1976);
      songwriters: Don Felder, Don Henley and Glenn Frey

231   "Hotel California" by Eagles from *Hotel California* (Asylum, 1976);
      songwriters: Don Felder, Don Henley and Glenn Frey

233   "Life in the Fast Lane" by Eagles from *Hotel California* (Asylum,
      1976); songwriters: Joe Walsh, Don Henley and Glenn Frey

249   "The Long Run" by Eagles from *The Long Run* (Asylum, 1979);
      songwriters: Don Henley and Glenn Frey

271   "Life's Been Good" by Joe Walsh from *But Seriously, Folks . . .*
      (Asylum, 1978); songwriter: Joe Walsh

277   "Heartache Tonight" by Eagles from *The Long Run* (Asylum,
      1979); songwriters: Bob Seger, Don Henley, Glenn Frey and J.D.
      Souther

278   "The Long Run" by Eagles from *The Long Run* (Asylum, 1979);
      songwriters: Don Henley and Glenn Frey

279   "In the City" by Eagles from *The Long Run* (Asylum, 1979);
      songwriters: Barry De Vorzon and Joe Walsh

280   "King of Hollywood" by Eagles from *The Long Run* (Asylum,
      1979); songwriters: Don Henley and Glenn Frey

280   "The Disco Strangler" by Eagles from *The Long Run* (Asylum,
      1979); songwriter: Don Henley

280   "Those Shoes" by Eagles from *The Long Run* (Asylum, 1979);
      songwriters: Don Henley, Glenn Frey and Don Felder

301–2 "The Boys of Summer" by Don Henley from *Building the Perfect
      Beast* (Geffen, 1984); songwriters: Don Henley and Mike Campbell

309   "Wichita Lineman" by Glen Campbell from *Wichita Lineman*
      (Capitol, 1968); songwriter: Jimmy Webb

ENDNOTES

To view the endnotes for *Life in the Fast Lane*, please visit
https://diversionbooks.com/books/endnotes-life-in-the-fast-lane/.

Or scan here:

ABOUT THE AUTHOR

MICK WALL is one of the world's best-known rock writers and the author of more than twenty-five internationally bestselling biographies and ghosted memoirs, including definitive titles on Led Zeppelin (*When Giants Walked the Earth*), Metallica (*Enter Night*), AC/DC (*Hell Ain't a Bad Place to Be*), Black Sabbath (*Symptom of the Universe*), Lou Reed, The Doors (*Love Becomes a Funeral Pyre*), Foo Fighters, Lemmy, and Guns N' Roses (*Last of the Giants*). During his long career in the music business, Mick worked with Dire Straits, Thin Lizzy, Journey, REO Speedwagon, Black Sabbath, The Damned, Willie Nelson, The Band, Kris Kristofferson, Motörhead, and many more. He lives in England.